CW00434763

LAKELAND **FELLRANGER**

THE **SOUTHERN** FELLS

by

Mark Richards

First edition by Cicerone Press 2009
ISBN-13: 978 1 85284 542 1
Reprinted 2014

Originally published under the same title by HarperCollins*Publishers* 2005
ISBN: 0 00 711367 6

Printed by KHL Printing, Singapore.
A catalogue record for this book is available from the British Library.

Artwork and photographs by the author unless otherwise credited.

Maps are reproduced with permission from HARVEY Maps, www.harveymaps.co.uk.

Dedicated to the memory of Alfred Wainwright – master, mentor and friend.

My first visit to Lakeland was in 1962 when I was 13. My parents took me on a day trip to the Langdales. Wandering into an Ambleside bookshop I spotted *The Southern Fells*, the fourth book in AW's *A Pictorial Guide to the Lakeland Fells*. That book was to change my life. It gave me a direction. First came a fascination with pen drawing which later, combined with a love of hill walking, grew into an ambition. Through a close friendship with AW, I was inspired to embark upon a lifetime of pleasure, creating illustrated walking guides and sharing my passion for the great outdoors.

ADVICE TO READERS

While every effort is made by our authors to ensure the accuracy of guidebooks as they go to print, changes can occur during the lifetime of an edition. If we know of any, there will be an Updates tab on this book's page on the Cicerone website (www.cicerone.co.uk), so please check before planning your trip. We also advise that you check information about such things as transport, accommodation and shops locally. Even rights of way can be altered over time. We are always grateful for information about any discrepancies between a guidebook and the facts on the ground, sent by email to info@cicerone.co.uk or by post to Cicerone, 2 Police Square, Milnthorpe LA7 7PY, United Kingdom.

Front cover: The Bell and Wetherlam from Walna Scar fell-gate
Title page: White Combe from Black Combe (Chapter 1)

CONTENTS

ABOUT THE AUTHOR

The Cumbrian fells have held a lifetime's attraction for me, as they have for many others. Brought up in the far-flung west Oxfordshire countryside, the romance of the high fells tugged at my emotions from my youth. In 2001 my wife and I were able to up sticks and make a permanent home within sight of Lakeland. The move was triggered by a sought-after commission to write and produce the Lakeland Fellranger series, an eight-part guide for HarperCollins. The series was also soon to find its natural Cumbrian home, with Cicerone Press, thus assuring completion of my task and a long-term future for the series.

My early experience of walking in fell country came in two guises. My mother's cousin was a farm manager on a fell estate near Kirkby Lonsdale. Hence summer holidays were spent gathering sheep and tending cattle. Though busman's holidays from my stockman's life in Oxfordshire, these were great experiences, developing my awareness of the magic of fell country.

By my late teens the lure of mountains for recreation had taken a real hold, and shortly after joining a mountaineering club I met, and became a regular house-guest of, Alfred Wainwright. Just being with such a gifted artist and writer was very special. We shared a delight in drawing and in poring over maps and walking guide ideas. He quickly saw my own appetite for pen and ink and my passion for the countryside, the fells in particular, and he encouraged me to consider creating my own illustrated guides.

My earliest guides were the *Cotswold Way* (1973), *Cornwall North Coast Path* (1974) and *Offa's Dyke Path* (1975). Cicerone commissioned a trio of hand-drawn walking guides to the Peak District that were published in the early 1980s (and subsequently revised). Other books followed, including – thanks to my fascination with historic landscapes – a guide to *Hadrian's Wall Path*.

After 14 years' dedicated research, the magnum opus Lakeland Fellranger series was officially completed in 2013, with all eight individual volumes now also available in a box set! So my attention turns southward to renew acquaintance with the spacious gritstone moors and edges of the Peak District, in order to produce a new volume of *Dark Peak Walks*, replacing my *High Peak Walks*, first published in 1982.

Mark Richards, 2014

Photo: Stephen Poulton LRPS

FROM FIRESIDE TO FELLSIDE

Packaging the Lakeland fells into neat fellwalking areas is not an exact science but the forces of nature are to be congratulated in giving some semblance of order to the high ridges. The one grey area in the region lies south and east of the Scafells where a wild tangle of upland merges with the Coniston fells. Here the Romans have come to our aid, in laying their military road from Ambleside to Ravenglass over the high passes of Wrynose and Hardknott – a deliciously juicy route adored (and feared) by motorised travellers to this day. Wainwright found it expedient to combine the fells south of Borrowdale with the higher fells of this southern group and turn a blind eye to the superb tramping to be found down the Duddon to Black Combe, denying the existence of a mid-western group altogether! The matter is now resolved; there are eight divisions of the Lakeland fells, including a mid-western group.

↑ Coniston Old Man from Great How Crags (Chapter 18)

THIS GUIDE

This guide therefore introduces a new consortium, a happy band of 23 fells: an intriguing mix of the wildly popular Coniston Old Man and Wetherlam, and the wild and solitary Stainton Pike and Black Combe. Hitherto unceremoniously divorced, none are unworthy of inclusion and all are here explored on trailworthy routes for the discerning fellwalker that should give you every cause to take a new look at, or break away from, the familiar areas of central Lakeland.

EIGHT DIVISIONS OF THE
ENGLISH LAKE DISTRICT

The purpose of this guide is to show the fullest complement of walking routes on each fell. The pressure of boots down the years has taken its toll and 'official' advice on your choice of routes has always been strict, limiting route information to the modern variations of traditional paths and thus concentrating walkers on limited

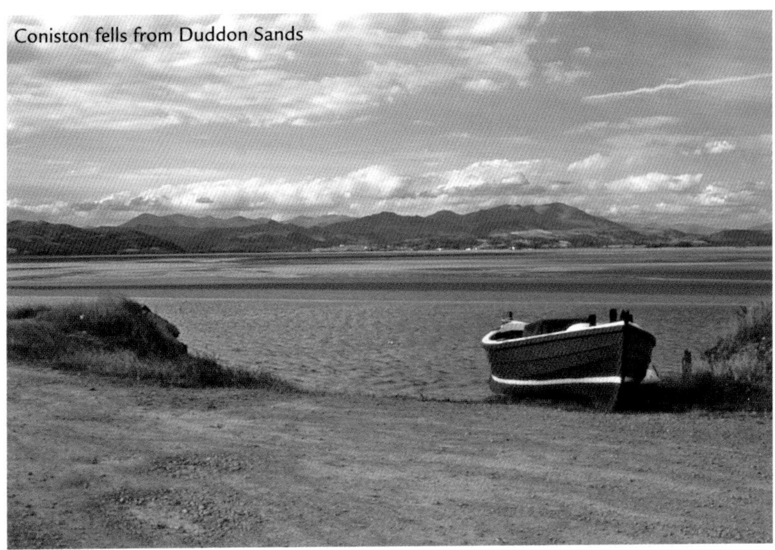
Coniston fells from Duddon Sands

routes. In contrast, the Lakeland Fellranger series provides a solid reference to the fullest range of reliable contemporary options, a valuable by-product being to spread the load more widely over the path network.

For ease of reference the 23 fell chapters are arranged in alphabetical order. Each chapter begins with a customised HARVEY map that illustrates the routes of ascent described in the guide, and shows ridge connections to neighbouring fells to assist in the planning of extended walks. The corresponding text describes routes up the fell from given valley starting points, identified on the map by a number (shown in a blue box). The starting points are listed in the 'Starting Points' table on page 16, and are also given in blue (in brackets) after the ascent route headings in the walks. In many instances there is also a diagram that shows the routes from a given perspective to assist visualisation.

KEY TO FELL MAPS

red dashed line	Route as a defined path
green dashed line	Route as an intermittent or undefined path
▲	Fell summit
25	Starting point
4	Route number

For other symbols see HARVEY map key p13.

The primary routes are described to the summit, with optional variations described to their natural point of connection with the more common route. Where a route follows a defined path this is shown in red dashes, and where the recommended route follows an intermittent path (or there is no path on the ground at all) this is shown in green dashes. Where a route follows a road it is not picked out by dashed lines.

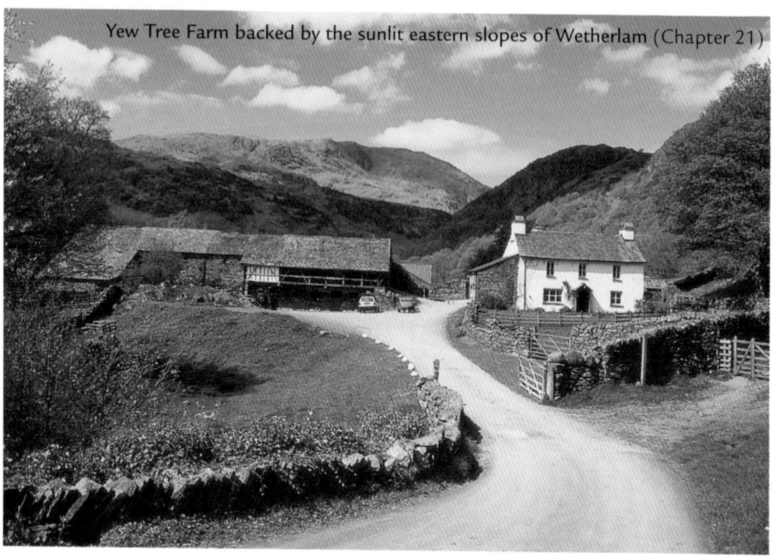
Yew Tree Farm backed by the sunlit eastern slopes of Wetherlam (Chapter 21)

There are many more paths on the fells than are shown on a conventional HARVEY map, and for clarity this guide only shows the paths/routes that are specifically described in a particular chapter. When undertaking these walks, you are advised to take a map and compass with you (and know how to use them). The map can enhance

Tarn on Holme Fell (Chapter 14)

your day by showing additional landscape features and setting your walk in its wider context, as well as being useful for your own safety. This is a guide not a hard and fast rulebook. The aim is to nurture free spirit and adventure.

As a good guide should also be a revelation, a full panorama is provided for each fell summit or better nearby viewpoint. This names the principal fells and picks out key features in their midst, including some more distant features beyond the national park to intrigue. Being aware of the safest lines of descent is important, and these are also carefully described. No two walkers follow exactly the same route, neither do they explore in the same way, so this guide is necessarily a very personal expression of the potential route structure for this area of fells. Nonetheless it is fundamentally reliable, and for fellwalkers who love to explore, it will provide a rich source of entertaining route-planning ideas.

FIX THE FELLS

This series highlights the work of the Fix the Fells project in pitching the most seriously damaged fell paths. The process has been a great learning curve and the more recent pitching is superb, ensuring a flat foot-fall where possible, and being easy to use in ascent and descent. However, invariably these trails are not rights of way, and are therefore beyond the statutory responsibility of the highway authority. Hence this partnership of the National Park Authority, National Trust and Natural England, with additional financial support from the Friends of the Lake District, has worked to make good the hill paths. The whole effort has been made possible by third-party match-funding from the Heritage Lottery Fund.

Caw (Chapter 5) from Baskell Farm

Much work remains to be done, most especially pre-emptive repair to stop paths from washing out in the first place. Nurture Lakeland (**www.nurturelakeland.org**) also contributes significantly to this work, but with a metre of path costing up to £100 there is every good reason to cultivate the involvement of fellwalkers in a cause that must be dear to their hearts… and soles! Make a beeline for **www.fixthefells.co.uk** to mark your commitment to the well-being of the fells by giving a modest donation. Clearly the occasional donation is welcome, but as yet this is still only a tiny injection. If it were the culture for regular fellwalkers to make small regular donations, so much the better.

ACCESS

May 2005 saw the implementation of the Countryside and Rights of Way (CROW) Act in Cumbria, from which time most rough open country became conditionally accessible to walkers. The so-called 'right to roam' legislation is in truth something of a sledge hammer to crack a nut. Quite the majority of fellwalkers only feel at ease when striding upon a clear path, especially one that has a time-honoured sense of purpose. The roving instinct, a broad-brush freedom to randomly explore trackless country, appeals to a narrow band of walkers. I love the liberty of exploring open country with a map, but being wedded to the preparation of practical guides, my liberty always has an eye on sensible routes that give the security that guidebook users expect. This guide shows only a few such 'roaming' routes.

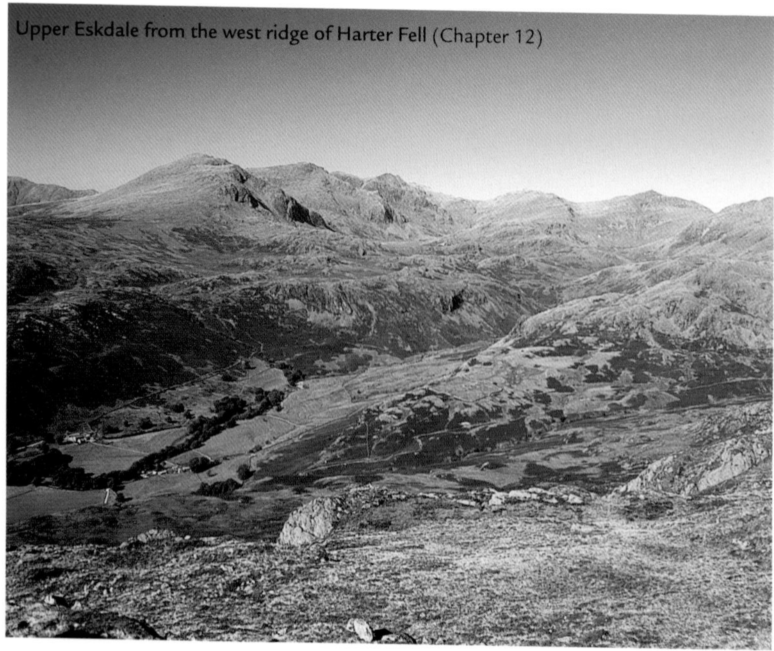

Upper Eskdale from the west ridge of Harter Fell (Chapter 12)

The mantra of Open Access should be stressed – Respect, Protect and Enjoy – for liberty to roam brings responsibilities. As wanderers we acknowledge that land has value, not confined to its ownership, and we above all should play our bit-part in its sustaining care. This new liberty has a further purpose, and is seen by Natural England as a flagship for a walking revolution. The notion of biophilia (a love of living things), and an inclusive joining up of natural heritage and people, has broadened the message, for alongside the well-being benefits of stepping out – see Walking the Way to Health (**www.whi.org.uk**) – Open Access brings new impetus for encouraging a wider range of people to experience the outdoors.

SAFETY

Being constantly alive to, and aware of, the potential dangers of walking in high fell country is essential for everyone, and most especially those who come new to this activity. The National Park Authority provides practical, up-to-date advice from daily weather checks (Weatherline 0844 846 2444, 24-hour fell forecast) to guided walks aimed at absolute beginners. As a first recourse obtain a copy of their leaflet 'Safety on the Fells' and consult their website: **www.lake-district.gov.uk**.

ADVISORY NOTE

The National Park have prepared a short advisory note for conscientious walkers:

- Place your feet thoughtfully; every single footstep causes wear and tear on the environment. The slow-growing plants that can survive on mountains are particularly vulnerable.
- Keep to the path surface; do not walk along the vegetation at the edge of the path.
- Do not build or add to cairns – paths need stones more than cairns.
- Do not take shortcuts – water will soon follow your tracks and an erosion scar will develop. Remember, there may be only one of you, but there are another 12 million pairs of feet treading Lake District paths every year.

Let us long love Lakeland and care for its future. May its magic remain an inspiration for each new generation.

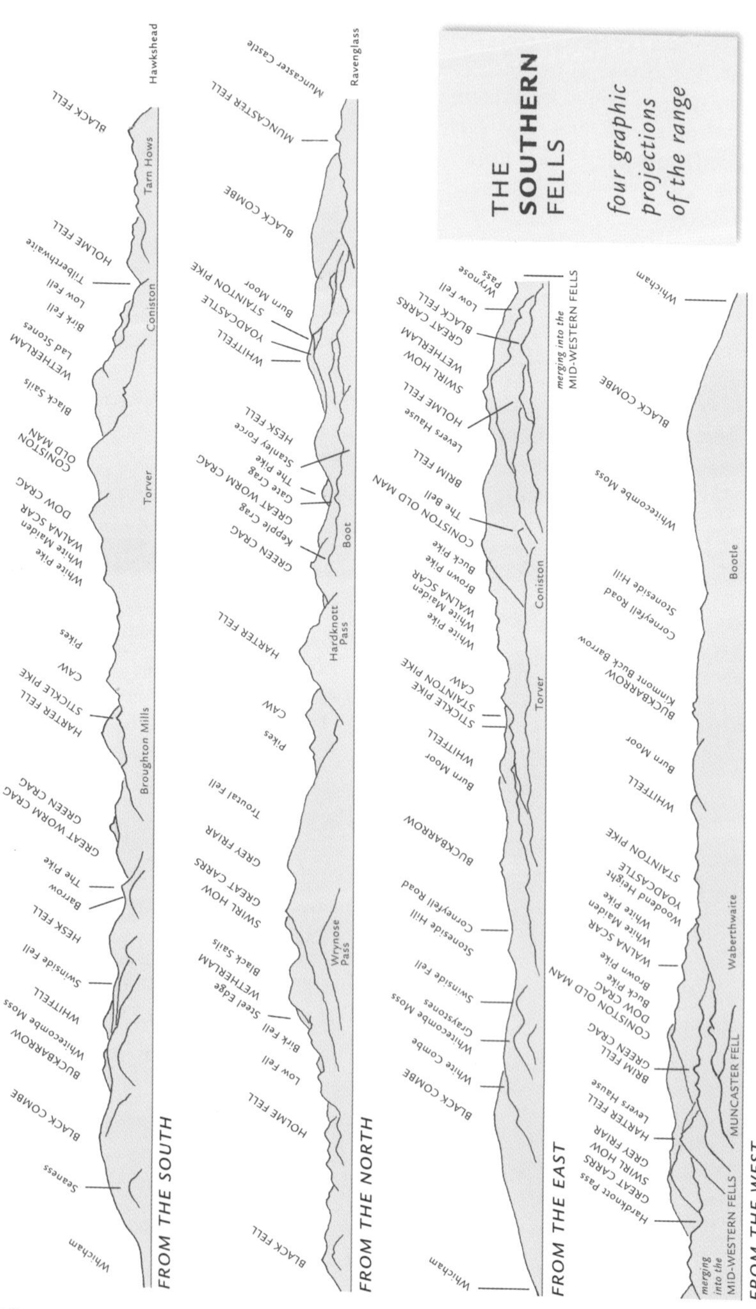
THE SOUTHERN FELLS
four graphic projections of the range
FROM THE SOUTH
Whicham
Seaness
BLACK COMBE
BUCKBARROW
Whitecombe Moss
WHITFELL
Swinside Fell
HESK FELL
Barrow
The Pike
GREAT WORM CRAG
GREEN CRAG
HARTER FELL
STICKLE PIKE
CAW
Pikes
White Pike
White Maiden
WALNA SCAR
DOW CRAG
CONISTON OLD MAN
Black Sails
WETHERLAM
Lad Stones
Birk Fell
Low Fell
Tilberthwaite
HOLME FELL
BLACK FELL
Broughton Mills
Torver
Coniston
Tarn Hows
Hawkshead
FROM THE NORTH
BLACK FELL
HOLME FELL
Low Fell
Birk Fell
Steel Edge
WETHERLAM
Black Sails
SWIRL HOW
GREAT CARRS
GREY FRIAR
Troutal Fell
Pikes
CAW
HARTER FELL
GREEN CRAG
Kepple Crag
GREAT WORM CRAG
Gate Crag
The Pike
The Crag
Stanley Force
HESK FELL
WHITFELL
YOADCASTLE
STAINTON PIKE
Burn Moor
BLACK COMBE
MUNCASTER FELL
Muncaster Castle
Wrynose Pass
Hardknott Pass
Boot
Ravenglass
FROM THE EAST
Whicham
BLACK COMBE
White Combe
Whitecombe Moss
Graystones
Swinside Fell
Stoneside Hill
Corneyfell Road
BUCKBARROW
Burn Moor
WHITFELL
STICKLE PIKE
STAINTON PIKE
CAW
White Pike
White Maiden
WALNA SCAR
Brown Pike
Buck Pike
CONISTON OLD MAN
The Bell
BRIM FELL
Levers Hause
HOLME FELL
SWIRL HOW
WETHERLAM
GREAT CARRS
BLACK FELL
Low Fell
Wrynose Pass
Torver
Coniston
merging into the MID-WESTERN FELLS
FROM THE WEST
merging into the MID-WESTERN FELLS
Hardknott Pass
GREAT CARRS
SWIRL HOW
GREY FRIAR
HARTER FELL
Levers Hause
BRIM FELL
GREEN CRAG
CONISTON
DOW CRAG
Buck Pike
Brown Pike
WALNA SCAR
White Maiden
White Pike
Woodend Height
YOADCASTLE
STAINTON PIKE
WHITFELL
Burn Moor
BUCKBARROW
Kinmont Buck Barrow
Corneyfell Road
Stoneside Hill
Whitecombe Moss
BLACK COMBE
Whicham
MUNCASTER FELL
Waberthwaite
Bootle

HARVEY MAP KEY

Lake, small tarn, pond
River, footbridge
Wide stream
Narrow stream
Peathags
Marshy ground

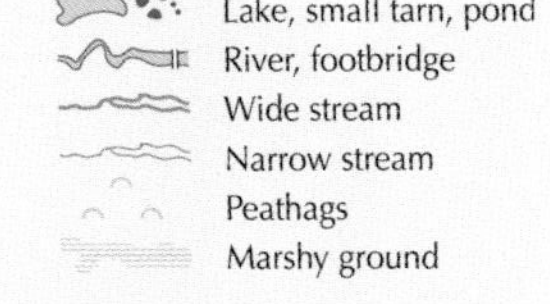

Contour (15m interval)
Index contour (75m interval)
Auxiliary contour
Scree, spoil heap
Boulder field
Scattered rock and boulders
Predominantly rocky ground
Major crag, large boulder
O.S. trig pillar, large cairn
Spot height (from air survey)

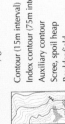

Contours change from brown to grey where the ground is predominantly rocky outcrops, small crags and other bare rock.

Farmland
Fell or moorland
Open forest or woodland
Dense forest or woodland
Felled or new plantation
Forest ride or firebreak
Settlement
Boundary, maintained
Boundary, remains

On moorland, walls, ruined walls and fences are shown. For farmland, only the outer boundary wall or fence is shown.

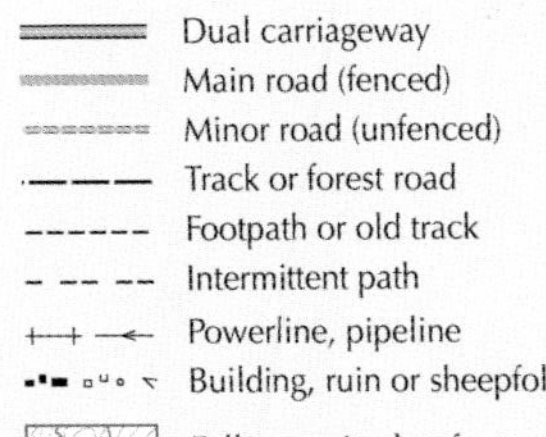

Dual carriageway
Main road (fenced)
Minor road (unfenced)
Track or forest road
Footpath or old track
Intermittent path
Powerline, pipeline
Building, ruin or sheepfold, shaft
Fell summits that feature as chapters in this guidebook.

The representation of a road, track or footpath is no evidence of the existence of a right of way.

SCALE 1 : 40,000

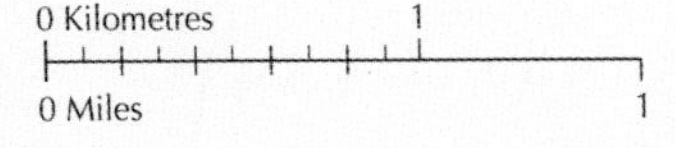
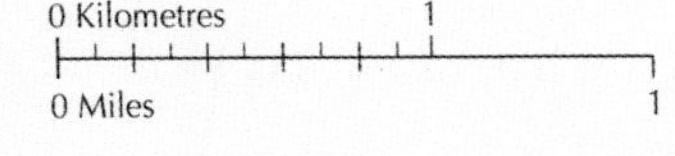

THE SOUTHERN FELLS

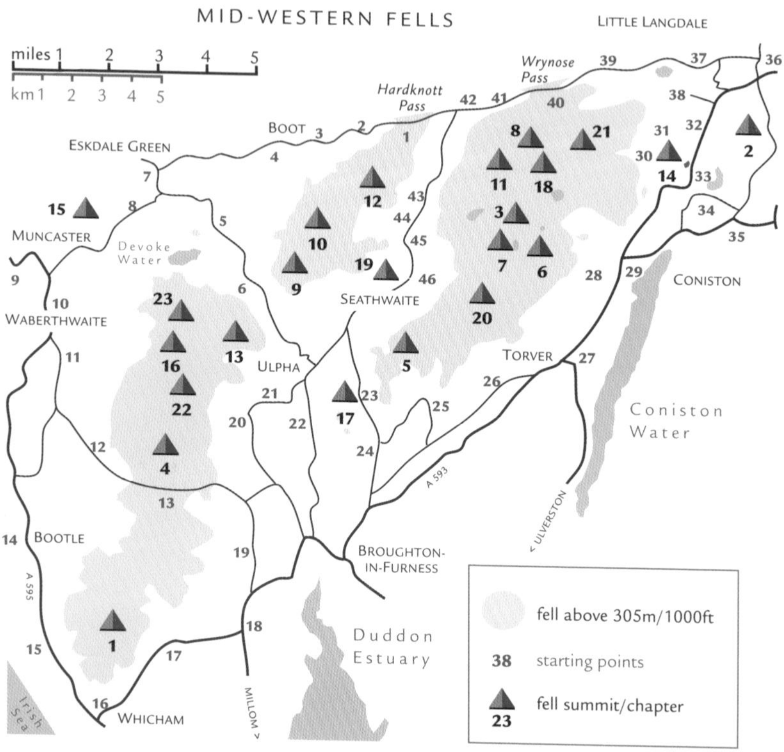

MID-WESTERN FELLS
LITTLE LANGDALE
miles 1 2 3 4 5
km 1 2 3 4 5
Wrynose Pass
Hardknott Pass
BOOT
ESKDALE GREEN
MUNCASTER
Devoke Water
WABERTHWAITE
SEATHWAITE
ULPHA
TORVER
CONISTON
Coniston Water
A 593
< ULVERSTON
BOOTLE
A 595
BROUGHTON-IN-FURNESS
Duddon Estuary
MILLOM >
WHICHAM
Irish Sea

fell above 305m/1000ft
38 starting points
23 fell summit/chapter

Green Crag from the track to Birkerthwaite (Chapter 10)

FELL MOSAIC

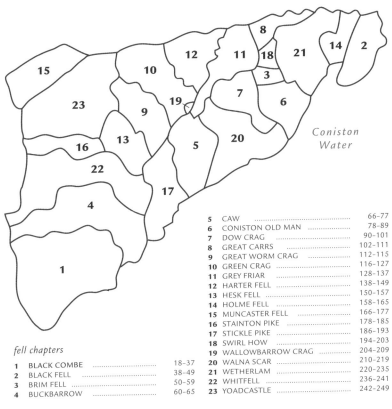

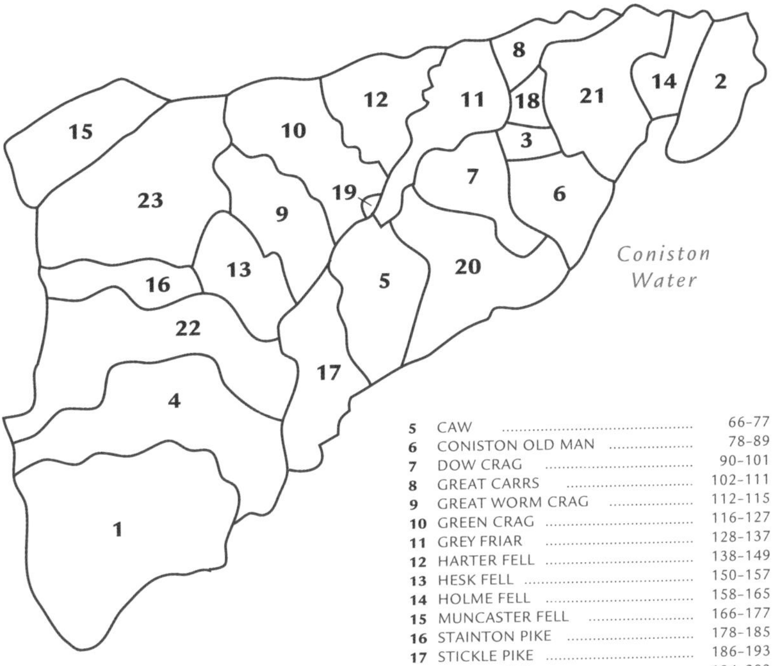

fell chapters

Slater Bridge spanning Little Langdale Beck (Chapter 21)

STARTING POINTS

Starting points for ascents are usually identified on the map for each fell by numbered parking symbols and also in each ascent title by number (in blue and in brackets).

	LOCATION	GRID REF	PARKING	BUS STOP
1	Hardknott Pass	228 015		
2	Jubilee Bridge	213 012	P	
3	Woolpack Inn	190 101	P	
4	Stanley Ghyll	171 003	P	
5	Birkerfell Road (Devoke Water track-end)	171 977		
6	Birkerfell Road (Woodend Bridge)	328 047		
7	Eskdale Green	146 996	P	
8	Brantrake	145 985		
9	Ravenglass	085 965	P	
10	Dyke	113 952		
11	Corneyfell Road (Fell Lane)	116 938		
12	Corneyfell Road (Buckbarrow Bridge)	134 904		
13	Corneyfell Road (road summit)	150 896		
14	Bootle	107 884		
15	Whitbeck	118 839		B
16	Whicham Church	135 826	P	B
17	Beckside	153 847		B
18	Hallthwaites	178 856		
19	Cragg Hall	181 877		
20	Brackenthwaite	178 922		
21	Bobbinmill Bridge	190 926		
22	Ulpha	199 919		
23	Kiln Bank Cross	214 933		
24	Broughton Mills	223 907		
25	Water Yeat (forest gate)	238 928		
26	Hummer Lane	268 934		
27	Torver (church hall)	285 944	P	
28	Walna Scar Road (fell-gate)	288 971	P	
29	Coniston (Lake Road)	307 973	P	B
30	Tilberthwaite	305 010	P	
31	Hodge Close	315 016	P	

	LOCATION	GRID REF	PARKING	BUS STOP
32	Oxen Fell (High Cross)	328 017		
33	Tom Gill	186 085	P	
34	Tarn Hows (NT)	326 996	P	
35	High Cross	333 985	P	B
36	Silverthwaite	341 037	P	B
37	Little Langdale	319 033		
38	Cathedral Quarry	315 028		
39	Castle How	296 032		
40	Wrynose Pass	277 027		
41	Wrynose Bottom	265 023		
42	Cockley Beck Bridge	246 016		
43	Birks Bridge	235 995	P	
44	Troutal	235 988		
45	Fickle Steps	231 974		
46	Seathwaite	229 963		

P – formal car parking facilities (some with coin meters) otherwise informal verge or lay-by parking.

B – serviced bus stop close by. Public transport to this area of Lakeland is not very helpful for walkers. There is a coastal railway service which gives access to Black Combe via Silecroft station, and Buckbarrow and Whitfell via Bootle station, while Stagecoach service X6 also runs up the A595 from Barrow to Whitehaven. However, regular buses do not penetrate the Duddon valley or Eskdale, although service 6 is useful, running from Whitehaven via Egremont to Ravenglass and thereby making a link with La'al Ratty. The most useful bus route is the Coniston Rambler service 505 from Windermere to Coniston via Hawkshead. Coniston is also connected with Ulverston by service X12, via Torver.

For current advice: TRAVELINE 0871 200 22 33 or **www.traveline.org.uk**.

The summit of Coniston Old Man (Chapter 6)

1 BLACK COMBE *(600m, 1969ft)*

Embracing the West Cumbrian seaboard, from Ravenglass down to the Whicham valley, the Lake District National Park takes in both a fascinating shore and a fine fell massif. Black Combe will forever draw admiration from those who live and work in its near shadow. It has a presence that might even delude the innocent into thinking it greater than the mighty Scafells. What it lacks in volcanicity it more than makes up for in solidity. It rests squat, resolute and reassuring, a cornerstone bulwark marking the fells' south-eastern limit.

For more than 50 years, A Harry Griffin wrote with huge affection about the craggy heights of central Lakeland. A Barrow man, his parochial favourite was Black Combe, a sentiment shared by Norman Nicholson from across the Duddon Estuary in Millom. William Wordsworth ventured to its summit and was profoundly elated by the view, as was Wainwright, AW concluding that this 'landmark' fell 'was made to be climbed'. Remote from common fellwalking affairs, Black Combe is deserving of more than a perfunctory inspection. Indeed, many walkers do make regular forays to the top, as the view of land and sea is quite stunning and infinitely variable through the time and tide.

Surveyed from the summit, the working world of south and west Cumbria displays a historic industrial scene from the Walney shipyards and the old Millom ironworks swinging round north beyond the Calder Hall/Sellafield complex to the headland of St Bees which shields the former marine coalfields of Workington and

↑ Black Combe from the Giant's Grave standing stones, Kirksanton

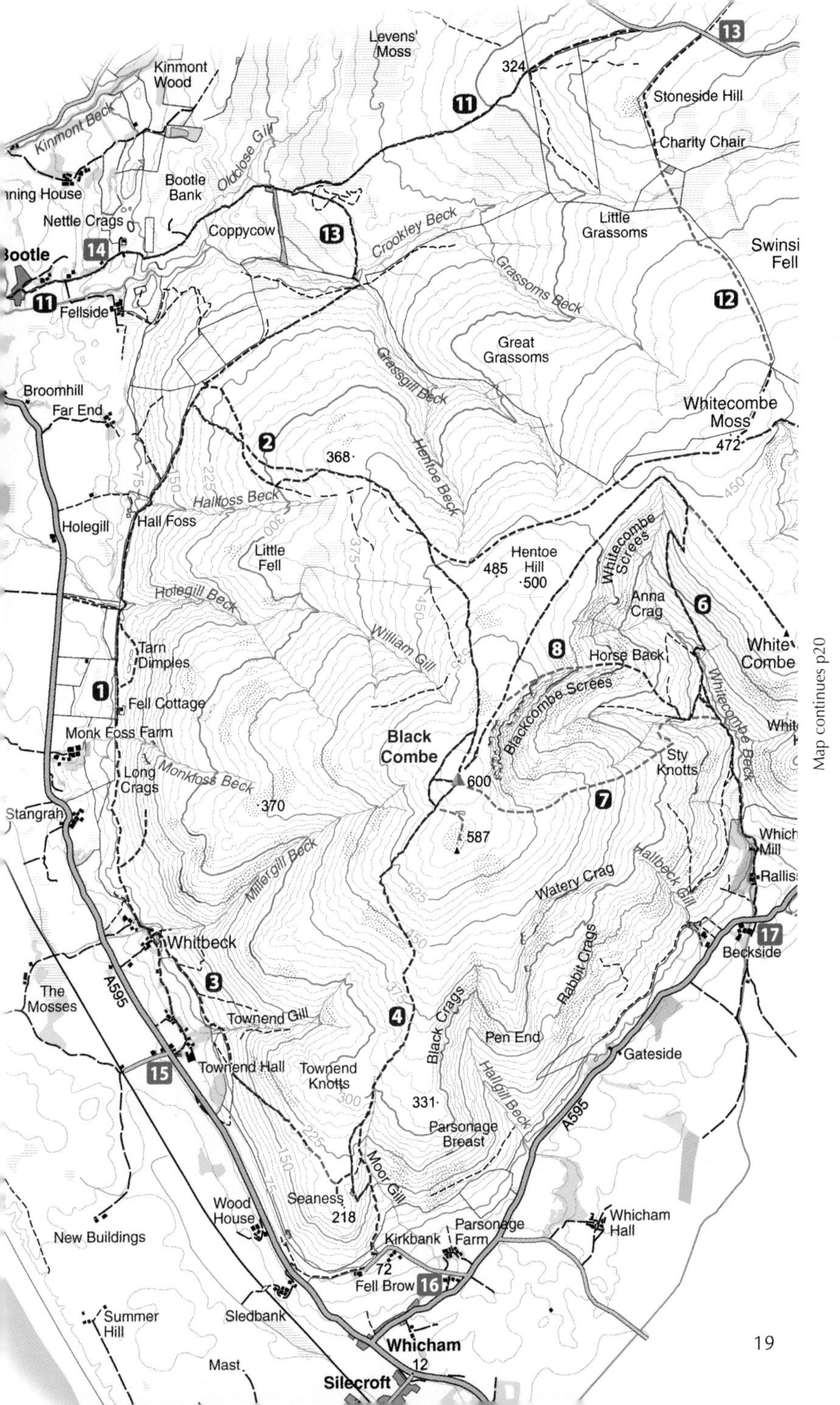

Map continues p20

Map continued from p19

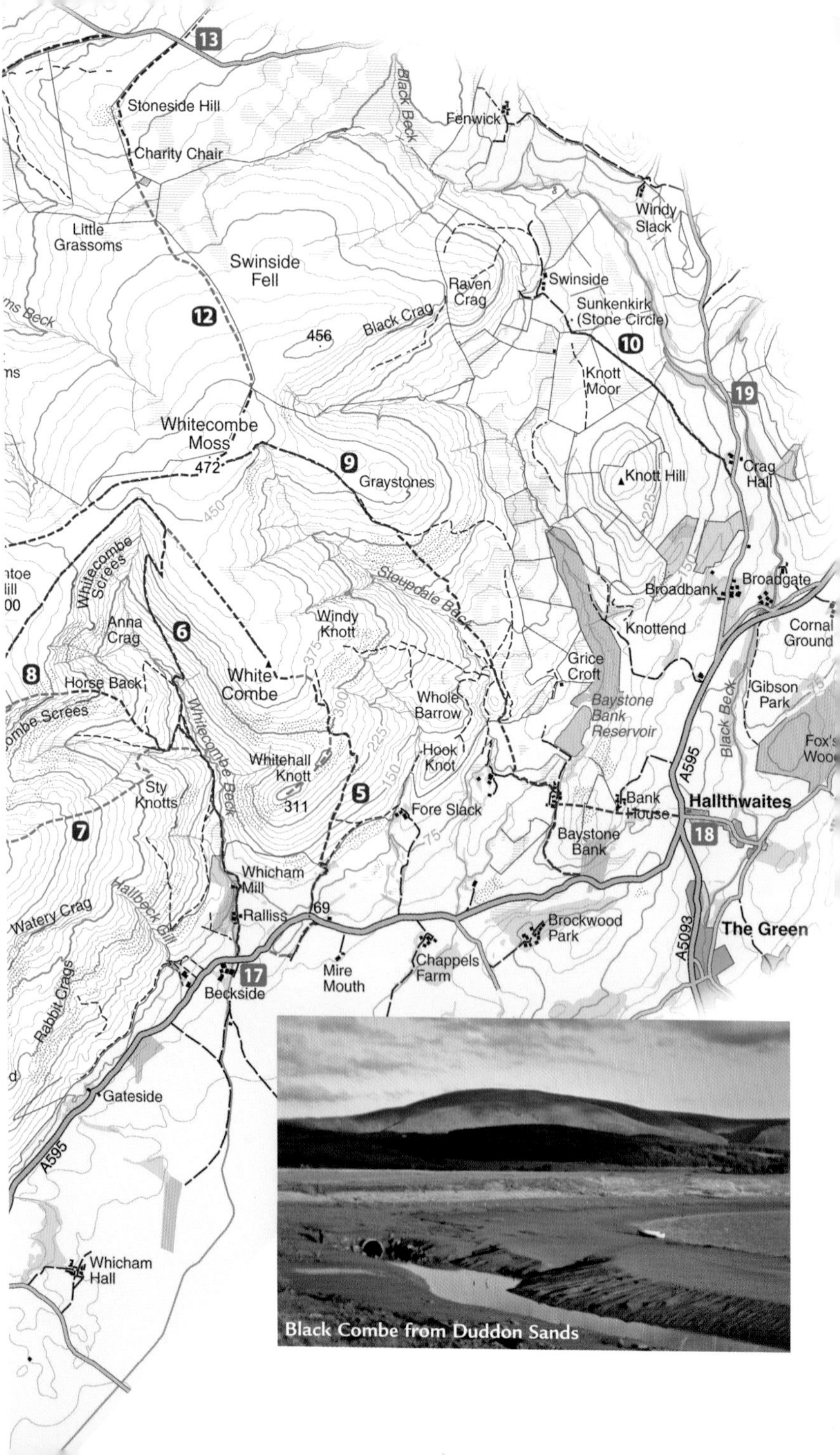

Black Combe from Duddon Sands

The southern aspect from Kirksanton, with the railway and Brocklebanks old brewery

Whitehaven. In shape, Black Combe is reminiscent of the Howgills – rounded ridges falling to the west and south with the northern slopes closer to Pennine in character. Whitecombe Beck etches deep into the southern slopes giving the fell its greatest dramatic statement – the splintered screes falling into eastern hollows, those nearest the summit most often in shade, giving rise to the blackness of the fell-name.

Most visitors climb the fell by the Whicham path; however, the fell's Christmas pudding shape means that anyone seeking to make a circular outing invariably chooses to advance up the Whitecombe Beck valley, wending to its head then leaving the summit by one or other of the ridges flanking Blackcombe Screes. Few walkers climb from Bootle, although there is a steady grassy way, useful in creating a circular outing beginning from Whitbeck. There is only one northern and one eastern approach, of value in grand traverses but awkward when it comes to making a tidy circuit. Walkers interested in ancient sites should make a point of visiting Sunkenkirk Stone Circle, although at present the natural ridge above Swinside Farm is not readily accessible. (It has a delicate ridge-top wall in need of a ladder-stile.)

The map shows the expanse of this fell – some 20 square miles of, for many fellwalkers, virgin territory. It is strange that so distinguished a fell should have no dedicated car park, though it does have railway stations comparatively close to its foot at Silecroft and Bootle, and there are regular services along the Cumbrian Coast Line.

Zermatt is to the Matterhorn what Coniston and Millom are respectively to the Old Man and Black Combe. Millom's man of letters, Norman Nicholson, had the fell very much in his sights, as did the author during the preparation of this guide. While I was operating many miles from my home, Millom proved a good base for creative expeditions, rekindling my affection for youth hostelling and teaching me the delights of the Duddon Estuary hostel, which is superb for purpose and especially well situated for Black Combe (see images on pages 7 and 20, taken from the shore in front of the hostel enclosure).

Along Millergill Beck rank bracken gives way to rock and dense heather

ASCENT FROM WHITBECK (15)

Via the north ridge 569m/1867ft 7km/4½ miles

Traffic shuttling along the A595 pays little heed to the charming little hamlet of Whitbeck but walkers intent on a satisfying circuit of Black Combe may consider it a fine spot to stop. The loop is effected by using the Seaness and Bootle paths. The old road forms a useful lay-by in front of the church. **1** For simplicity and gentler walking the recommended route takes a clockwise course. Follow the lane by Townend Hall passing the old mill at the foot of Millergill Beck. Although 80 years have elapsed since corn was ground here, the gearing and over-shot wheel remarkably remain. Even the old header pond survives beneath the cascades and narrow ravine (with no effective passage to the fell top) and a small turbine has recently been tried to modest effect. It's heartening to see sensitive renovation to the fabric of the mill continuing. The bridleway proceeds northbound initially with the intake wall close on the left. It then crosses an undulating section, a clear way firmly striking through the dense bracken with the hint of a shepherd's path veering right at the first rise which climbs onto a natural shelf of the near ridge. (This may be a good direct line of ascent or descent but route has not been tested.) The circuit keeps faith with the lower path passing the derelict Fell Cottage and a curious ridge feature with an even more intriguing name – Tarn Dimples. Just before the path fords Holegill Beck a footpath enters from the field-gate left. **2** This path begins at a gate off the busy A595 opposite the Barfield Tarn lane. (A lay-by exists 500m north opposite Holegill Farm, but the verges are mean and the traffic even meaner!) The path traverses the cattle pasture and goes

A hazy Isle of Man from the Bootle path

through successive gates to the open fell at the ford. Go left over the ford and look out for the hay-turner on your left. It must be 40 years since it did June duty in the neighbouring hay meadows but it is made of sterling iron and will last many a year yet. The ruined Hall Foss can be seen over the wall left as the path next fords Hallfoss Beck and begins to rise beside the wall, then fence, onto the fell. Go right up the ridge as the ground levels opposite a gate in the intake wall. Route 13 from Bootle joins at this point. The main ascending path winds up the shallow ridge eastward, mounting above a ruined fold and all-too-briefly through heather, onto Hentoe Hill and thence to the summit of Black Combe. (Just before the summit of Hentoe Hill, a lovely old shepherd's path breaks left across the northern slopes by the ruined square of Charley Fold enabling you to take in the full sweep of Whitecombe and Blackcombe Screes in an extended ascent if you so wish.)

Link to Whicham path via Seaness 2.3km/1½ miles

3 The alternative start from Whitbeck turns immediately before the mill. Rise up the garden edge almost to the pond to veer right on a clear path above the enclosure wall. Ford Townend Gill, continue beside the fence on a firm farm track that duly angles up the slope petering out on the fell shoulder – a quad-bike track dwindles to

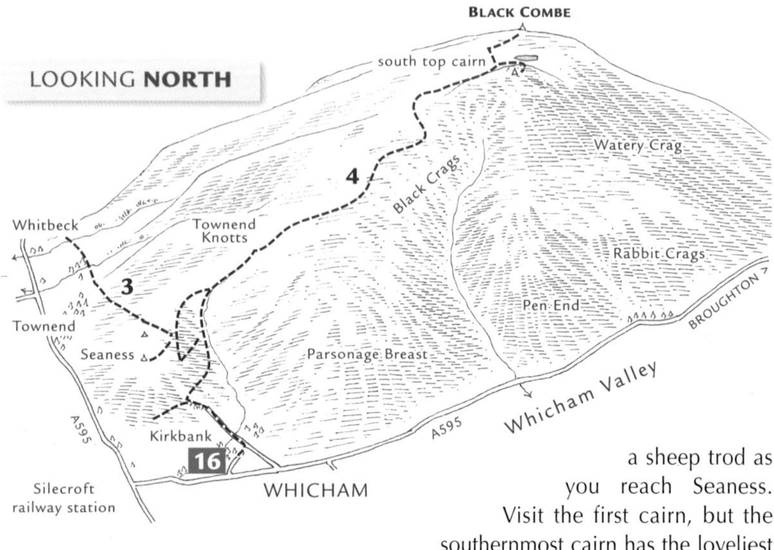

a sheep trod as you reach Seaness. Visit the first cairn, but the southernmost cairn has the loveliest view down the coastal margin to the cluster of wind turbines adjacent to Haverigg prison. (The luckless inmates must hate the overbearing blades.) Bear left regaining a clear path to join the popular path (Route 4) rising north from Kirkbank.

St Mary's Church, Whicham

ASCENT FROM WHICHAM (16)

Direct 565m/1850ft 3.2km/2 miles

4 This is the way of the many. Stories of multiple ascents abound, including sunrise and sunset treks. It's the peoples' way up Black Combe without question. Begin from the church car park (there is a lay-by just before the turn into the church should a service be in progress). Slip through between the old school and the church to join the byway beyond. Go left to rise behind Kirkbank as the road becomes a track. Find a gate/stile after a fenced recess to gain access to the open fell. Ascend the shallow combe merging with the Seaness path, for a pleasant, steady plod on firm turf. When you get to the head of the Millergill Beck valley, take the opportunity to break right to the tarn and then veer back right and south over stony ground to reach the plump cairn on the south top, for the perfect bird's eye view over the Millom and Barrow district. Backtrack to the fell summit, from where the prospect of Lakeland to the north will tantalise.

ASCENT FROM BECKSIDE (17)

Via White Combe 555m/1820ft 5.6km/3½ miles

The Whitecombe Beck valley gets right to the dark heart of the fell and not surprisingly offers the most impressive routes but few walkers appear to take advantage of this fantastic arena. **5** Horseshoe ridge walks are especially delectable and the ridges on the valley rim make the perfect highway. From the generous lay-by close to

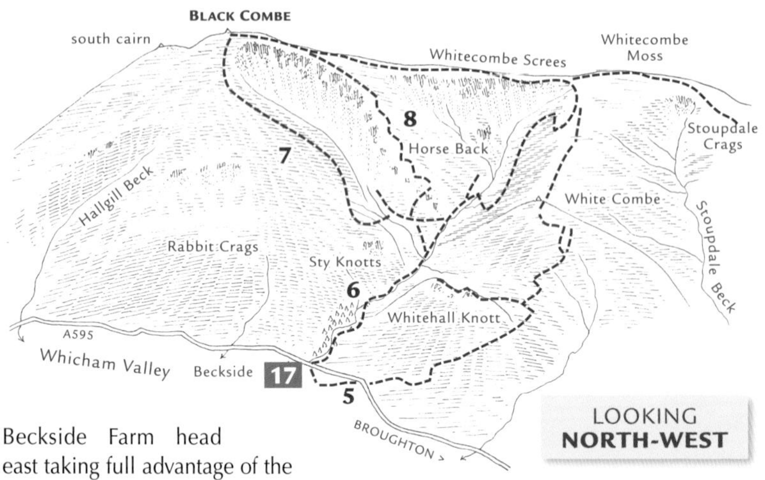

Beckside Farm head east taking full advantage of the field path via Cross Bank to the south of the vergeless main road, newly equipped with hand-gates. As you regain the road take the leafy lane from a gate at the bend above Fox & Goose Cottages. The lane leads to a gate onto the bracken slope of Whitehall Knott. Go up left then diagonally across the slope on a grooved track mounting onto the northern shoulder. (The short ridge of Whitehall Knott itself is worthy of a detour. It's a fine spot from which to peruse the Whicham valley and consider the fat ridge of Sty Knotts climbing to the

White Combe from the brink of Blackcombe Screes

North-east into the heart of Lakeland from Blackcombe Screes

top of Black Combe.) As the path continues on up by stunted gorse shrubs, it gleefully fends off the bracken, being a drove-way, but it does not go to the ridge-end summit of White Combe. Watch to break left on a path that peters out. The shelter cairn at the summit is a fine place to halt and delve into your rucksack for a bite to eat, with the great scoured hillsides of Blackcombe and Whitecombe Screes the focus of attention. A narrow ridge path leads purposefully north-westward from here, fading as it approaches the junction with the path at the valley head.

6 This path starts from the foot of the valley. Follow the gated lane direct from the main road at Beckside. Pass the old farmhouse of Ralliss, keeping right to avoid the immediate environs of Whicham Mill. As the woodland ends a gate leads into the combe's inner sanctuary. The path skips over a plank footbridge, keeping to the west side of the beck until an obvious switch right over a broader plank footbridge. The path switches left again as it begins to climb up the valley-head slope, zig-zagging towards the end to curve naturally around the rim and make the final good mile of ascent south-westerly over easy ground.

Two ridges take in Blackcombe Screes; Horse Back (**8**) is the better climb and Sty Knotts (**7**) the better descent. To ascend on either look left after fording Black Combe gill, and join the first path that keeps above its north bank. The Sty Knotts route is barely visible on the ground, so the only advice is to follow the clearer path into the combe until you can devise a line that avoids the worst of the bracken to climb south to gain the ridge and then west up to the summit. The Horse Back ridge, by contrast, has a certain clientele, and a path is faintly evident, mounting above a small fenced area. As the ridge narrows the path threads up through rocks and climbs impressively in steps – exciting situations abound.

The meat and matter of Black Combe from White Combe

ASCENT FROM HALLTHWAITES (18)

Via Graystones 615m/2020ft 6.8km/4¼ miles

9 Approaches from the east have traditionally drawn up the Graystones ridge from the vicinity of Baystone Bank Reservoir. Car parking for anglers at the farm might, if you ask, be extended to walkers. Guests at Brockwood Hall have the best option –

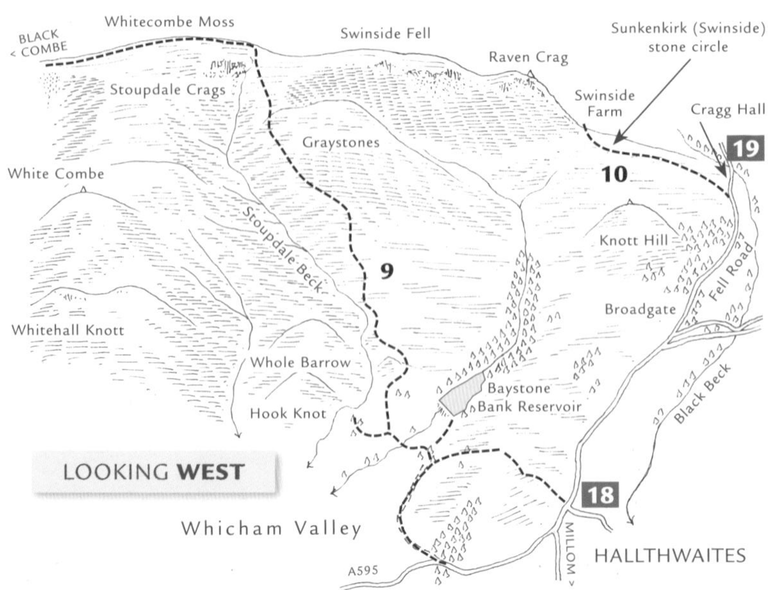

simply to follow the footpath from Lanthwaite Bridge. Otherwise walkers are obliged to begin at Hallthwaites, traversing the intermediate ridge on a footpath served by ladder-stiles via Bank House (hand-gate in tangled dip). The view from above Baystone Bank Farm is a delight. Joining the farm roadway, at a stile, go right. (Notice, in passing the farmhouse, a curious animal motif set high upon the facing wall. Is it a boar or badger?)

Follow the lane towards Whirlpippin. Short of the cottage find a footpath signed right. Go through the gate and brief lane opening into a pasture, the invisible path keeping close company with the left-hand wall. Towards the end go through a dip, cross a ditch and then a ladder-stile onto the open fell. For all its best endeavours bracken fails to subsume the path. Slip over the wave-like knoll of Force Knott and keep on along the top of the bank to the east of Stoupdale Beck. To begin with, marshy ground makes the going soft, but firmer ground eventually arrives and the path rises purposefully onto the western slope of Graystones. The facing fellside, known as Leadmine Breast, is a reminder of the days of small-scale prospecting, for copper as well as lead. The path passes by gorse rising onto the ridge high above Stoupdale. (A stoup was a form of Cumbrian stone gatepost, and the name may refer to a source of such stone.) At the dale head a small broken slope bears the ambitious name of Stoupdale Crags. The path skirts the top of the gullies and you are rewarded with a fine view down the valley before heading over Whitecombe Moss's peaty plateau, slightly south of west, to meet the path climbing out of the Whitecombe Beck valley. (In mist, keep within the fence which runs along on the north side of the plateau.)

White Combe from Baystone Bank Reservoir

WALK FROM CRAGG HALL (19)

To Sunkenkirk stone circle 80m/262ft 1.6km/1 mile

The most easterly ridge on the Black Combe massif, Swinside Fell, has no tradition of access, despite the presence of cairns on the skyline of Raven Crag. So while open access will eventually bring freedoms even here, the lack of an adequate ladder-stile crossing the ridge-top wall above Raven Crag presently rules out any approach route to Black Combe along this narrow moorland ridge. **10** However, there is considerable cause to consider tracing the bridleway and open trackway from the vicinity of Cragg Hall towards Swinside Farm. Located close to the farm buildings there rests a genuine Bronze Age stone circle, composed of some 40 or 50 stones (everyone comes up with a different number). The old name Sunkenkirk shows awareness of its ceremonial origins, although there is no hint of a ditch. (Did 'sunken' mean 'stooped', comparing the stones to a reverential religious gathering?) There is no sign of rock art, which may have been erased by centuries of livestock rubbing. The fragmentary nature of the stones suggest the circle may be a Victorian reconstruction.

Via the Old Road 655m/2150ft 9.7km/6 miles

11 The Bootle Fell byway gives a grand insight into the style of roads before the advent of tarmac. Where feasible it is flanked with neat ditches (or a *fosse*) to allow run-off and minimise wash-out. The Romans were adept at incorporating them on their engineered military roads, hence the Fosse Way, which sliced diagonally across Britannia between Exeter and Lincoln, forming the first Roman frontier of their island

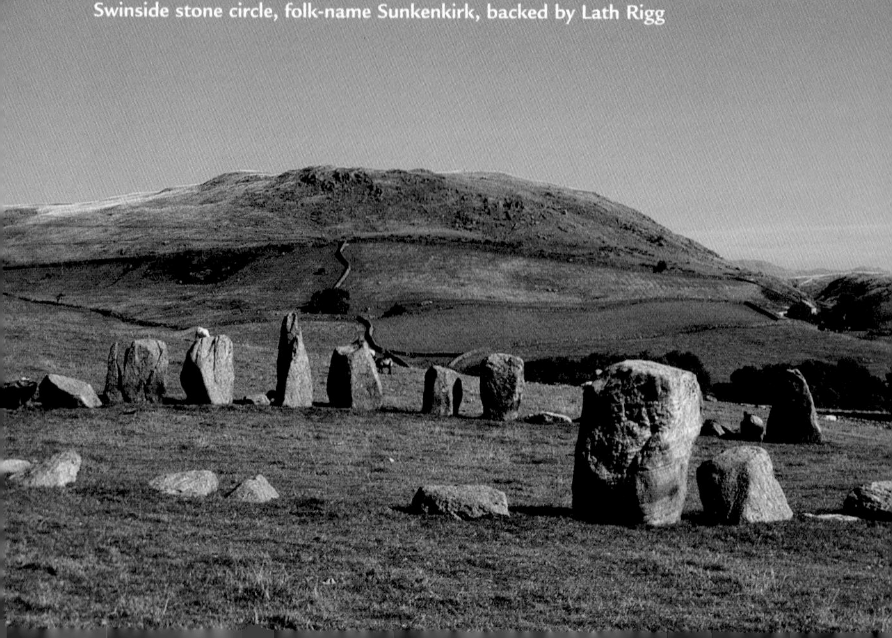
Swinside stone circle, folk-name Sunkenkirk, backed by Lath Rigg

Black Combe from Bootle main street

province. After Route 13 has curled up the fell to the right, at a stile/gate the road becomes confined as it progresses onto the Corneyfell Road, heading on up to the road summit where the fell opens up once more. **12** From this point join the ridge wall over Stoneside Hill, and, from the depression beyond, follow the ridge fence onto Whitecombe Moss and on to the summit – see the Buckbarrow ridge route description. (A good circular walk can be created by turning NE at the road summit instead to traverse Buckbarrow and Whitfell and then cross Burn Moor to follow the bridleway down over the Corneyfell Road into the Kinmont Beck valley and by Kinmont Wood to the minor road leading back into Bootle.)

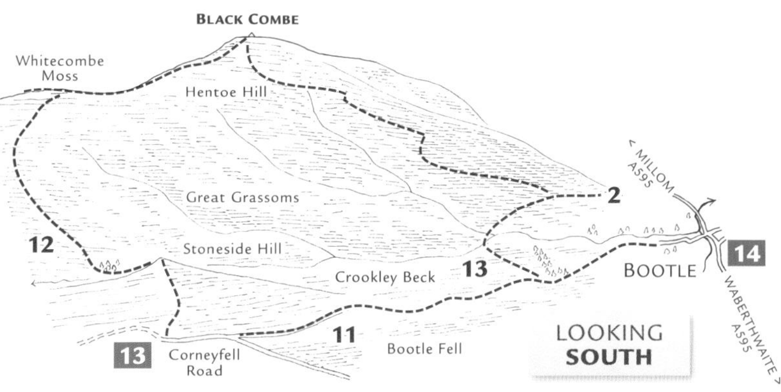

Black Combe from Buckbarrow Beck

ASCENT FROM BOOTLE (14)

Via Crookley Beck and the north ridge path 605m/1985ft 6.7km/4¼ miles

13 Park in the village off the main street opposite the church or, failing that, with due sensitivity, on Fellgreen, above Fell Gate Cottage (GR116885). The road running up from the village is a pleasure to tread. (Notice the neat Cumbrian dyke walling at Underwood Cottage.) From Fellgreen the old Bootle Fell byway proceeds through a gate. Passing Nettle Crags, winding up then down through the Oldclose Gill dell, spot Gibson's Spout over to the right in Crookley Beck. The old road climbs to pass the top end of Coppycow (coppy: 'coppiced woodland', now sadly replaced by conifers). Immediately beyond the trees, find a huge granite erratic block known as the Resting Stone. There is a fat finger-sized hole in the upper south side, presumably an example of Bronze Age cup and ring symbolism. (You could imagine it as a talisman for which, perhaps, 'they who insert their right thumb in this hole are blessed with longevity'. If you do insert your thumb, you will know that you have at least one thing in common with the author!) The open fell flanking the byway also has Bronze Age field systems, but there isn't much to see. As the open track bends left take the second green path rising right. This crosses over the bracken bank and slices through a cross-path to avoid the broad sphagnum marsh. Descend into the Crookley Beck valley to a ford the beck, passing over the hurdle gate, smartly followed by a concrete culvert of Grassgill Beck. Now heading south-west, keep to the higher of the two subsequent green paths, slanting across the fellside, duly coming alongside the top of the enclosure wall. As a field-gate is spotted, just before the path begins to descend, take the obvious path left, up the gently rising ridge to join Route 2 – most commonly used as a descent route, so expect to meet someone. The author encountered two couples sitting in the heather midway up. They were taking a breather on their way down, but the women claimed, amid much laughter, that they were waiting for a bus!

THE SUMMIT

Retiring and something of an enigma, the gently domed top of Black Combe ensures that, even from afar, the actual summit is barely perceived and only hoves into view at the last moment of any ascent. Seen from the south, notably Kirksanton, the portly south cairn pricks the skyline as the sham summit, the convex slope hiding the true top. Coming upon the shallow domed table-top, with the wind whistling off the ocean, the crude wind shelter has a greater than usual value. You may wonder who gathered

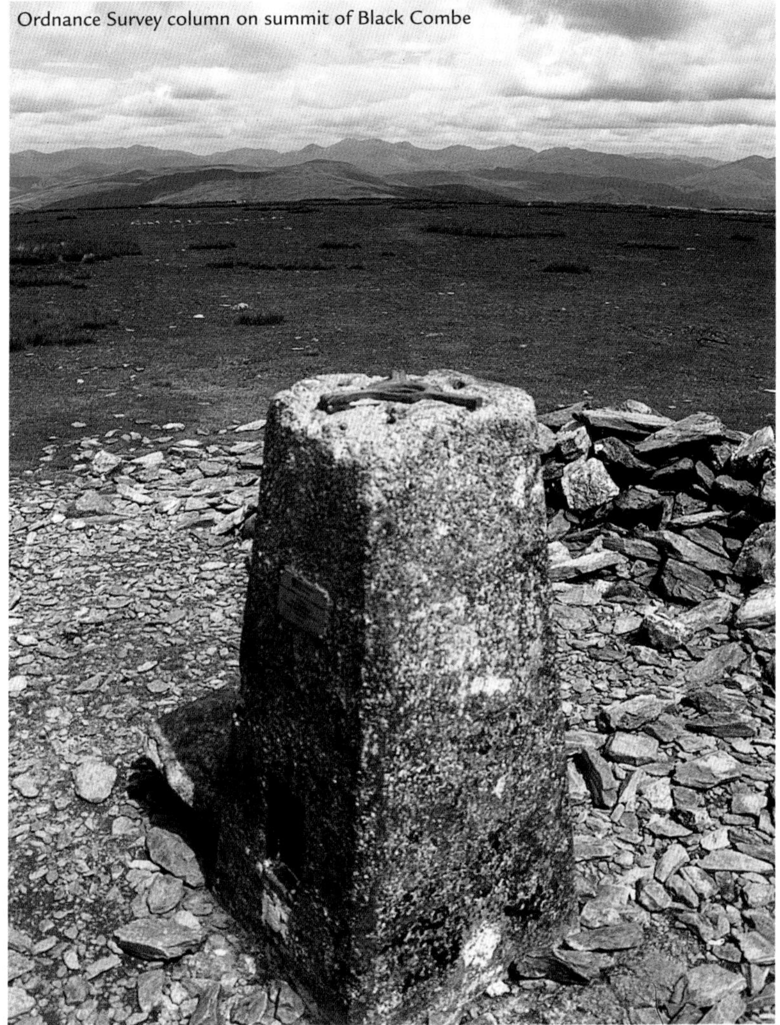

Ordnance Survey column on summit of Black Combe

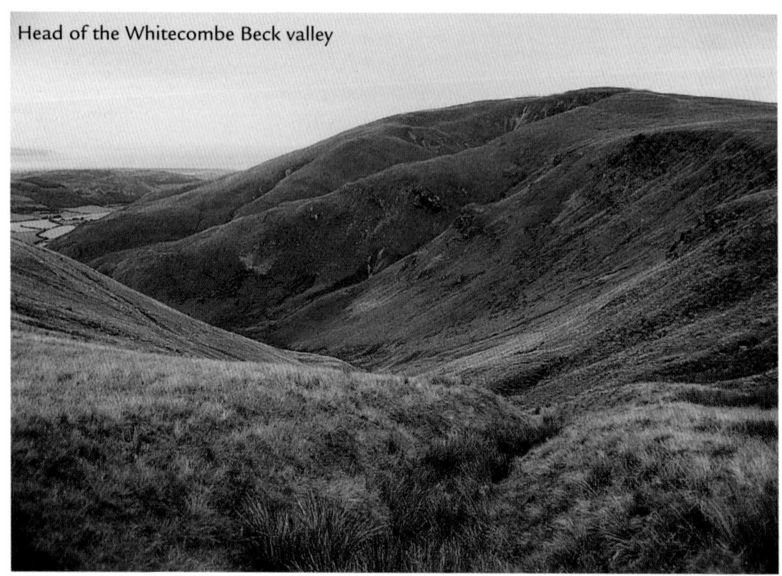
Head of the Whitecombe Beck valley

the stones and over what period, but you'll be more grateful than quizzical. The OS column gains permanent benefit from this humble huddle of boulders. The majority of such pillars have become redundant but this one still serves cartographers as a strategic point in the network of the global positioning system. And the south cairn, beyond the tarn in the intermediate dip, is not to be outdone, playing its part in the informal games of GPS users as an unofficial GPS geocache station with the treasure discreetly stashed under a slate. (Don't go stealing anything – you're on your honour!).

William Wordsworth described the summit of Black Combe as a place where 'the amplest range of unobstructed prospect may be seen that British ground commands' and no wonder with so much ocean to the south and west. But the view worthiest of admiration lies to the north-east, with the 'Four-Threes' (fells over 3000ft) – Sca Fell, Scafell Pike, Skiddaw and Helvellyn – in view. It's the best of Lakeland telescoped into a narrow mass a long arm's length away. In his collected poems *Sea to the West*, that great Cumbrian observer Norman Nicholson, gazing from his Millom study window, expressed the fell's propensity to gather its own cap of cloud – 'Black Combe alone still hides' and 'beneath the Herdwick-fleece of mist you can feel the heave of the hill'. Beware Black Combe's poetry-inspiring micro-climate before you commit to an ascent when all else in Lakeland is clear.

SAFE DESCENTS

The immediate concern on descending Black Combe is the broken precipice of Blackcombe Screes which lurks unseen close under the eastern lip of the summit plateau. As the majority of visitors will have come by the Whicham path their minds will naturally turn to a straightforward retreat, although many wisely make a circuit upon the continuing bridleway down the broad N ridge, cutting back S to Whitbeck (and Seaness for Whicham Church). Those that have come up the Whitecombe Beck valley may be lured into descending either side of Blackcombe Screes. In mist, beware of the fall of the ground.

RIDGE ROUTE

BUCKBARROW ↓290m/955ft ↑230m/760ft 7km/4¼ miles

Follow the emerging path leading NE watchful to keep a safe distance from the profound declivity overlooking the Whitecombe Beck valley. As the ground levels a narrow peaty trod draws close to a wire fence traversing Whitecombe Moss (tension causing it to emit a high-pitched hum during a strong wind). As a barbed fence intervenes step over the plain fence, and keep to the west side of the continuing fence, to avoid the even wetter ground on Swinside Fell indicated by the rushes. The semblance of a path descends to cross a tall fence at a fence junction. Head straight on, keeping just left of the dwarf conifer shrubbery coming up to the netting fence beside the rising wall. (A stile needs inserting adjacent to the Charity Chair sheepfold.) Climb to the stony top of Stoneside Hill, a really good viewpoint for Buckbarrow. Descend keeping the wall left and advancing to the summit of the Corneyfell Road (where there is a car parking space). Cross directly over, keep the wall close left and clamber over Great Paddy Crag before slanting half-right, weaving through boulders and outcrops to reach the summit cairn.

White Combe and the pastoral Whicham Valley from above Po House

PANORAMA

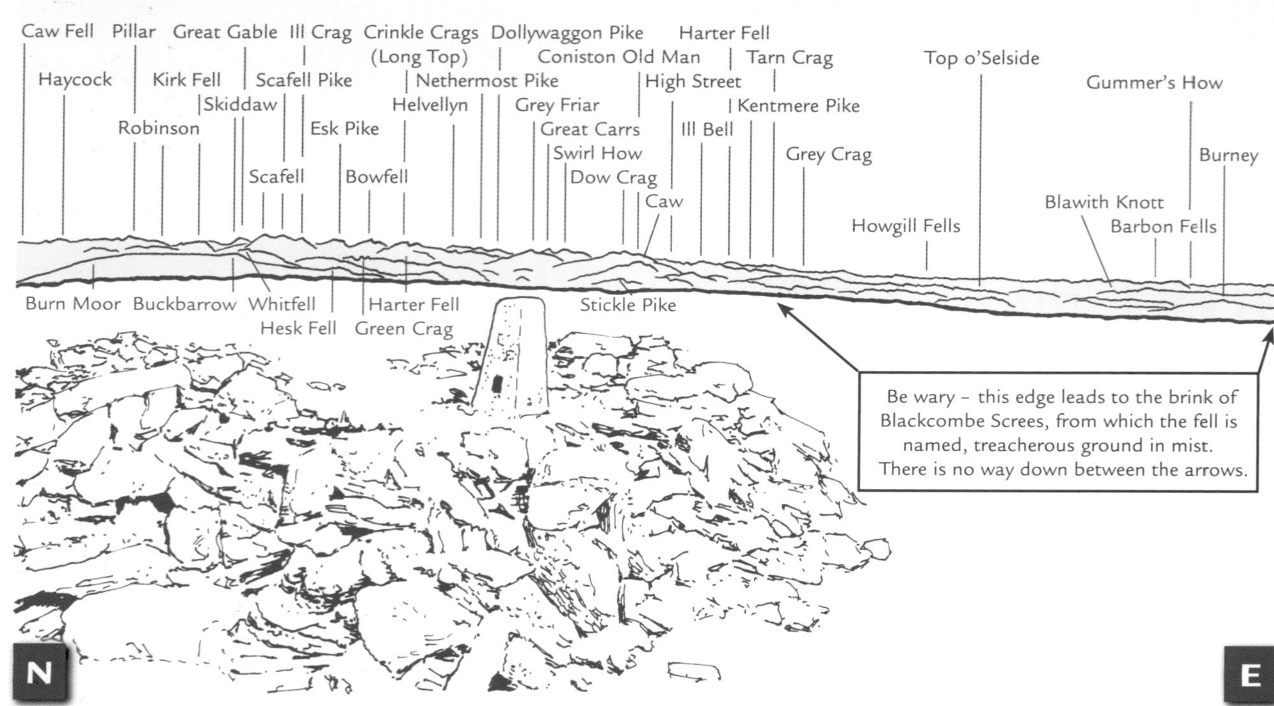
Caw Fell
Pillar
Great Gable
Ill Crag
Crinkle Crags (Long Top)
Dollywaggon Pike
Harter Fell
Coniston Old Man
Tarn Crag
Top o'Selside
Haycock
Kirk Fell
Scafell Pike
Nethermost Pike
High Street
Gummer's How
Skiddaw
Helvellyn
Grey Friar
Kentmere Pike
Robinson
Esk Pike
Great Carrs
Ill Bell
Swirl How
Grey Crag
Burney
Scafell
Bowfell
Dow Crag
Caw
Blawith Knott
Howgill Fells
Barbon Fells
Burn Moor
Buckbarrow
Whitfell
Harter Fell
Stickle Pike
Hesk Fell
Green Crag
Be wary – this edge leads to the brink of Blackcombe Screes, from which the fell is named, treacherous ground in mist. There is no way down between the arrows.
N
E

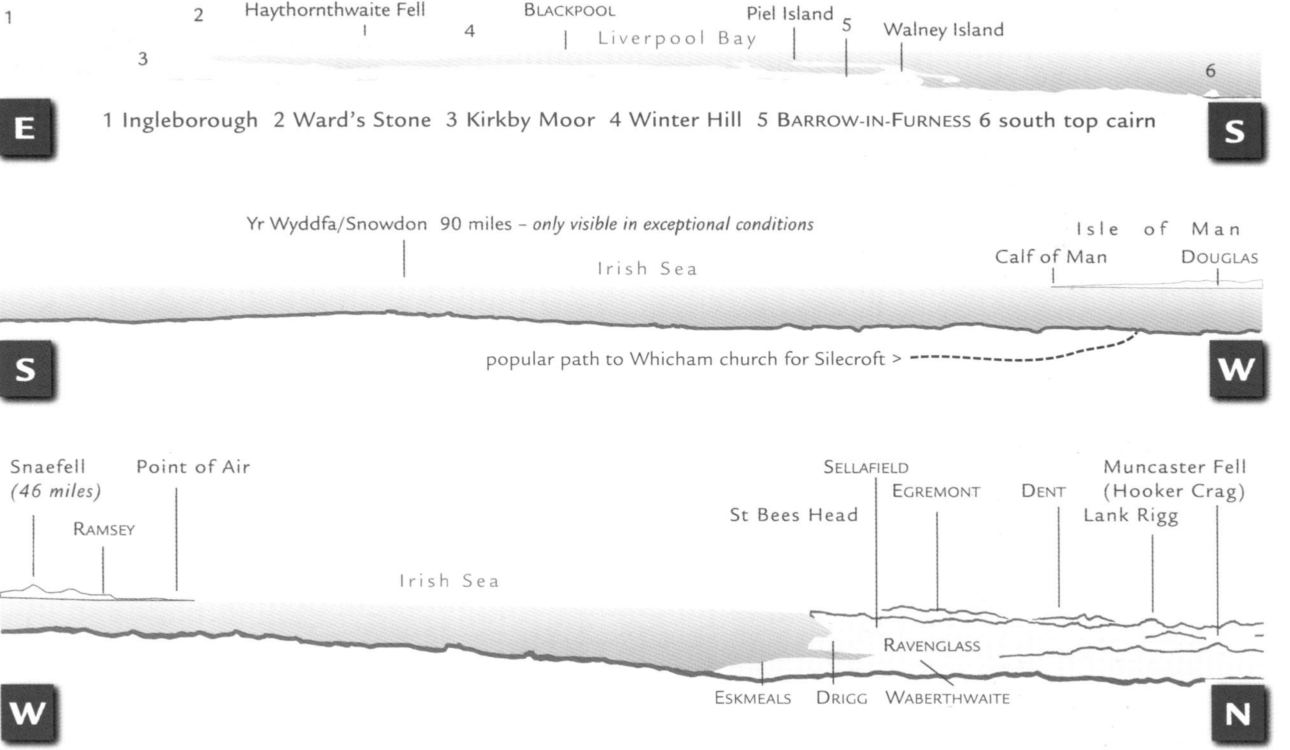
1
2
Haythornthwaite Fell
Blackpool
Piel Island
5
Walney Island
4
Liverpool Bay
3
6
E
1 Ingleborough 2 Ward's Stone 3 Kirkby Moor 4 Winter Hill 5 Barrow-in-Furness 6 south top cairn
S
Yr Wyddfa/Snowdon 90 miles – *only visible in exceptional conditions*
Isle of Man
Calf of Man
Douglas
Irish Sea
S
popular path to Whicham church for Silecroft >
W
Snaefell
(*46 miles*)
Point of Air
Ramsey
Sellafield
Egremont
Dent
Muncaster Fell
(Hooker Crag)
St Bees Head
Lank Rigg
Irish Sea
Ravenglass
W
Eskmeals
Drigg
Waberthwaite
N

2 BLACK FELL *(322m, 1056ft)*

Lying within the triangle of Skelwith Bridge, Hawkshead and Coniston, Black Fell forms the northerly backdrop to the comparatively low, intrinsically wild, undulating ridge on which sits the ever-popular Tarn Hows. A perfect embodiment of the picturesque, enhanced by unabashed human intervention, this magical mix of trees, rock and water was the brainchild of James Marshall, a wealthy linen magnate and Leeds MP who moved to Monk Coniston in the 1860s.

The landscaping was inspired but not without its problems for Marshall. He stocked the tarns with trout, only to have them consumed by pike. Frustrated, he drained the tarns, re-filling after two years, but the damp ground harboured pike eggs and the voracious aquatic monster took any new stock. In 1920 a new dam was constructed just above Yew Tree Farm, the snag this time being that it was built on a geological fault and so every twenty years or so the leaking dam needs some re-engineering. In the time of the Marshall family there was only a linear path running along the east side of Tarn Hows to Rose Castle – a folly that was once also home to quarrymen.

Today this wonderful place has been made thoroughly accessible for all levels of visitor from the wheelchair-bound to lively imps. The National Trust has embarked on a programme to re-create James Marshall's original vistas. Beatrix Heelis (née Potter) purchased the estate when the Marshall family were selling it to recoup family losses after the First World War and sold it, at cost, to Sir Samuel Scott of Windermere in 1930. He acquired it for the Trust to keep the estate intact and his generosity and far-

 ↑ Black Fell backing Tarn Hows

sightedness are marked by a plaque set on the headland east of the tarns beyond the disabled car park. Anyone who wanders from off the Hawkshead/Coniston road will know and adore the stately majesty of this estate, nurtured by the Marshalls and lovingly sustained by the Trust.

Evidently the fell-name Black Fell derived from the eastern perspective, from where afternoon and evening light cast shadows down its steep slopes,

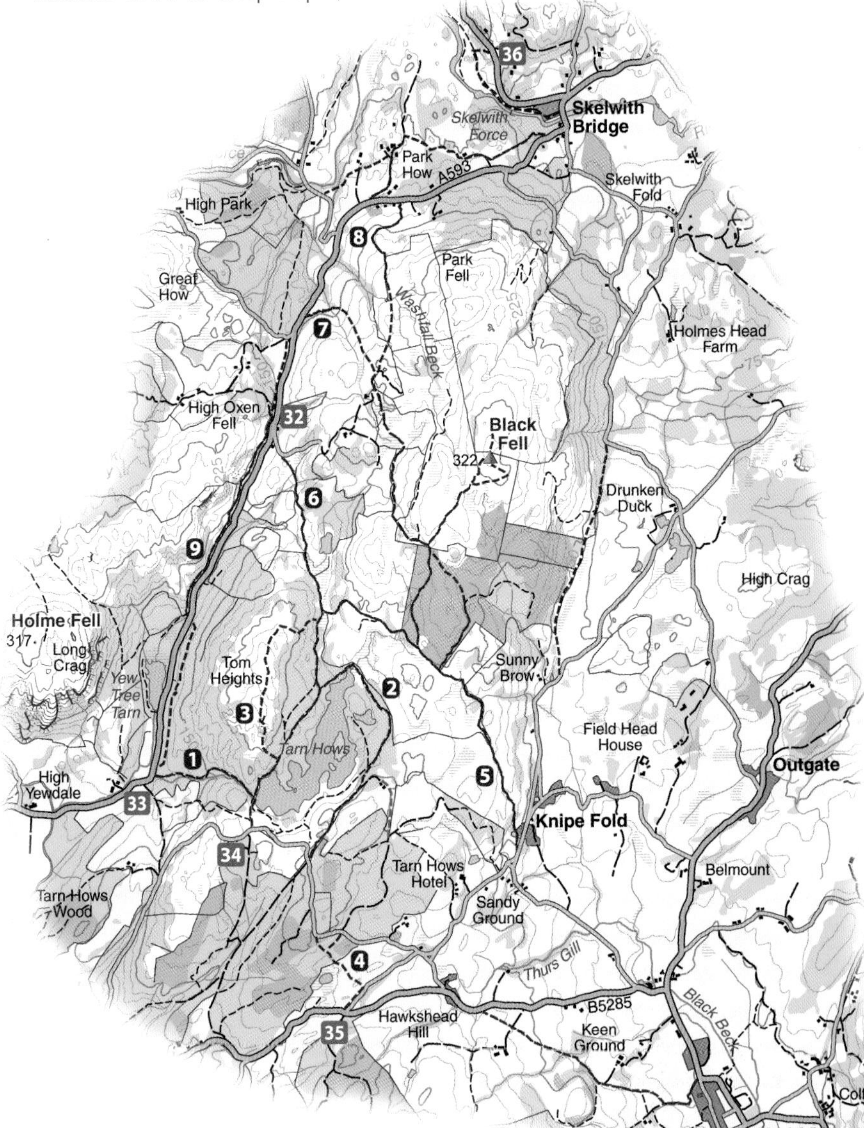

Wetherlam from Tarn Hows

View over Tarn Hows to Black Fell from the Scott Memorial

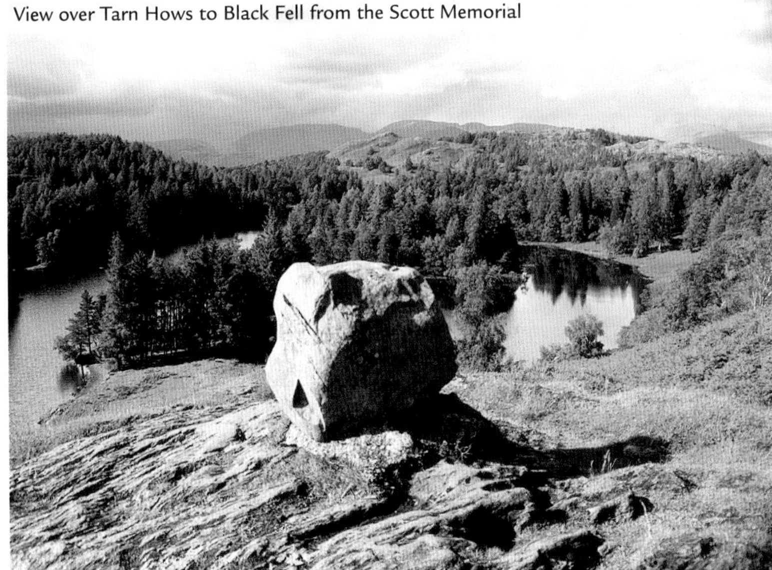

clearly visible to patrons tumbling out of the fashionable Drunken Duck Inn about half a mile away to the east.

Walkers enjoying the Cumbria Way, heading north from Coniston, understandably relish their encounter with Tarn Hows, but the majority are unaware of Black Fell. Cross-country routes have that knack of missing great locations when they fit awkwardly with their overall thrust. The lack of wear on the one path to the top shows that the actual number of visitors is quite modest, restricted to a small, discerning proportion of the multitude who stroll in the environs of Tarn Hows, but this summit is the perfect place to come for a first inspection of this marvellous landscape, the lie of both high land and low land superbly displayed.

ASCENT FROM TOM GILL (33) AND TARN HOWS (34)

Via Tom Heights 224m/735ft 4km/2½ miles

1 Visitors are naturally drawn to park at the main Tarn Hows car park. However, the far more exciting walk sets off from the smaller car park at Tom Gill. A stepped path climbs in harmony with the north bank of the beck in woodland, particularly revelling in the graceful waterfall in the upper section, below the dam. Of the two paths climbing on the south side, directly from the car park, one in the stony lane joins the one-way road, the other branches left, winding up pasture. Both have their special merit for easy descents. **2** From the dam a broad path, fit for an urban park, proceeds north. Every Tom, Dick and Harry, with canine accomplice or without, comes this way, the

The Mountain Road

majority simply enacting a clockwise circumnavigation of the tarn, admiring the rocky, marshy wild periphery from a distance. The northern continuation leads on to meet the fell-crossing lane, known as the Mountain Road, where Black Fell proper begins. **3** Readers of this guide, however, will need no second invitation to venture onto the wonderfully undulating top of Tom Heights. As the path makes the first rise into woodland go sharp left under an ageing larch. An obvious path climbing the bank winds up onto the rising ridge gaily decked with birch, each stepped knoll inevitably marked with a cairn. The cairned summit is a place to pause – perhaps wondering where all the people have gone. Gaze westward over Holme Fell to Wetherlam and north-eastward to Black Fell with the Near Eastern Fells behind. It seems no height has been climbed, but the wildness is profound. The ridge path threads on down north and then east through the tough growth. Taking damp ground in your stride, pass another prominent cairn to reach the broad path from The Tarns at the ladder-stile/gate entry into the Mountain Road. Follow this lane right (east), bound for an enclosure (marked as Iron Keld or 'iron well' on OS maps) with two access points.

The Windermere cairn

North to Helvellyn and Fairfield from Great Cobble

ASCENT FROM HAWKSHEAD (35)

Walkers approaching Black Fell from Hawkshead village can follow a footpath up to Hawkshead Hill (1.6km/1 mile) for either High Cross or the minor road via Borwick Lodge to enter the Mountain Road.

High Cross via Tarn Hows — 3.6km/2¼ miles

4 Bus travellers can alight from the Coniston Rambler service at High Cross at the northern tip of Grizedale Forest (Forest Enterprise car park). A well-defined path leads by Wharton Tarn via hand-gates through woodland, joining the formal trail passing Tarn Hows on either side to enter the Mountain Road at a hand-gate. Turn right to enter the enclosure at the next gate left, following the track uphill to exit onto the fell proper and climb the ridge path mounting NNE to the prominent fell-top pillar.

Hawkshead Hill via Borwick Lodge — 5.2km/3¼ miles

5 From the hamlet of Hawkshead Hill follow the minor road to Borwick Lodge, just before Knipe Fold. Fork left onto the Mountain Road and walk up the walled lane, taking the first kissing-gate on the right into the enclosure. Keep to the track and then the path which sweeps up north-westward to meet the main track at the kissing-gate at the top of the enclosure and complete the climb (as described above).

ASCENT FROM OXEN FELL (32)

Via the Mountain Road — 164m/540ft — 2.7km/1¾ miles

Sheep-wash fold near the Park Fell bridleway

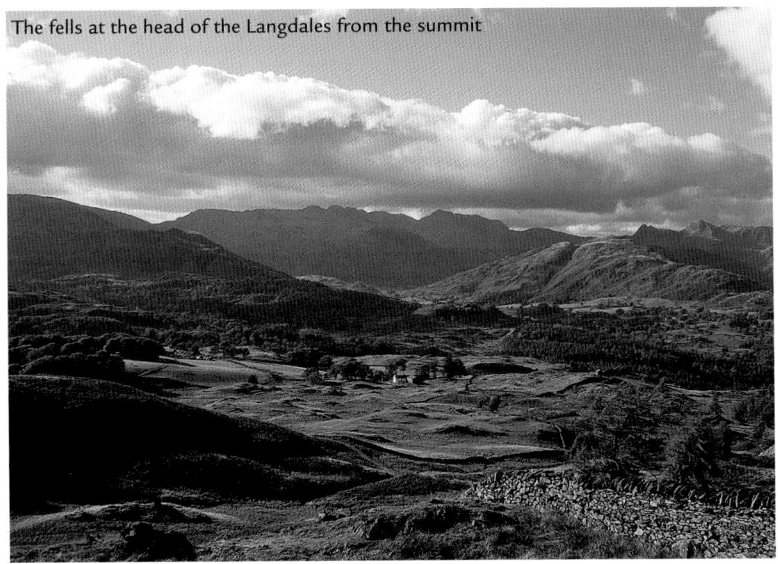
The fells at the head of the Langdales from the summit

6 From Oxen Fell High Cross the Mountain Road begins as a proper road, being access for High Arnside Farm, but quickly turns into a gravel trackway. This is a lovely walk with a succession of scenic turns. Passing the Tarn Hows access gate the lane winds up and levels under Arnside Intake advancing to a gate entry, left, into the enclosure. The National Trust has made considerable strides in removing most of the misfit conifer trees in the enclosure, to restore a more natural wooded habitat within context of the overall estate. They certainly take their custodianship of this national treasure seriously.

ASCENT FROM HIGH PARK ROAD-END AND SKELWITH BRIDGE (36)

Direct 2km/1¼ miles

7 An excellent 'quick way to the top' embarks from the High Park road-end upon a footpath commencing from a gate and short wooded lane, leading east. This descends momentarily with a wall left, then, where another footpath joins at a gate, climbs the pasture beside the same wall to a gate, coming up to merge with the Park Farm bridleway (Route 8).

Via Park Farm 6km/3¾ miles

8 From Skelwith Bridge and the Brathay Vale the National Trust Silverthwaite car park is the best starting point. This gives access to the riverbank path heading serenely downstream. Entering woodland, tight by the busy road, the river becomes tumultuous.

Skelwith Force is a real force to be reckoned with – and to admire. The fuming falls can be viewed from both banks. The footpath passes on by the Kirkstone Quarry workshops to cross Skelwith Bridge. Keeping company with the Cumbria Way head west via Park Farm to Low Colwith. Go left up the road to meet the A593, then to turn left along the main road and branch right after a bus shelter, through a gate onto the bridleway climbing the north-western side of Park Fell. The open track winds up with excellent views back to Lingmoor Fell and the great swelling heights about Great Langdale. By gates the track passes a sheepwash fold on the right and winds on by Low Arnside cottage. Coming up to the top of the enclosure find the path to the summit branching left.

9 Walkers wishing to complete an off-road circuit of the fell having begun at Tom Gill can follow a footpath as they come off Route 7. It rises, fenced, inside the pasture on the west side of the A593 at the High Park road-end and continues directly over at Oxen Fell High Cross, dipping down into the wooded dell beneath Holme Fell. You can then either cross the road at a ladder-stile before Yew Tree Tarn to trace the woodland path under Tom Heights, or follow the path on the western side of the tarn.

THE SUMMIT

Black Fell has a conclusive rock summit, adorned with a stone-built OS pillar. Old maps give it the somewhat over-dramatic name Black Crag. While it may be generally true that it is better to travel than to arrive, this is a spot well worth arriving at. Black Fell has its aficionados, regulars who readily extol its virtues as a place to soak up a rejuvenating view, time and again. In the course of the preparation of this guide the author made just two visits, each time meeting regulars whose love of the landscape

Black Fell summit

Black Fell from Holme Fell

was reinvigorated by this one place. The view is an utter joy. The Coniston Fells loom large to the west with the fells simply crowding into the great northerly arc, Scafell Pike and Great End making sneaky guest appearances either side of Bowfell. Also in view are the Langdale Pikes and Blencathra through the Thirlmere trench, with Helvellyn and Fairfield, Red Screes and the Kentmere fells leading to a long Pennine skyline beyond Windermere. Arguably the best views in that direction are to be found on the ridge over the ladder-stile, purposefully installed to facilitate visitors' desire to venture onto the headland. There is no means of reaching a public road from this northerly enclosure, and for all the cairns on the lower north top of Park Fell, walkers are encouraged to step back over the ladder-stile and retreat the way they came, perhaps with a slight detour to enjoy a prominent viewpoint cairn down on the eastern shoulder of the fell, less than 200m away – definitely a place to frequent and enjoy the wooded vale towards Windermere. Although this cairn is flagging from age, its retains much of its original fine construction, so at busy times walkers have at least three excellent viewing stations to share out between them.

SAFE DESCENTS

Take care not to clamber over walls or stray from paths. Woodland thicket and giraffe-high bracken await the wayward wanderer. Simply backtrack to the enclosure then either take the Park Fell bridleway to go north, or pass on down through the enclosure to join the Mountain Road for points east, west or south.

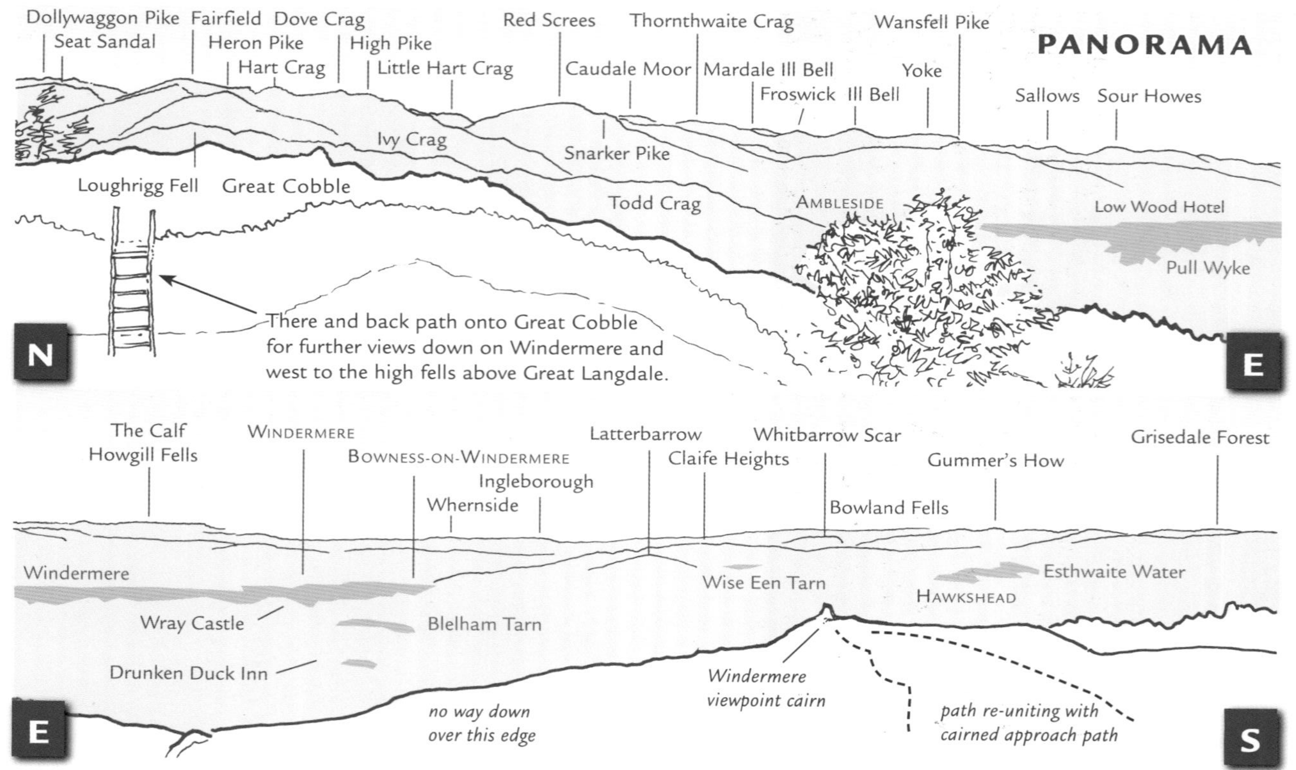
PANORAMA
Dollywaggon Pike
Seat Sandal
Fairfield
Heron Pike
Dove Crag
Hart Crag
High Pike
Little Hart Crag
Red Screes
Caudale Moor
Thornthwaite Crag
Mardale Ill Bell
Froswick
Ill Bell
Yoke
Wansfell Pike
Sallows
Sour Howes
Ivy Crag
Snarker Pike
Loughrigg Fell
Great Cobble
Todd Crag
Ambleside
Low Wood Hotel
Pull Wyke
There and back path onto Great Cobble for further views down on Windermere and west to the high fells above Great Langdale.
N
E
The Calf
Howgill Fells
Windermere
Bowness-on-Windermere
Ingleborough
Whernside
Latterbarrow
Claife Heights
Whitbarrow Scar
Bowland Fells
Gummer's How
Grisedale Forest
Windermere
Wise Een Tarn
Esthwaite Water
Hawkshead
Wray Castle
Blelham Tarn
Drunken Duck Inn
no way down over this edge
Windermere viewpoint cairn
path re-uniting with cairned approach path
E
S

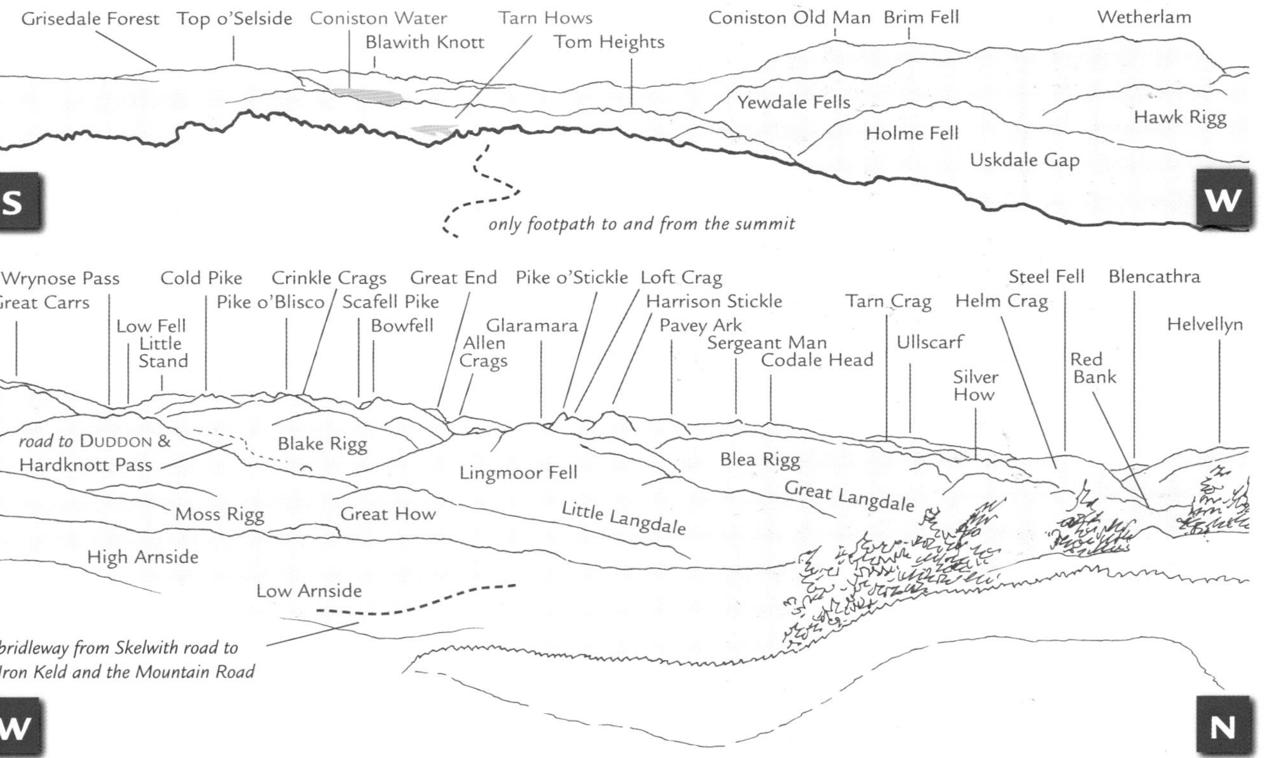
Grisedale Forest
Top o'Selside
Coniston Water
Blawith Knott
Tarn Hows
Tom Heights
Coniston Old Man
Brim Fell
Wetherlam
Yewdale Fells
Hawk Rigg
Holme Fell
Uskdale Gap
S
W
only footpath to and from the summit
Wrynose Pass
Great Carrs
Cold Pike
Low Fell
Little Stand
Crinkle Crags
Pike o'Blisco
Scafell Pike
Bowfell
Great End
Allen Crags
Glaramara
Pike o'Stickle
Loft Crag
Harrison Stickle
Pavey Ark
Sergeant Man
Codale Head
Tarn Crag
Ullscarf
Silver How
Helm Crag
Steel Fell
Red Bank
Blencathra
Helvellyn
road to DUDDON &
Hardknott Pass
Blake Rigg
Lingmoor Fell
Blea Rigg
Great Langdale
Moss Rigg
Great How
Little Langdale
High Arnside
Low Arnside
bridleway from Skelwith road to
Iron Keld and the Mountain Road
W
N

3 BRIM FELL *(795m, 2608ft)*

Literally the 'brim' of the Coppermines Valley skyline, comprising the lion's share of the Old Man ridge yet subjugated to ancillary rank on grounds of altitude, Brim Fell cradles two wind-whipped tarns, Levers Water and Low Water, either side of a blunt ridge which ends abruptly at Raven Tor. Below the cliff runs the lateral Boulder Valley, which in its lower portion harbours some extraordinary chunks of rock, of which The Pudding Stone is the biggest. (It has one easy scrambling ascent for those with the aptitude and inclination.) At the head of the Boulder Valley lie fenced clefts associated with possibly the oldest coppermine in the area, Paddy End. The most striking feature here is Simon's Nick, prominent as you climb up Leverswater Beck, beneath which characteristic brown iron oxide spoil scree spills out.

With so much attention directed at the Old Man of Coniston it seems likely that anyone seen climbing Brim Fell is there by mistake. I certainly have twice encountered walkers on the upper slopes of Brim Fell in glorious sunshine nervously enquiring whether 'this is the way to the Old Man'. Some walkers clearly reach Low Water, walk over to its outflow thinking that they are on the main path and, then having crossed the outflow, find that any hint of a path disappears. Instead of backtracking they head on up the inviting grassy slope to the saddle to the rear of Raven Tor and climb Brim Fell, oblivious of their error. In fact it is a master-stroke, for this is definitely the finest way onto the main ridge.

 ↑ Brim Fell from Great How Crags

Viewed from the west, Brim Fell has few endearing qualities. Its shattered cliff and scree provide a conclusive eastern headwall of the Seathwaite Tarn valley. The unrealistic marking of a footpath into this wild hollow from Levers Hawse is a cruel mystery that Ordnance Survey mapping should rectify for the sake of delicate ankles and necks. One hopes that not too many walkers have relied on their otherwise meticulous cartography in hostile conditions and presumed this a safe recourse. It isn't!

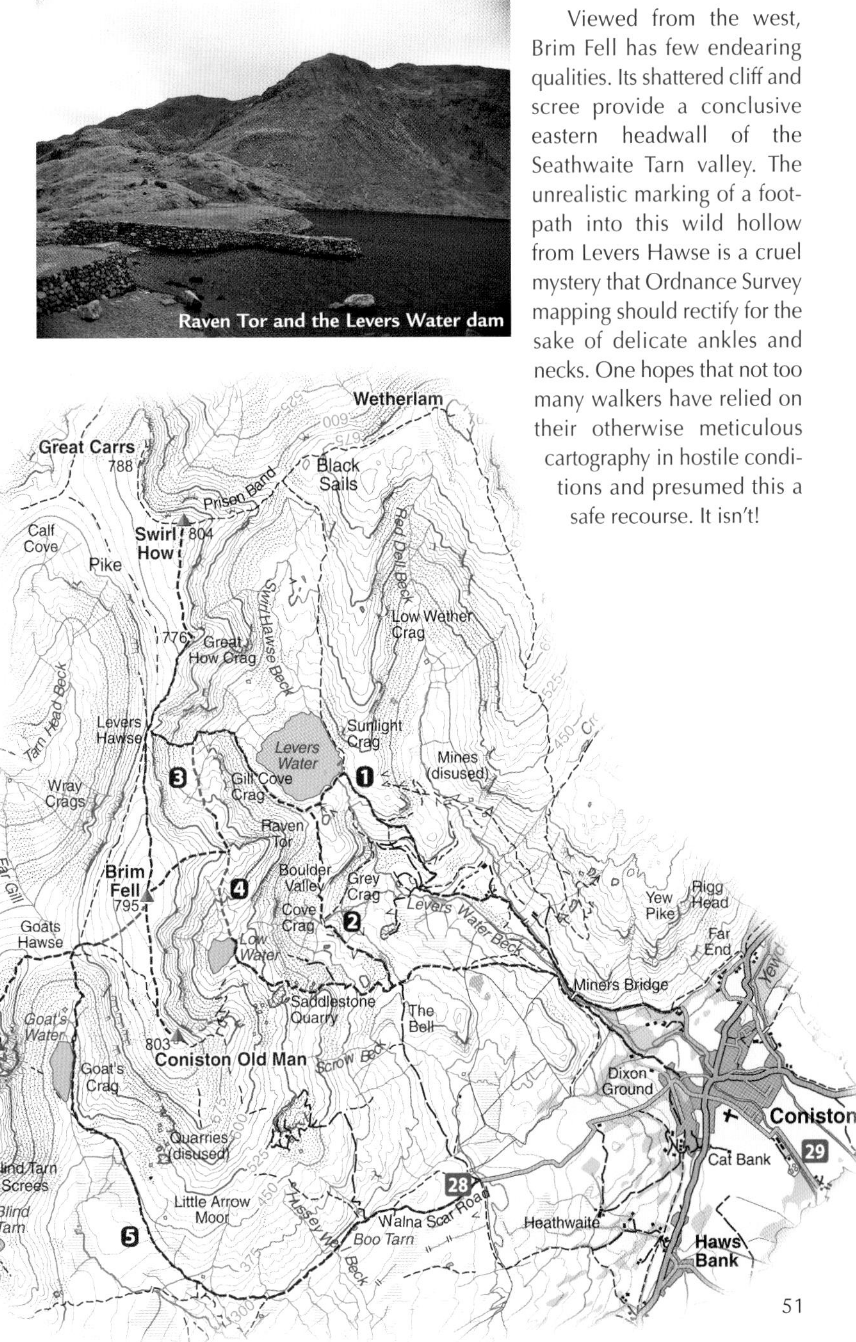

Raven Tor and the Levers Water dam

ASCENT FROM CONISTON (29)

Via Levers Water 746m/2450ft 5km/3 miles

1 Start from the bridge in the centre, beside the Black Bull Hotel and brewery in Coniston main street. Follow either the road and open valley access track on the north side of Church Beck, or cross the beck and turn right, beginning along the Walna Scar Road and turning right after the Sun Hotel following a signpost to the 'Old Man' via Dixon's Ground. From either route, at Miners Bridge join the main valley track on the right bank of Levers Water Beck that leads on to the Coppermines Youth Hostel, the former coppermine captain's office. The continuing track winds on up, dominated towards the end by the massive cleft of Simon's Nick, part of the Paddy End copper workings. Finally it reaches the outflow and dam of Levers Water, cradled in a wild corrie rimmed with crags, where the large boulder sitting in the tarn

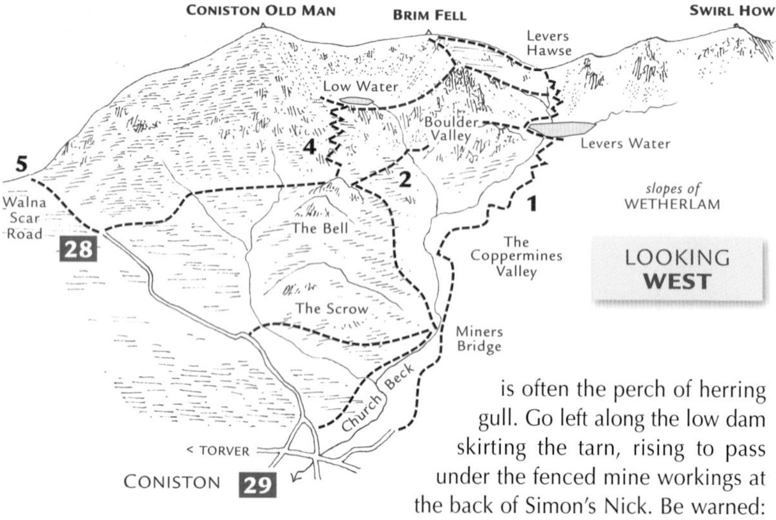

is often the perch of herring gull. Go left along the low dam skirting the tarn, rising to pass under the fenced mine workings at the back of Simon's Nick. Be warned: the mine workings are a death trap, shafts running many hundreds of feet down into the fell, tracing the rich veins of copper sulphite and the preserve of well-equipped speleologists only. **2** A popular path veers left at this point, crossing the brow left and wending down the intriguing Boulder Valley to pass the Pudding Stone after a plank footbridge. It then joins an old quarrymen's track leading back to The Bell cutting.

Otherwise, follow the clear, if rough, path contouring above the tarn beneath Raven Tor. After fording one gill it veers uphill with Cove Gill, steeper sections suitably pitched. Little How Crags are up to the right. Keep to the well-made path as it rises, avoiding the loose scree which appears to offer a more direct route. The ground

Mine enthusiast abseiling into the Simon's Nick/Paddy End coppermine, adjacent to Levers Water

Swirl How from the north ridge

steepens still further with consistent pitching zig-zagging to Levers Hawse, where the main ridge route is joined. Turn left, due south to reach the summit cairn. **3** An intriguing alternative branches south before the main stepped section begins and accompanies Cove Gill into the cove recess, slipping over a saddle to find a faint path across a loose section leading to the skyline col directly behind Raven Tor. The going is all easy but in mist you should stay with the main path to Levers Hawse.

Via Raven Tor 5.7km/3½ miles

4 The way up from Low Water is a splendid route, predominately on grass, something one cannot say about the quarryman's path onto the Old Man. Follow the walkers' highway to Low Water (see CONISTON OLD MAN Route 1 (page 81)). Branch right upon arrival at the tarn, threading through the large boulders haphazardly gathered among the moraine and cross the outflow. Head north up the grassy slope to the saddle to the rear of Raven Tor. Make a brief detour up the bank right to the cairned top of the Tor and look through the notch across the airy gulf to Great How Crags. Back at the saddle turn left (due west). Minor broken outcrops lead onto the plateau. Pass a large cairn amongst clitter ('fragmented bedrock'), en route to the main summit cairn.

Seathwaite Tarn and Harter Fell from the north ridge

ASCENT FROM WALNA SCAR ROAD FELL-GATE (28)

Via Goat's Hawse 570m/1870ft 4.8km/3 miles

5 By normal convention this route is used as an easy-on-the-knees descent, ideal for the round trip (see CONISTON OLD MAN Route 4 (page 85)). Follow the regular path from the Walna Scar Road to Goat's Water and up to Goats Hawse. Take the main path towards Coniston Old Man, curving up from the hawse, but then branch half-left and climb the grass slope direct to the summit.

Brim Fell summit cairn

Great How Crags from Raven Tor

THE SUMMIT

Although the fell-top of Brim Fell is gently domed and almost bereft of surface features, the summit cairn, composed of thick wafers of bedrock slate, is a gem, a solid pile far grander than the cairn on Swirl How. The view is only hampered by the extent of the plateau but it is brimful of detail as the panorama shows.

SAFE DESCENTS

In misty conditions put your faith in either Levers Hawse, due N, with its well-pitched path E leading down to Levers Water, or Goats Hawse SW, with a steady descent S down by Goat's Water and The Cove to join the Walna Scar Road, in both instances seeking the shelter of Coniston. Goats Hawse also provides a safe line NW into the Seathwaite Tarn valley for the Duddon Valley.

RIDGE ROUTES

CONISTON OLD MAN ↓25m/80ft ↑30m/100ft 0.8km/½ mile

Head S keeping steep ground several strides length to the left.

DOW CRAG ↓150m/490ft ↑130m/425ft 1.2km/¾ mile

Descend the grassy slope SW to Goats Hawse joining the regular path curving round from W to S to the summit bastion.

SWIRL HOW ↓110m/360ft ↑120m/390ft 2.4km/1½ miles

Follow the ridge on its steady descent to Levers Hawse, which, like Link Hause on the Fairfield Horseshoe, is not a cross-over pass! A definite path contours above Calf Cove towards the namesake Fairfield saddle beneath Grey Friar, while the actual ridge route climbs NNE glancing by the consecutive tops of Little How Crag and then the more significant Great How Crag. Beyond weave through the irregular surface outcrops to the summit.

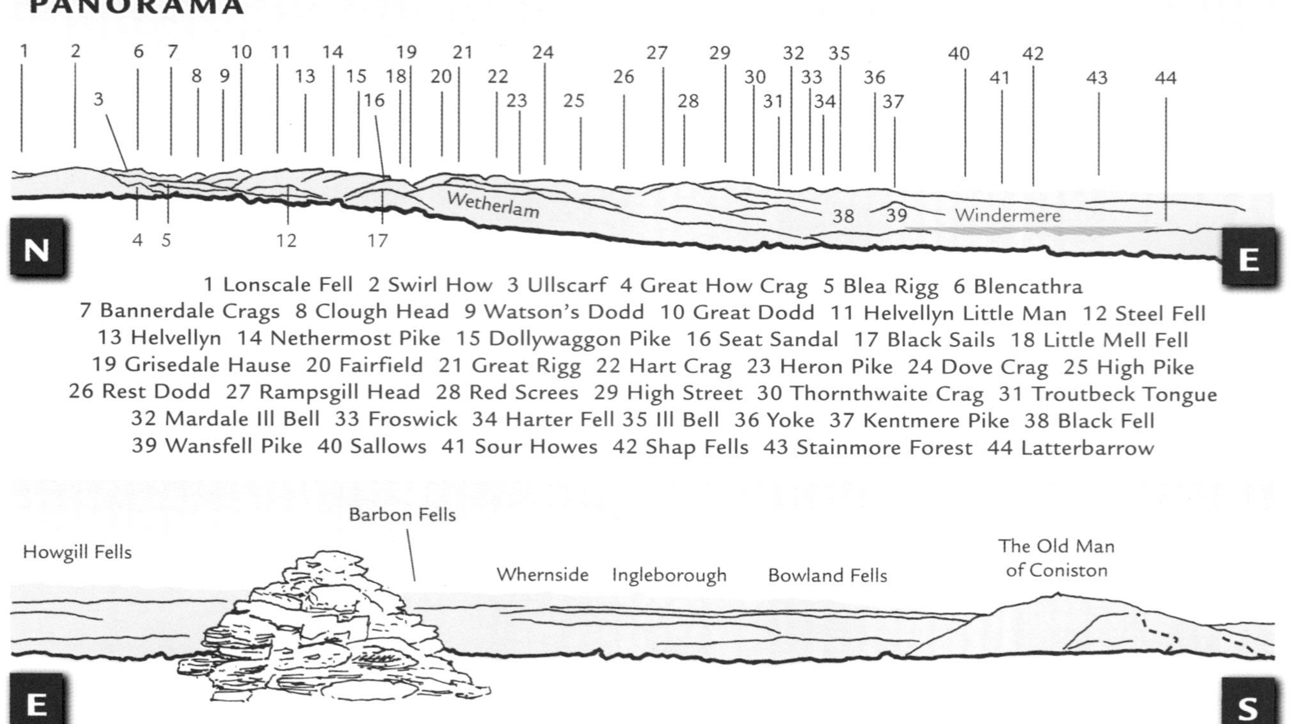
PANORAMA
N
E
Wetherlam
Windermere
1 Lonscale Fell 2 Swirl How 3 Ullscarf 4 Great How Crag 5 Blea Rigg 6 Blencathra
7 Bannerdale Crags 8 Clough Head 9 Watson's Dodd 10 Great Dodd 11 Helvellyn Little Man 12 Steel Fell
13 Helvellyn 14 Nethermost Pike 15 Dollywaggon Pike 16 Seat Sandal 17 Black Sails 18 Little Mell Fell
19 Grisedale Hause 20 Fairfield 21 Great Rigg 22 Hart Crag 23 Heron Pike 24 Dove Crag 25 High Pike
26 Rest Dodd 27 Rampsgill Head 28 Red Screes 29 High Street 30 Thornthwaite Crag 31 Troutbeck Tongue
32 Mardale Ill Bell 33 Froswick 34 Harter Fell 35 Ill Bell 36 Yoke 37 Kentmere Pike 38 Black Fell
39 Wansfell Pike 40 Sallows 41 Sour Howes 42 Shap Fells 43 Stainmore Forest 44 Latterbarrow
Barbon Fells
Howgill Fells
Whernside
Ingleborough
Bowland Fells
The Old Man
of Coniston
E
S

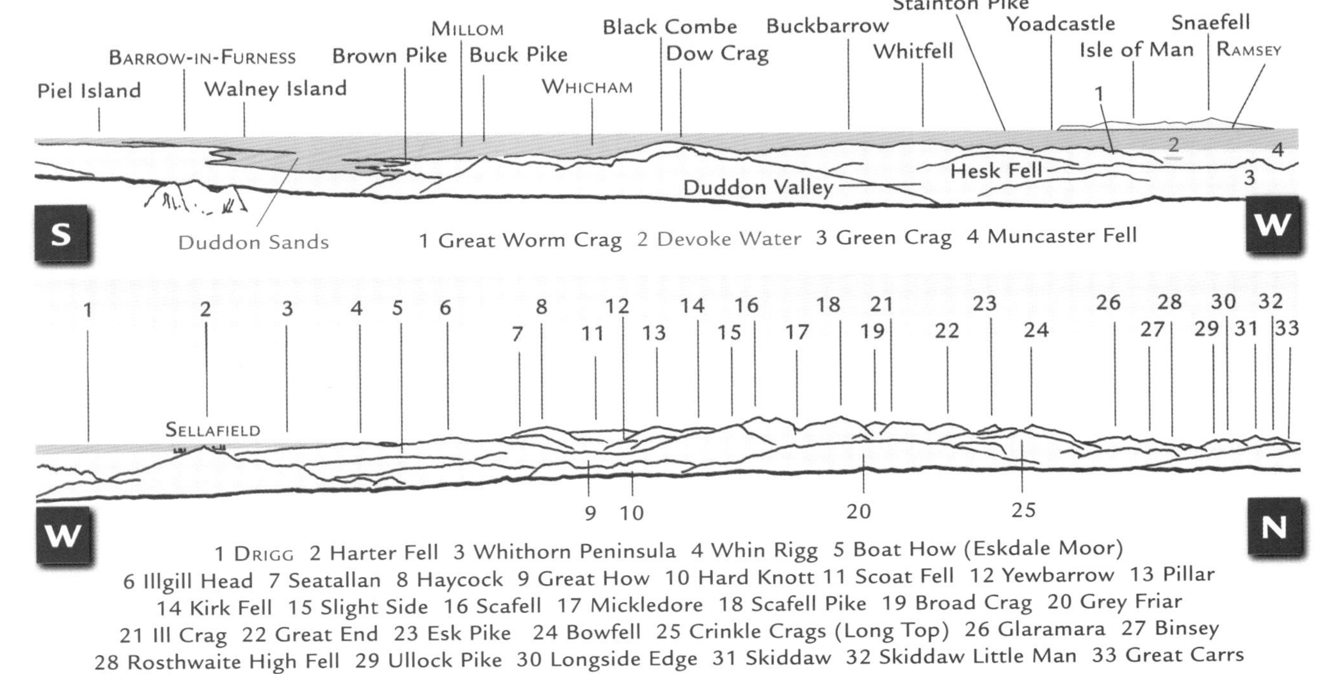

Sellafield (formerly known as Windscale and Calder Hall) appears either side of the summit of Harter Fell

↑ Looking south from the summit of Buckbarrow

4 BUCKBARROW *(549m, 1801ft)*

The name Buckbarrow means 'the gathering place of young bucks' (red deer) but older bucks (*Homo sapiens*) now have the run of the place – the deer have fled. The summit area is an oasis of mountain lakeland, with three, if not four, rocky tops to explore. It shares with the crest of Stoneside Hill a sense of rugged wildness, a welcome contrast to the sleeker lines of Black Combe and Whitfell. Access to this felltop could not easier; a gently rising ridge-wall leads from the Corneyfell Road summit straight into the midriff of the summit mass on Great Paddy Crag, but the summit itself is well-defended with rocky ground.

Fellwalkers eyeing linear outings will see the pleasure in a 'Bootle to Boot' connection, or the 'Black Combe to Devoke Water' ridge route, and in either case Buckbarrow makes a most satisfying early objective. From the Corneyfell Road rise the uninviting fenced western slopes of Prior Park – the name indicative of medieval monastic deer enclosure. The eastern slopes run down over the unlikely tilled Plough Fell, angling south over Thwaites Fell to end in the old coppice woodland at the foot of the Duddon Valley. Here is possibly the fell's greatest treasure, namely the remarkably extant remains of Duddon Bridge iron blast furnace which ran on locally sourced charcoal, succumbing to the greater efficiency of coke in 1867. A bridleway from the site climbs onto the fell, via the subsidiary top, Barrow.

ASCENT FROM THE CORNEYFELL ROAD (13)

Direct 150m/490ft 2 km/1¼ miles

1 Park at the road summit, follow the clear path north in harmony with the ridge wall. As Great Paddy Crag rears there is the element of choice. Either slant up right threading through boulders and outcrops onto the summit with only spasmodic hints of a path, or bear left, keeping beside the fence under the boulder bank, passing a curious wind-shelter-like object. Then head west-north-west to a gateway and mount the easy slope to reach the western scarp-top summit of Kinmont Buck Barrow. The cairn here, which rests upon a more ancient predecessor, is a smaller version of one on Whitfell summit, although this top surveys a great sweep of land and ocean. Backtrack to the gateway and slant half-left

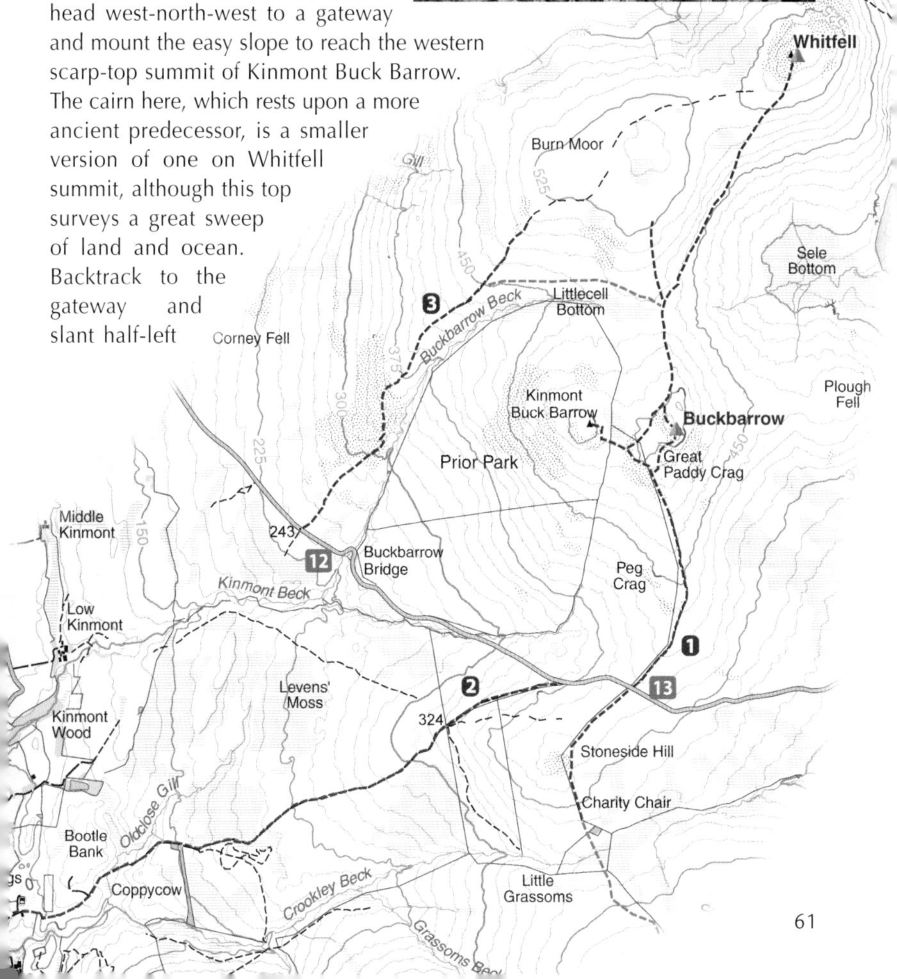

Black Combe from Kinmont Buck Barrow

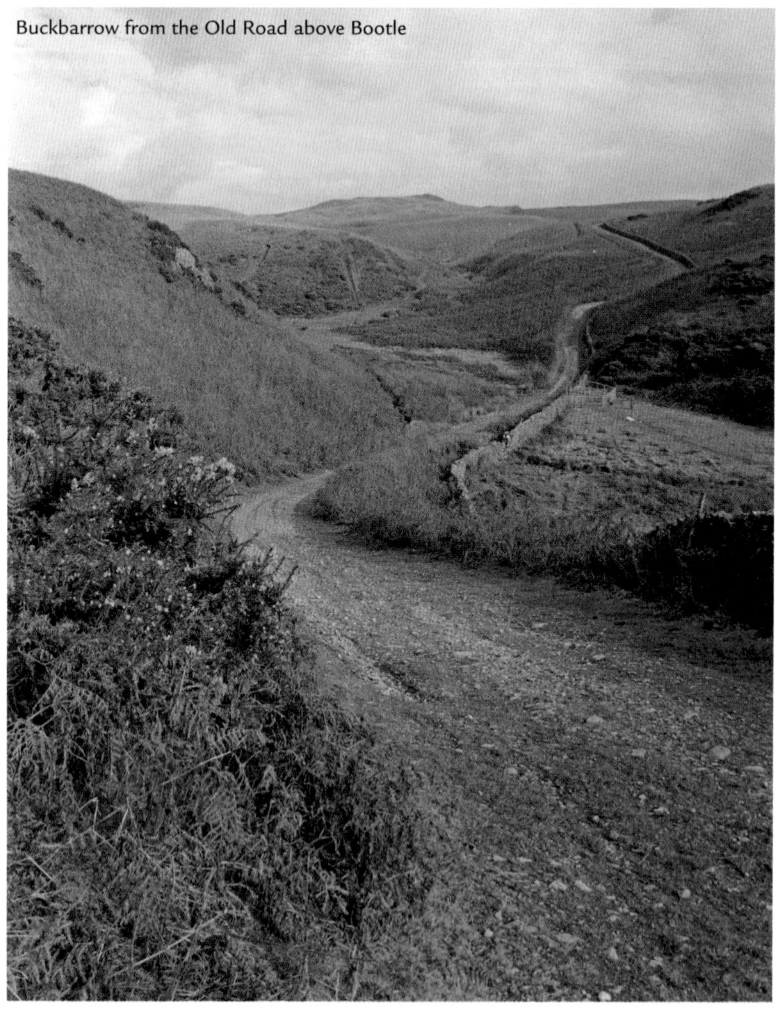

Buckbarrow from the Old Road above Bootle

via a broken wall to reach the main summit of Buckbarrow up the boulder slope, or continue with the ridge path down towards Littlecell Bottom and Whitfell.

Ascent from Bootle (14) 530m/1740ft 8km/5 miles

2 The honest ascent starts from Bootle following the old road up from Fellgreen. A pleasure to stride along, the open byway is a firm green ribbon winding up into a lane to meet the Corneyfell Road some 250m west of the road summit. From the road summit follow Route 1.

Ascent from Buckbarrow Bridge **(12)** 330m/1080ft 3.7km/2¼ miles

3 Follow the green track, originally made for peat extraction on the plateau of Burn Moor, directly up from the open road. Watch for the shepherd's quad bike marks forking right off the green-way short of Hare Raise – if you meet the perpetrator in misty conditions it could indeed be hair-raising! Contour round the northern side of the Littlecell Bottom marsh linking up with the ridge path coming from the north off Burn Moor. Head south, perhaps keeping among the outcrops for greater interest up to the summit.

THE SUMMIT

This rocky crest would not be out of place anywhere in Lakeland. In fact, it is very reminiscent of Cold Pike, but with a rather different view. Take time to savour it, particularly northwards towards Whitfell drawing attention to the majesty of the central Lakes.

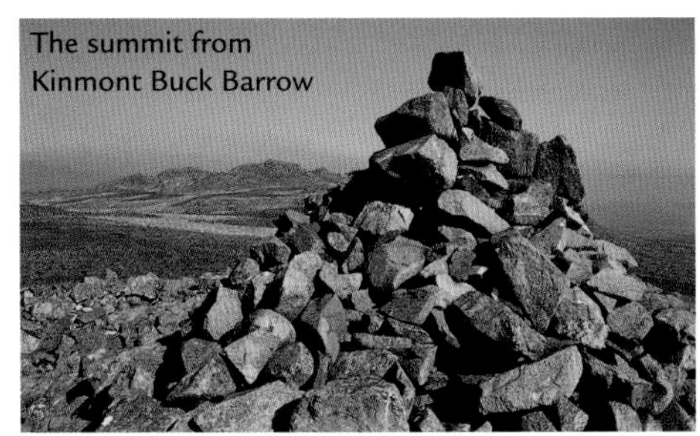
The summit from Kinmont Buck Barrow

SAFE DESCENTS

Follow the ridge wall S off Great Paddy Crag ('frog's rocks') to the summit of the Corneyfell Road. (The traffic is so frequent that you may be tempted to thumb a lift!) The nearest settlement is Bootle down the Old Fell Road which branches into a lane going WSW some 200m from the road summit.

RIDGE ROUTES

BLACK COMBE **↓230m/760ft** **↑290m/955ft** **7km/4¼ miles**

For much of the way a wall, then a fence, act as guides. Although this land is open access there are, as yet, no stiles. Follow the ridge wall off Great Paddy Crag crossing the Corneyfell Road and mounting onto the rocky hillock of Stoneside Hill. Descend S looking for a suitable gap through the decrepit wall and netting fence near the sheepfold at Charity Chair. Pass the stunted conifer spinney, and skip over the ditch to follow a low bank to a fence junction. Step over this tall obstacle and continue up the rough moorland with the fence to the left. Near the brow step over the plain fence immediately beyond the barbed fence junction and continue over Whitecombe Moss, to join with the path from the Whitecombe Beck valley that runs above the steep escarpment of Whitecombe Screes and rises onto the summit SW.

WHITFELL **↓70m/230ft** **↑95m/310ft** **2.4km/1½ miles**

Head N, crossing Littlecell Bottom, and contour across Burn Moor's eastern slopes before rising to the summit.

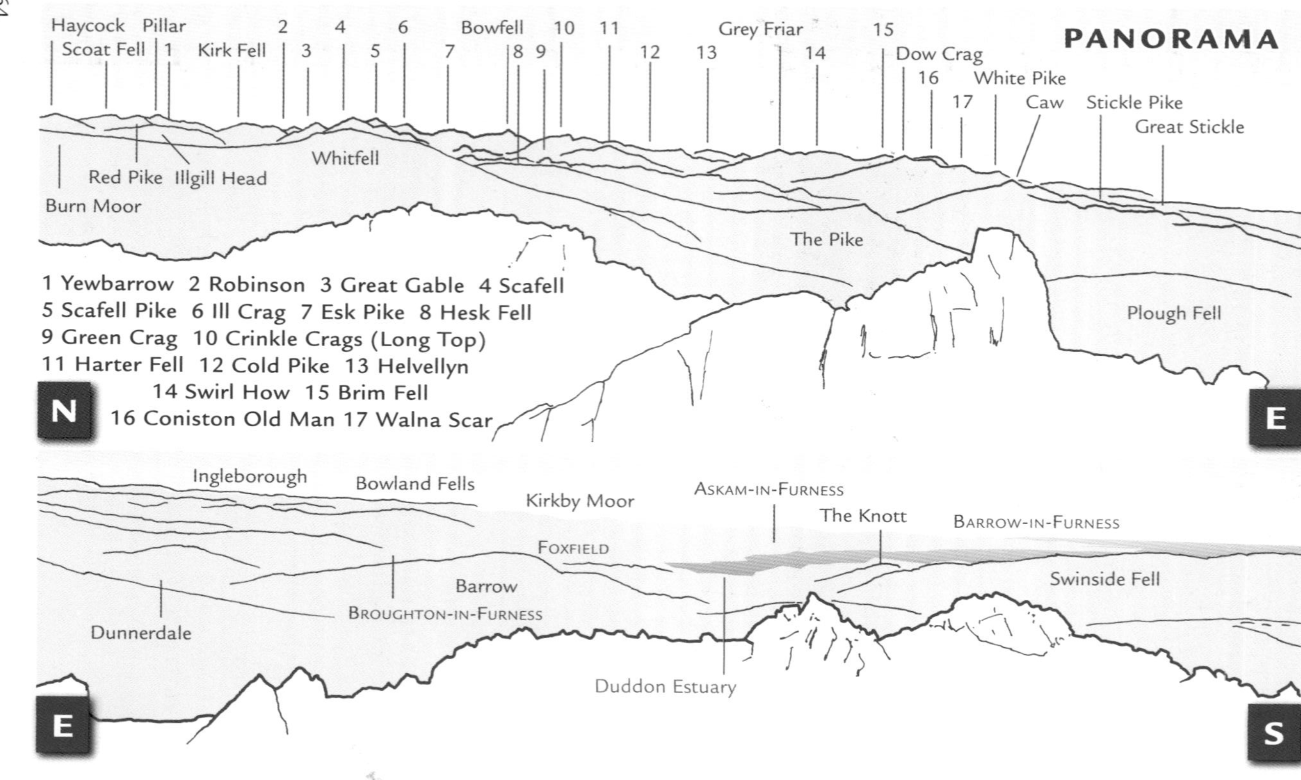
PANORAMA
Haycock
Scoat Fell
Pillar
1
Kirk Fell
2
3
4
5
6
7
Bowfell
8
9
10
11
12
13
Grey Friar
14
15
Dow Crag
16
17
White Pike
Caw
Stickle Pike
Great Stickle
Red Pike
Illgill Head
Burn Moor
Whitfell
The Pike
Plough Fell
1 Yewbarrow 2 Robinson 3 Great Gable 4 Scafell
5 Scafell Pike 6 Ill Crag 7 Esk Pike 8 Hesk Fell
9 Green Crag 10 Crinkle Crags (Long Top)
11 Harter Fell 12 Cold Pike 13 Helvellyn
14 Swirl How 15 Brim Fell
16 Coniston Old Man 17 Walna Scar
N
E
Ingleborough
Bowland Fells
Kirkby Moor
Askam-in-Furness
The Knott
Barrow-in-Furness
Foxfield
Swinside Fell
Barrow
Broughton-in-Furness
Dunnerdale
Duddon Estuary
E
S

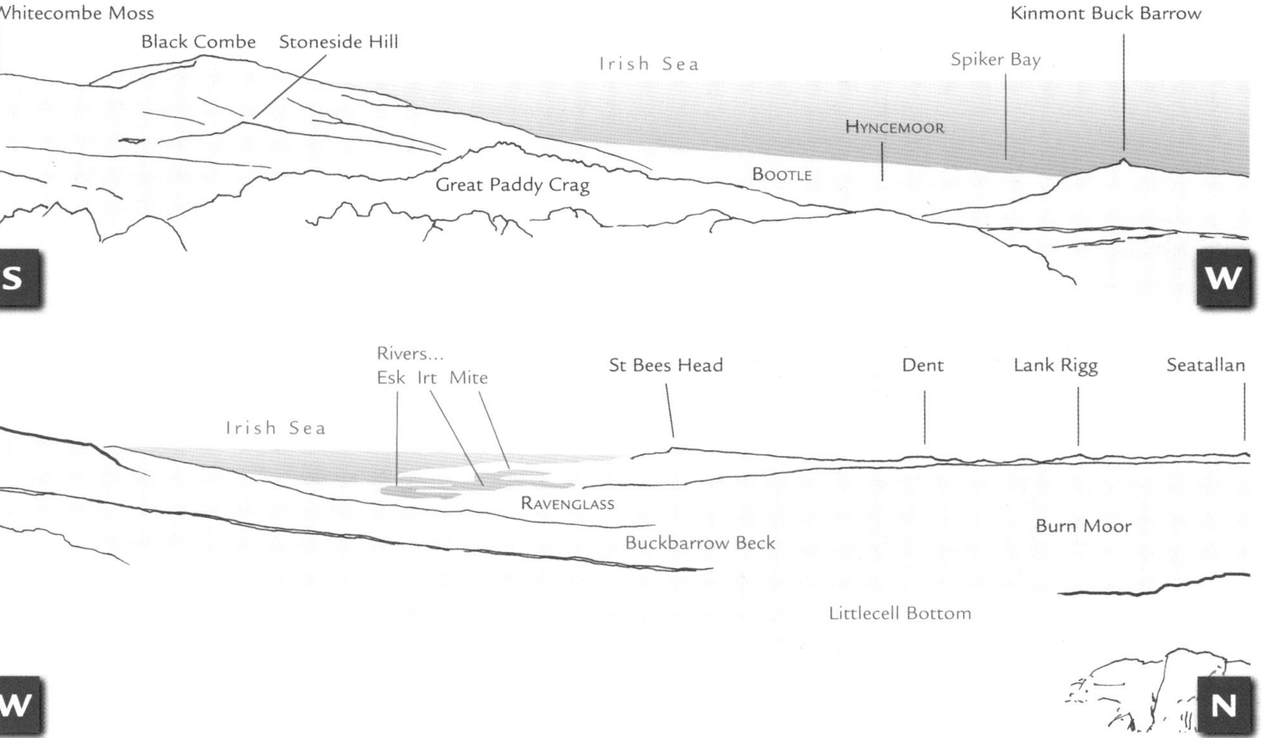
Whitecombe Moss
Black Combe
Stoneside Hill
Irish Sea
Spiker Bay
Kinmont Buck Barrow
Hyncemoor
Bootle
Great Paddy Crag
S
W
Rivers...
Esk Irt Mite
St Bees Head
Dent
Lank Rigg
Seatallan
Irish Sea
Ravenglass
Buckbarrow Beck
Burn Moor
Littlecell Bottom
W
N

5 CAW *(529m, 1736ft)*

Viewed from Ulpha this is a real peak, a fell that simply demands to be climbed. Caw is highly individual with a presence disproportionate to its size, catching the eye from as far away as the M6. From within the Duddon Valley its gracefully chiselled profile looms even larger. If you stand on its summit you can see its central importance to an appreciation of that most beautiful of dales, as the northern slopes fall quickly away beneath your feet, giving a fabulous outlook towards the Scafells.

The fell-name sounds corvine, though is probably associated with a former breeding ground of red deer. It is defined to the east and west by the Rivers Lickle (a unique name, the earliest known spelling (c1180 'Licul') and Duddon respectively. Bridleways flank it on both sides, giving interesting approach options, and there is much rock on all sides, its several subsidiary pikes adding immeasurably to any ascent.

The Duddon from the Caw slate mine

 ↑ Caw from Bobbinmill Bridge

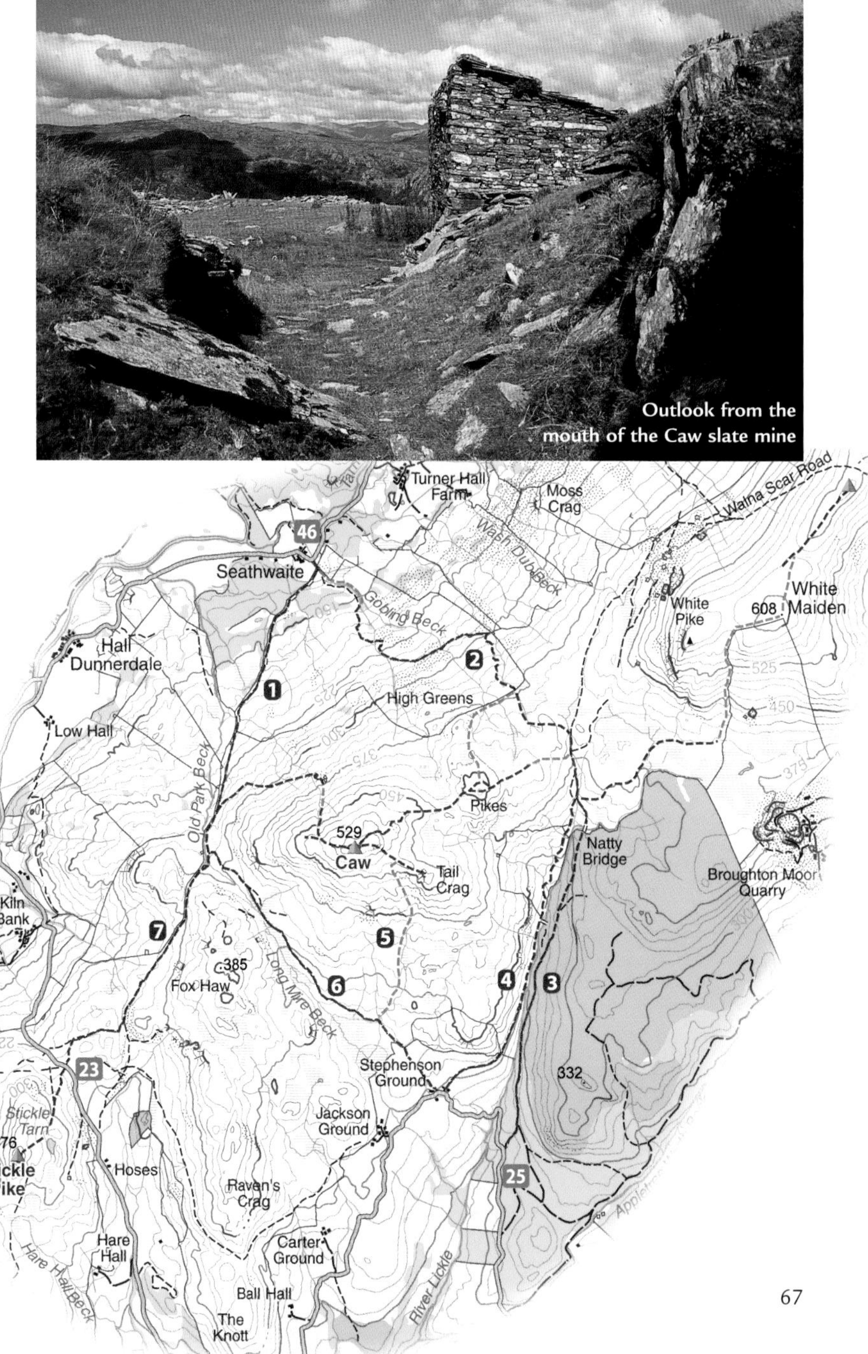

Outlook from the mouth of the Caw slate mine

Caw slate mine incline

ASCENT FROM SEATHWAITE (46)

Via Park Head Road 425m/1395ft 2.5km/1½ miles

1 From the road bend 100m east of the Newfield Inn, pass through the gated sheep pen onto the rough cart track of Park Head Road up by a gate, close to Old Park Beck, and look for the stone-retained incline branching up left. Stride at ease up the soft turf, in contrast to the grinding graft of the hobnail booted slate quarrymen and their ponies for whom this steep way was a laborious trod. The tooling shed and spoil heap mark the end of the original path. The mine level invites a tentative peer – to judge by the quantity of slate in the heap it must run deep into the fell. The hint of a continuing path now mounts the grassy rake above (south-south-west), eventually bending left to the summit.

Via Pikes 455m/1490ft 3.3km/2 miles

2 A less than obvious drove-way branches off the Park Head Road left immediately clear of the sheep pens. Keep Gobling Beck to the left as you rise over marshy ground, then climb a bracken bank, fording the beck left, to curve around a rush patch now onto a far clearer green path. This slips through a gateway (note the old stoup stone lying here) and contours north-east before winding up the enclosure to a hurdle in the boundary wall. Either trend right along the wall and south to clamber over Green Pikes or keep with the continuing path up Yaud Mire to embark on the easier ridge heading south-west to the summit of Pikes. Descend, via a ramp, into the hollow with more than the hint of a ridge path advancing to the main summit mass.

ASCENT FROM THE LICKLE VALLEY (25)

Via Natty Bridge 262m/860ft 4km/2½ miles

Four routes stem from the vicinity of Water Leat Bridge (GR239930), situated two miles upstream of Broughton Mills, at the edge of the Broughton Moor Forest Enterprise estate. **3** From the forest gate, 300m to the south of the bridge (GR239928), enter the part-cleared plantation beneath The Knott, on a clear if infrequently used forest track. Three wheeling buzzards indignantly responded to the author's presence above the tall conifer stand. The track wends up the valley nearing the juvenile Lickle with the rough slopes of Caw clearly in view. (As the mature plantation gives way to younger stock you will see a path branching down left which leads to an elegant flag footbridge otherwise hidden from the track. If you take this, you can proceed along the west bank path and pass through a wall and join the continuation of the forest track on the open fell beyond Natty Bridge.)

Keeping with your forest track, pause at the next turning space to admire, to your left, the waterfall spilling from the combe south of Pikes – a prominent summit later in this ascent. Shortly the track ends at a stile just before an attractive ravine. A serviceable wooden bridge has replaced the old stone-arched Natty Bridge, now almost entirely washed away with only a fragment remaining. Pause again on the bridge to appreciate the cascades – the term 'natty' here meaning 'chattering stream'.

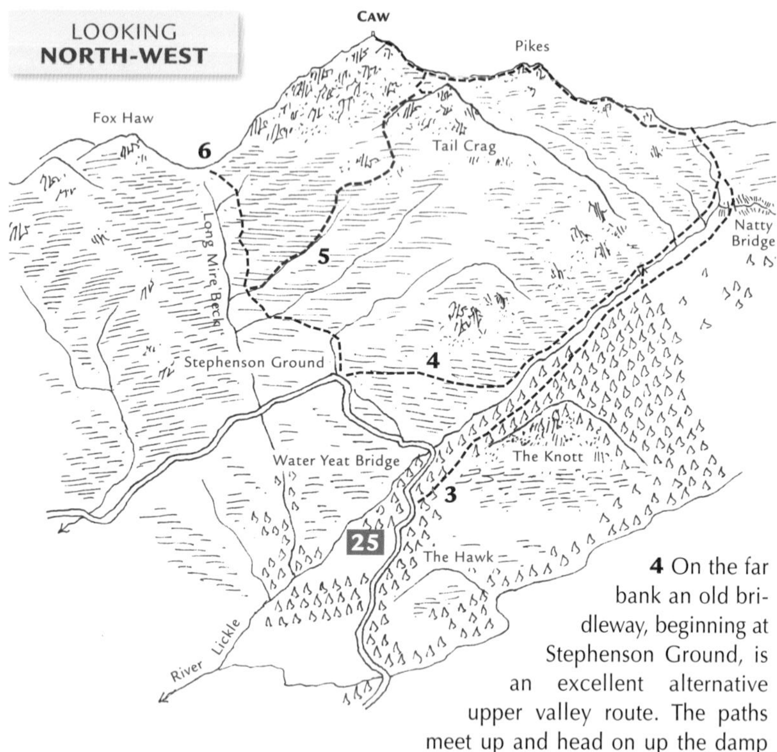

4 On the far bank an old bridleway, beginning at Stephenson Ground, is an excellent alternative upper valley route. The paths meet up and head on up the damp fell towards a shallow pass, whose ultimate destination is the old Walna Scar Quarry. Carry on until you reach a point where a path bears sharply right off the main path, across from a small outcrop on your left. Leave the main path to round the outcrop, in a westerly direction with no hint of a path. Clamber onto the top of the first rise and look north-eastward to the dominant peak of White Pike, the prow of Walna Scar and southern limit of the principal mountain mass of the Coniston group – a most impressive sight. With only the slightest hint of a path, walk on up the south-westerly trending ridge, passing a lovely pool en route to the rocky peak of Pikes. This makes a good intermediate point to rest and consider the Duddon scene. Continuing on, a path trends down right, into the hollow, before setting its sights on the main summit. (This path would be unreliable in mist.) The path becomes clearer and then splits momentarily before the steep final pull to the pillar.

Via Tail Crag **370m/1215ft 2.2km/1½ miles**

5 From the forest gate parking space walk along the road to cross Water Yeat Bridge. The road winds uphill, closing eventually on the farmhouse at Stephenson Ground. Take the gate right immediately short of the farmhouse, where two bridleways start,

Mountain bikers on the road up to Stephenson Ground

Black Combe from Tail Crag

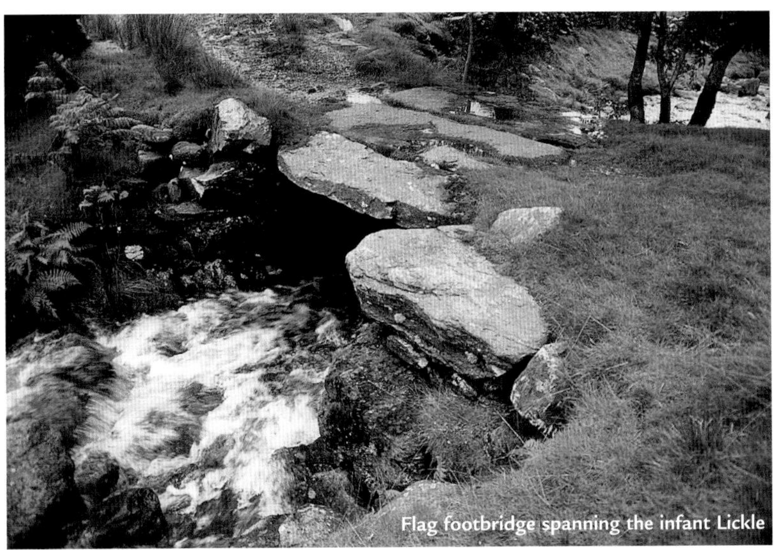
Flag footbridge spanning the infant Lickle

signed 'Walna Scar' and 'Seathwaite'. Take the latter path, passing up by the house to enter a walled lane. The walling deserves a close look, particularly after the ford mid-way up, see how the gill is ushered through and admire the corresponding wall stiles (neither relevant to ramblers) and sheep creeps, the left-hand an unusual arched form with original blocking stone in situ. After the hand-gate exit the lane. Follow Broadslack Beck up through the bracken and outcrops onto the ridge between Tail Crag and Caw, detour right for Tail Crag and return north-west to rise to the summit.

Via Long Mire Beck 400m/1310ft 3.7km/2¼ miles

6 Follow Route 5 from Water Yeat Bridge to the end of lane, and then follow Long Mire Beck north-west up to the turf trail over the hause to merge with the Park Head Road, bearing up the quarry incline, just south of Route 1.

ASCENT FROM DUNNERDALE BECK VALLEY (23)

Direct 320m/1050ft 3.5km/2¼ miles

A further link approach, **7**, starts at the Kiln Bank Cross hause at the head of the Dunnerdale Beck valley. Follow the Park Head Road green-way to the Caw slate mine incline and join Route 1.

THE SUMMIT

Caw has the perfect summit, but for the imposition of a now-redundant white concrete triangulation pillar – redundant, except in a strong breeze when balancing a camera steady for the classic view towards the Scafells.

SAFE DESCENTS

There are crags on all fronts, the most notable being Goat Crags on the blunt western end, so sticking to a path is important. If heading for the Duddon aim for the Park Head Road, though look out for your right-hand fork some 50m down the north slope. This leads into a grassy rake and down to the slate mine. Bear left here with the incline. The broken southern slope has not a single path, outcrops and later bracken hampering progress down by Broadslack Beck to join the Long Mire bridleway, leading into the green lane and the road at Stephenson Ground.

RIDGE ROUTES

STICKLE PIKE ↓300m/960ft ↑150m/480ft 3.6km/2¼ miles

Heed the advice on descent to Park Head Road via Caw slate mine (see Safe Descents), then keep with the track SSW over Brock Barrow hause to the open road at Kiln Bank Cross. Cross the road and continue on a clear path heading up the bank in the same direction, climbing to the compact summit.

Caw summit

The Duddon from the drove-way

WALNA SCAR ↓60m/190ft ↑85m/270ft 4km/2½ miles

There are two options. Firstly, follow the ridge NE over Pikes to meet the bridleway emerging from the head of the Lickle Valley. Then, either follow its continuation north passing below Walna Scar Quarry to join the Walna Scar Road up to the pass, or link with the ascent of White Maiden from the vicinity of Natty Bridge, via Caw Moss (see WALNA SCAR Route 3 (page 213)).

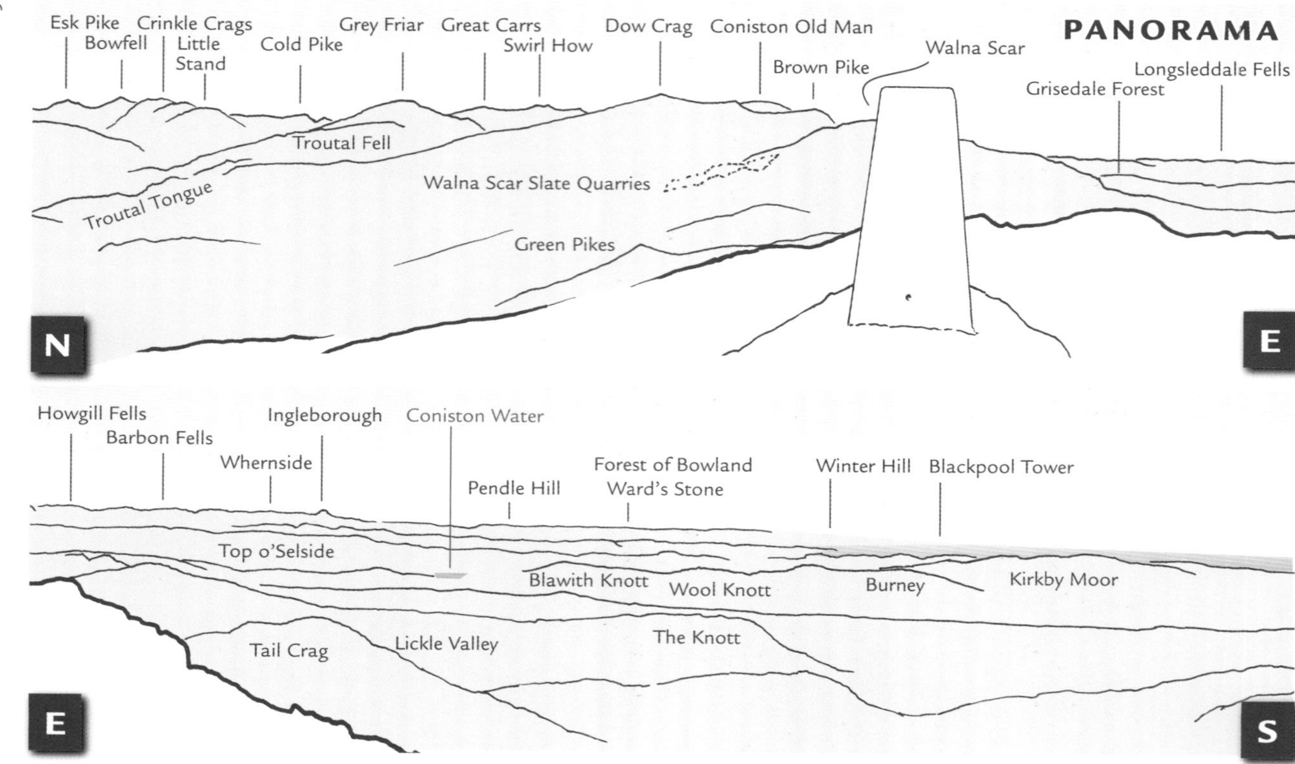
PANORAMA
Esk Pike
Bowfell
Crinkle Crags
Little Stand
Cold Pike
Grey Friar
Great Carrs
Swirl How
Dow Crag
Coniston Old Man
Brown Pike
Walna Scar
Grisedale Forest
Longsleddale Fells
Troutal Fell
Troutal Tongue
Walna Scar Slate Quarries
Green Pikes
N
E
Howgill Fells
Barbon Fells
Whernside
Ingleborough
Coniston Water
Pendle Hill
Forest of Bowland
Ward's Stone
Winter Hill
Blackpool Tower
Top o'Selside
Blawith Knott
Wool Knott
Burney
Kirkby Moor
Tail Crag
Lickle Valley
The Knott
E
S

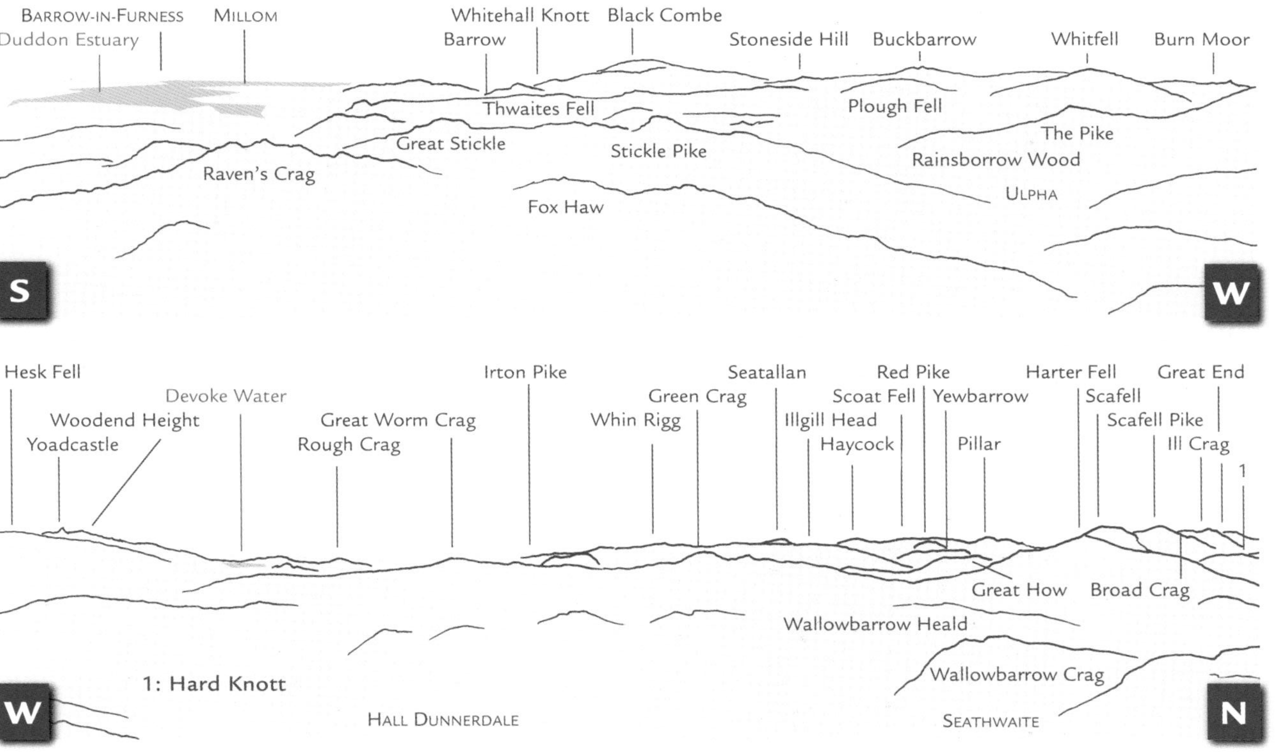
Barrow-in-Furness
Millom
Duddon Estuary
Whitehall Knott
Black Combe
Barrow
Stoneside Hill
Buckbarrow
Whitfell
Burn Moor
Thwaites Fell
Plough Fell
Great Stickle
Stickle Pike
The Pike
Raven's Crag
Rainsborrow Wood
Ulpha
Fox Haw
S
W
Hesk Fell
Irton Pike
Seatallan
Red Pike
Harter Fell
Great End
Devoke Water
Green Crag
Scoat Fell
Yewbarrow
Scafell
Woodend Height
Great Worm Crag
Whin Rigg
Illgill Head
Scafell Pike
Yoadcastle
Rough Crag
Haycock
Pillar
Ill Crag
1
Great How
Broad Crag
Wallowbarrow Heald
Wallowbarrow Crag
W
Hall Dunnerdale
Seathwaite
N

1: Hard Knott

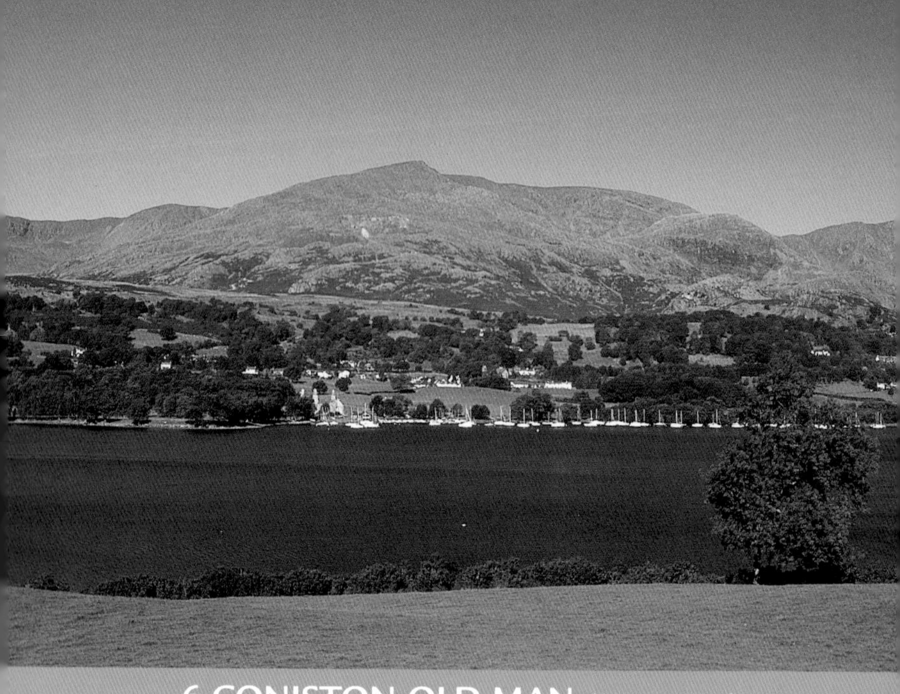

6 CONISTON OLD MAN *(803m, 2635ft)*

As life turns fads and fashions change, but not so readily mountains. The old allure lingers and such a distinguished fell as the Old Man of Coniston has laid claim to regular, even daily, visits from time immemorial. The climb up this long slate staircase is always rewarded by a life-enhancing sensation of being on top of a worthier world. An industrial wasteland of mineral and slate extraction fades away as the fellwalker's eyes take in the sumptuous panorama of mountain Lakeland. Yet this ever-popular summit is only the start of a magnificent line of fells which reaches its culmination a little under two miles further north on Swirl How. Walkers are naturally drawn to follow a clockwise horseshoe from Coniston ending with the descent from Wetherlam back into the Coppermines Valley. Mercifully the intrinsic qualities of the eastern combes leading down to the village of Coniston have not been spoilt by stone extraction, and there is even much to intrigue in what remains of the workings.

Visitors curious to know more about the history of mining in the valley should consult Eric G. Holland's *Coniston Copper Mines: A field guide* and, for greater depth, his *Coniston Copper – A history* both published by Cicerone Press, although the latter is now out of print.

The correct name for the fell is the Old Man of Coniston, although it is colloquially known, and labelled on many maps, as Coniston Old Man. Harry Griffin called it the 'kindly monarch', an appropriate image as the fell-name literally meant 'high boundary stone' for a small Viking kingdom centred upon Coniston Water. John

 ↑ Coniston Old Man from Brantwood

Ruskin took daily delight in the view of the Old Man from his home, Brantwood, across the lake. One of the most important influences on Victorian attitudes to the natural world, Ruskin would be in tune with contemporary taste with his love of this mountain. He felt that mountains were the beginning and end of all that is truly scenic and pilgrims to Brantwood will see no cause to doubt his judgement.

Coniston is a service centre village, rare in Lakeland, where the visitor and the local can find most things to meet their needs – from launches to lunches, micro-brewing to cultural exhibitions – the principal attraction,

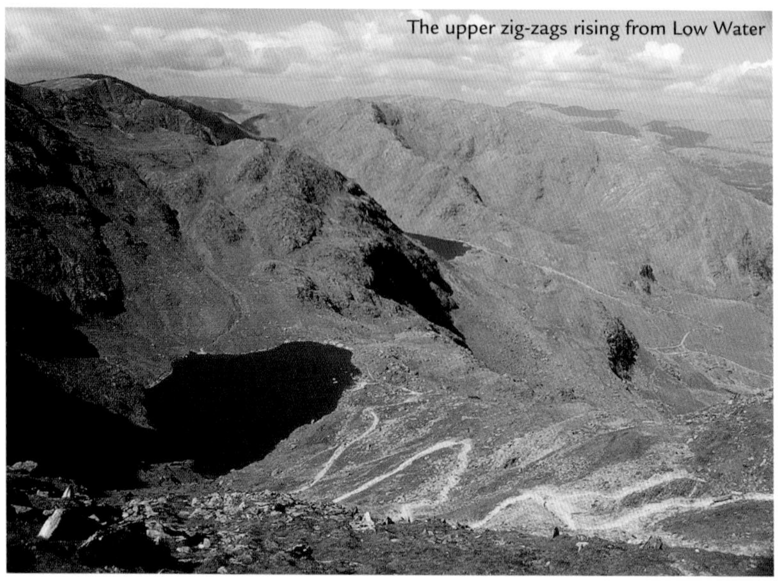
The upper zig-zags rising from Low Water

the Ruskin Museum, quite the most absorbing of its kind. Here you can learn not just the robust detail of an agrarian and industrial heritage, but witness the influence of great people on the locality, from Donald Campbell to Ruskin himself. Visit and be inspired!

Coniston from the Old Man

There are three principal routes to the summit of the Old Man, its position at the end of the ridge giving more scope for tortuous trails than many walkers realise. Invariably large parties of walkers traipse up the fell directly on Routes 1 and 2; the discerning, in their ones and twos, find the best of the fell by starting from the Walna Scar Road and either following Route 3 to wind up the whale-back south ridge above Burstingstone, or approaching from the west by The Cove and Goats Hawse on Route 4.

ASCENT FROM CONISTON (29)

Direct 753m/2470ft 4.3km/2½ miles

The Old Man in springtime

1 From the bridge in the middle of the village you have two routes to Miners Bridge. Either take the road past the Black Bull (the Old Man Ale can wait) and turn left by the Ruskin Museum on a road which rises to become an open track, or cross the bridge and climb the lane, turning right behind the Sun Hotel to a gate at Dixon Ground and an open path advancing to a kissing-gate, with Church Beck close right. At the gate on Miners Bridge the two routes come together. Keep to the south bank soon to climb diagonally up the slope through hand-gates, with open views of the extensive spoil and remaining buildings of the Coppermines Valley (including the youth hostel) over to the right. At the saddle between The Bell and the main fell, join the track coming up from the Walna Scar Road fell-gate (Route 2).

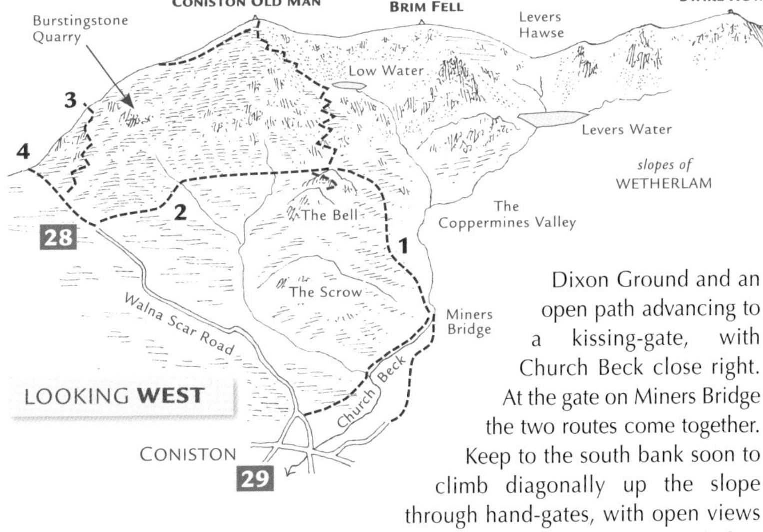

Saddlestone Quarry

Climb up the main ascending quarryman's track, passing various features of the Saddlestone Quarry – working platforms with track, winding gear and ruined tooling steds – stark reminders of hard toil of another age. The massive Saddlestone Quarry (fenced to ward off casual visitors) has an eerie interior, with much loose rock. Mercifully, the nature of the slate here was inferior to the regular planes of Snowdonian slate, so the level of development was nowhere near as great. Arrival at Low Water gives a final excuse to pause before tackling the final narrow, winding quarry path up the northern slope. For all the repair work that is done on this popular path, loose slate continues to give discomfort.

ASCENT FROM THE WALNA SCAR ROAD FELL-GATE (28)

One wonders how many walkers come to Coniston, park down Lakes Road, flog up the long, narrow Walna Scar Road to reach the fell-gate and then stare in dismay – not at the massive bulk of the fell ahead, but rather at the large car parking area in front of them. If you do leave your car at the bottom, you can console yourself that the climb thus far was a good warm-up for the rigours ahead. From the car park two options are apparent. **2** Go right along the open track to link with the direct Route 1. This gives you an opportunity to visit the top of The Bell, a mini-mountain and a superb situation offering an intimate view of the Coppermines Valley and a modest objective to have under your belt if mist scuppers the rest of the day.

Via Little Arrow Moor — 555m/1820ft — 3.2km/2 miles

3 Quite the better option follows the Walna Scar Road (an open cart track) westward. Passing the foot of the Burstingstone Quarry track – the quarry is still occasionally active, hence the metal barrier – notice a footpath sign directing right for the 'Old Man'. This climbs the bank drifting leftward onto a shoulder of Little Arrow Moor. An older path runs on across the eastern slope above the quarry, but this has fallen from favour and is now rarely used. The popular path comes close to the edge overlooking The Cove, then bears up right onto the upper ridge, with no hazards.

The Old Man from Low Water

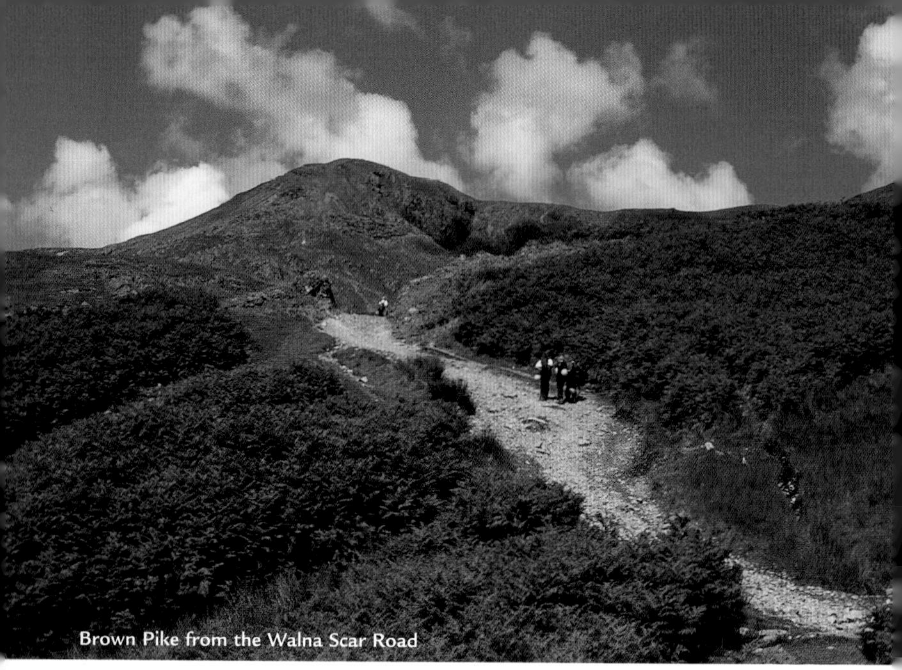

Brown Pike from the Walna Scar Road

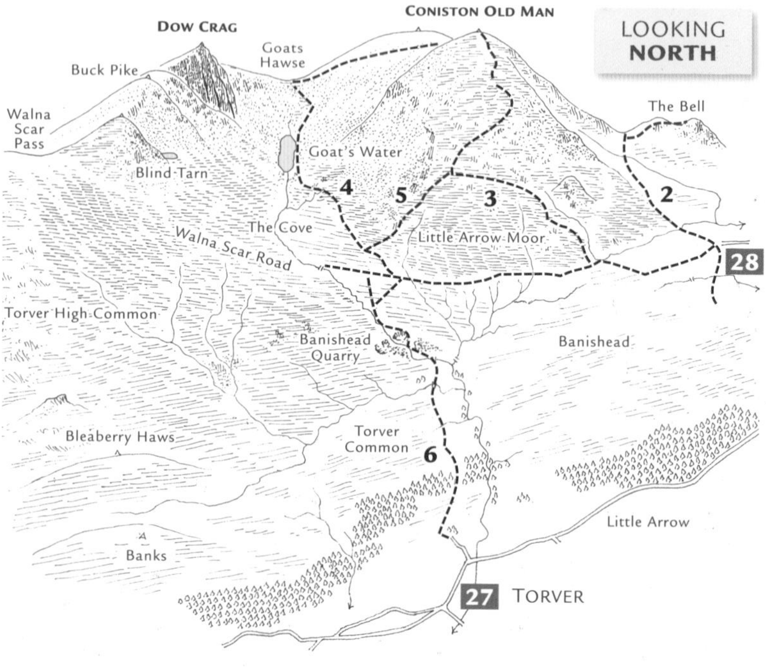

DOW CRAG
CONISTON OLD MAN
LOOKING NORTH
Goats Hawse
Buck Pike
Walna Scar Pass
The Bell
Goat's Water
Blind Tarn
4
5
3
2
The Cove
Little Arrow Moor
Walna Scar Road
28
Torver High Common
Banishead Quarry
Banishead
Bleaberry Haws
Torver Common
6
Little Arrow
Banks
27 TORVER

Via The Cove 560m/1840ft 5km/3 miles

4 Alternatively, continue with the Walna Scar track as it rises through two rock cuttings to branch right up steps onto a clear, part-pitched path traversing into The Cove. **5** An old green path can be followed right up to a ruin. This was originally an access route to the old quarries high up on the SW slope of the Old Man. When this path bends left at the ruin, carry straight on up the pathless slope from the ruin to the skyline to join the Little Arrow Moor path, just where it hits the edge. To stay with Route 4, follow the more popular path up The Cove, over the Goat Crag rock step and along the eastern shore of Goat's Water. The pitched path winds up to Goats Hawse depression, then swings naturally up right to the summit, the path never in doubt. Sadly, the erosion is all too apparent. This route is most frequently used as an easy descent for jaded knees.

ASCENT FROM TORVER (27)

Via Banishead Quarry 695m/2280ft 6.4km/4 miles

Banishead Quarry with Torver Beck spilling into the pool to soak away mysteriously

6 At Torver park at the Church Hall (£1 donation requested) next to St Luke's and the Church House Inn, or at the road-end off the bend of the main road (GR285945). Follow the lane up by Scarr Head entering a gated bridle lane signed to 'Walna Scar'. Pass ruined barns following another sign to 'Tranearth'. Cross a concrete bridge, with Tranearth Climbers' Hut over to left. (Tranearth meant 'ground frequented by great cranes', now only found in continental Europe.) Continue to a hand-gate through sheep-handling pens to a gate and over the wooden bridge. Keep to the main track, up through the slate tips to swing round the fenced Banishead Quarry.

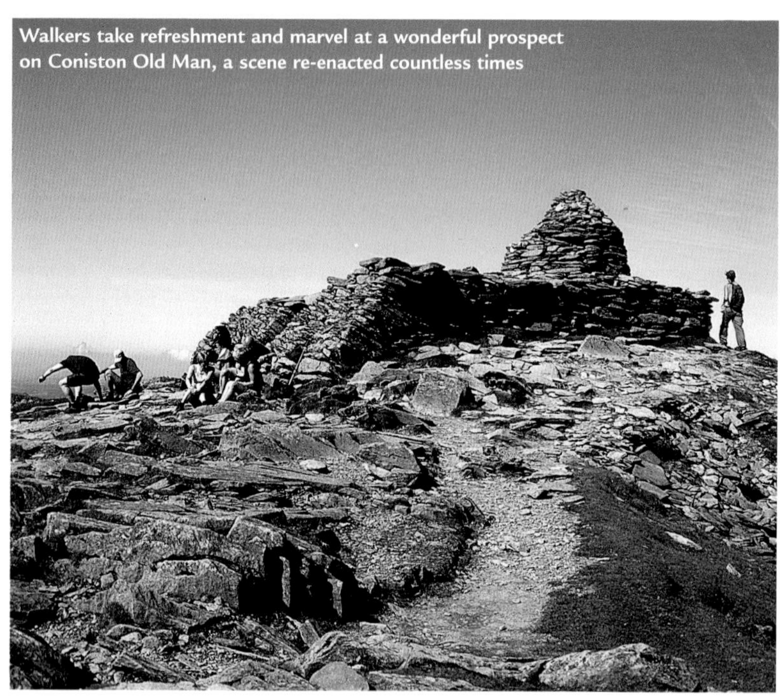
Walkers take refreshment and marvel at a wonderful prospect on Coniston Old Man, a scene re-enacted countless times

At the western end Torver Beck falls into the pool at the base of the quarry and soaks away through a cave. The route ascends the bracken bank, with several green ways to choose from to merge with the Walna Scar track (Route 4).

THE SUMMIT

The drystone viewing platform and cairn are now depleted (the old cairn was a handsome edifice twice the height of the present one) and in need of a serious facelift. There is also a stone-built OS column, an ideal leaning post while you gaze awestruck, the profound drop beneath your feet into the hanging valley of Low Water making you feel as if you're above the clouds. This is the best view in the Coniston group, across the Coppermines Valley to Wetherlam, backed by ridge after ridge of wonderful fells, with the majestic Scafells appearing half-left. Wander left to look across at the face of Dow Crag. The ridge-edge location gives a sense of isolation and finality, with the fells one way and the wooded lowlands about Coniston Water and the sea southward. Some will also look down Morecambe Bay and spot the square block of Heysham Power Station and even stretch their gaze to Blackpool Tower, but the majority, having climbed this enigmatic height, will look north-east and feel on top of the world and thankful that they committed themselves to the climb, the pain melting away the instant they reached the brink.

SAFE DESCENTS

Wind is always a nuisance and, on occasion, a real danger on the fells. Prevailing south-westerlies encourage walkers to seek the shelter of the popular slate staircase down by Low Water heading directly for Church Beck. The most pleasant descent is without question by Goat's Water on the path heading NW from the summit. This curves down to the broad saddle of Goats Hawse, turns due S down the pitched path to skim the shores of Goat's Water and ventures on down The Cove to meet the Walna Scar Road. There, turn left for Coniston or straight on, by Banishead Quarry, for Torver.

RIDGE ROUTES

BRIM FELL **↓30m/100ft** **↑25m/80ft** **0.8km/½ mile**

There are no logs on the ridge, but the walk to Brim Fell is as easy as falling off one. The one concern is to keep the steep ground of the corrie a comfortable distance to the right. Take care that you are not drawn down the popular path NW to Goats Hawse. The ridge broadens, as does the path, as it advances north to the large solitary cairn.

DOW CRAG **↓150m/480ft** **↑145m/465ft** **1.6km/1 mile**

This is an exciting walk linking two compatriate summits. The clear path leads NW curving down to Goats Hawse. From here, climb naturally round the scarp W, turning to S to climb to the magnificent summit bastion.

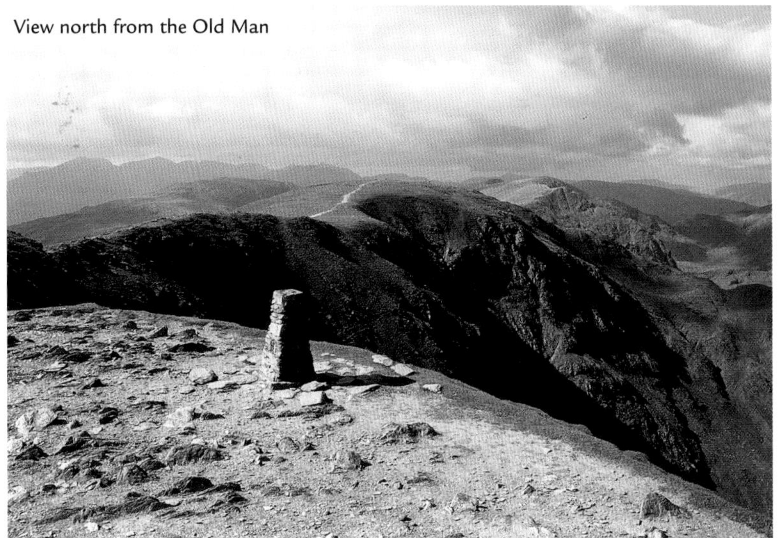

View north from the Old Man

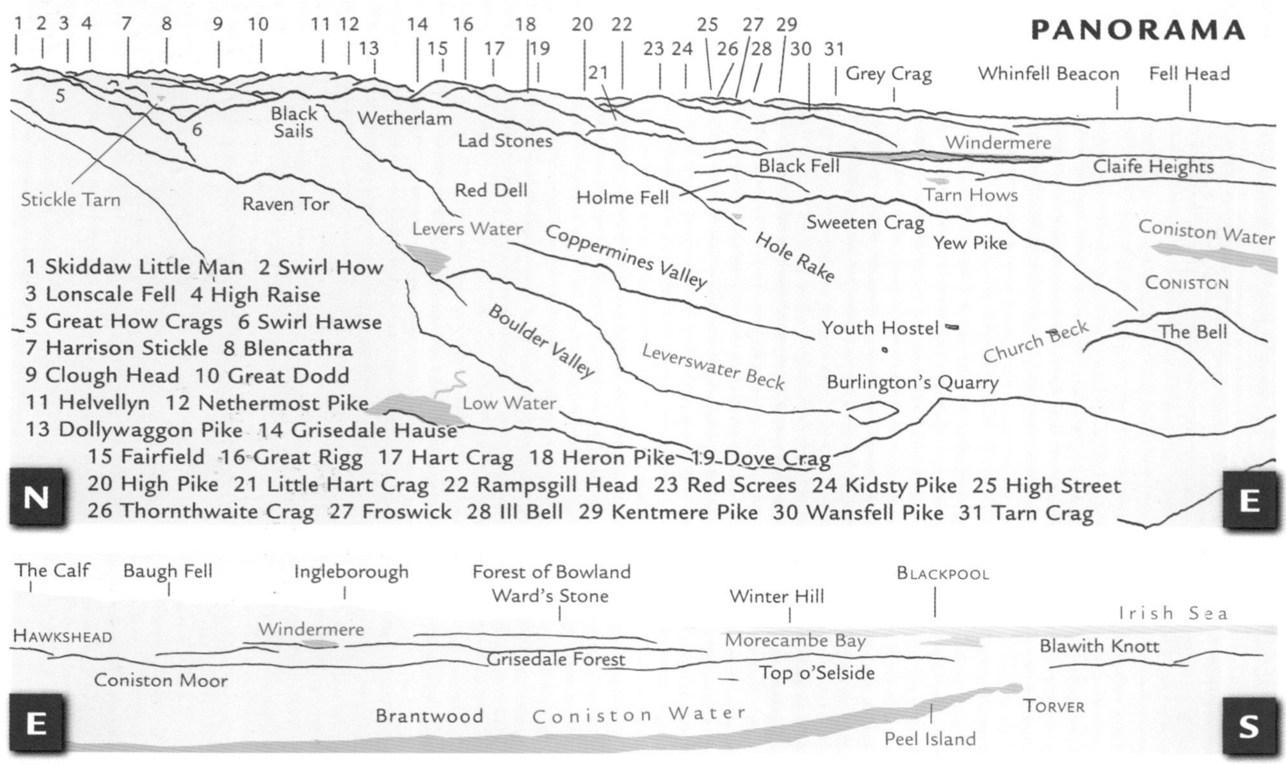
PANORAMA
1 2 3 4 7 8 9 10 11 12 13 14 15 16 17 18 19 20 21 22 23 24 25 26 27 28 29 30 31
Grey Crag
Whinfell Beacon
Fell Head
5
6
Black Sails
Wetherlam
Lad Stones
Windermere
Black Fell
Claife Heights
Stickle Tarn
Raven Tor
Red Dell
Holme Fell
Tarn Hows
Levers Water
Coppermines Valley
Hole Rake
Sweeten Crag
Yew Pike
Coniston Water
Coniston
Boulder Valley
Youth Hostel
Church Beck
The Bell
Leverswater Beck
Burlington's Quarry
Low Water
1 Skiddaw Little Man 2 Swirl How
3 Lonscale Fell 4 High Raise
5 Great How Crags 6 Swirl Hawse
7 Harrison Stickle 8 Blencathra
9 Clough Head 10 Great Dodd
11 Helvellyn 12 Nethermost Pike
13 Dollywaggon Pike 14 Grisedale Hause
15 Fairfield 16 Great Rigg 17 Hart Crag 18 Heron Pike 19 Dove Crag
20 High Pike 21 Little Hart Crag 22 Rampsgill Head 23 Red Screes 24 Kidsty Pike 25 High Street
26 Thornthwaite Crag 27 Froswick 28 Ill Bell 29 Kentmere Pike 30 Wansfell Pike 31 Tarn Crag
N
E
The Calf
Baugh Fell
Ingleborough
Forest of Bowland
Ward's Stone
Winter Hill
Blackpool
Irish Sea
Hawkshead
Windermere
Morecambe Bay
Blawith Knott
Grisedale Forest
Top o'Selside
Coniston Moor
Brantwood
Coniston Water
Torver
Peel Island
E
S

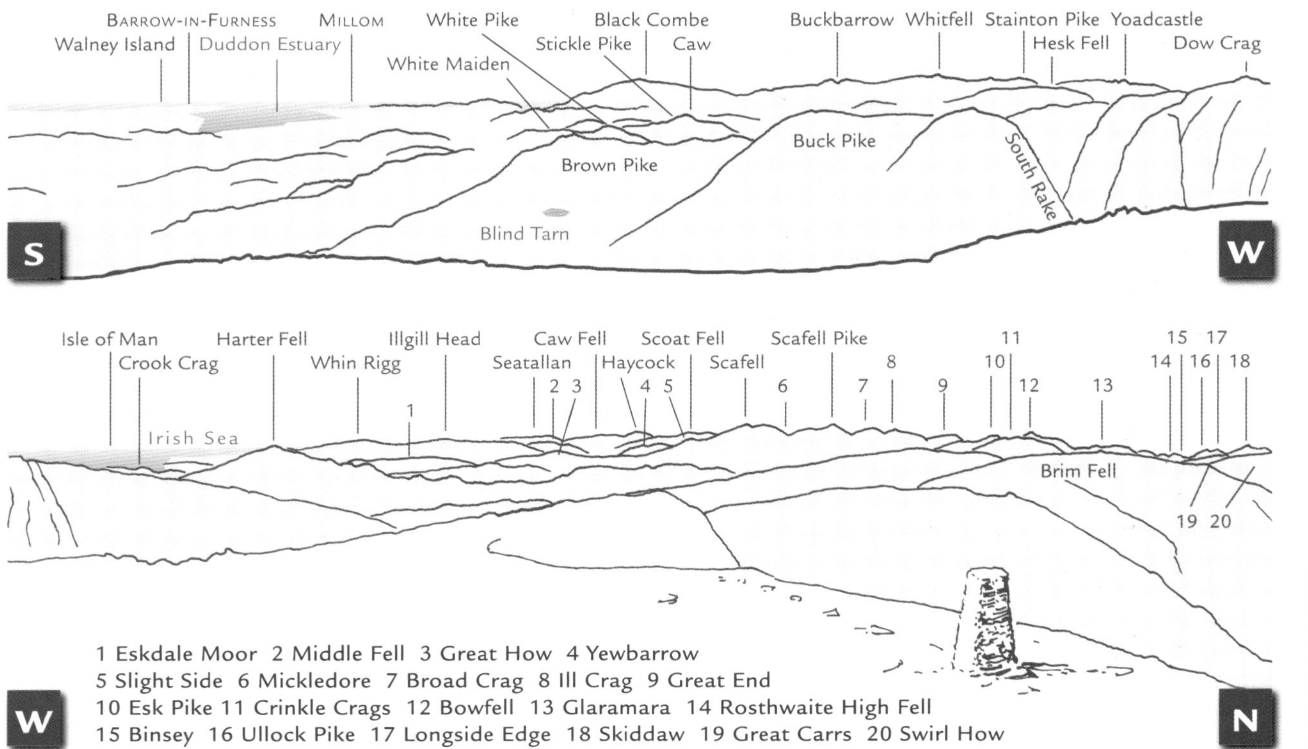
Barrow-in-Furness
Millom
White Pike
Black Combe
Buckbarrow
Whitfell
Stainton Pike
Yoadcastle
Walney Island
Duddon Estuary
Stickle Pike
Caw
Hesk Fell
Dow Crag
White Maiden
Buck Pike
South Rake
Brown Pike
Blind Tarn
S
W
Isle of Man
Harter Fell
Illgill Head
Caw Fell
Scoat Fell
Scafell Pike
Crook Crag
Whin Rigg
Seatallan
Haycock
Scafell
1 2 3 4 5 6 7 8 9 10 11 12 13 14 15 16 17 18
Irish Sea
Brim Fell
19 20
1 Eskdale Moor 2 Middle Fell 3 Great How 4 Yewbarrow
5 Slight Side 6 Mickledore 7 Broad Crag 8 Ill Crag 9 Great End
10 Esk Pike 11 Crinkle Crags 12 Bowfell 13 Glaramara 14 Rosthwaite High Fell
15 Binsey 16 Ullock Pike 17 Longside Edge 18 Skiddaw 19 Great Carrs 20 Swirl How
W
N

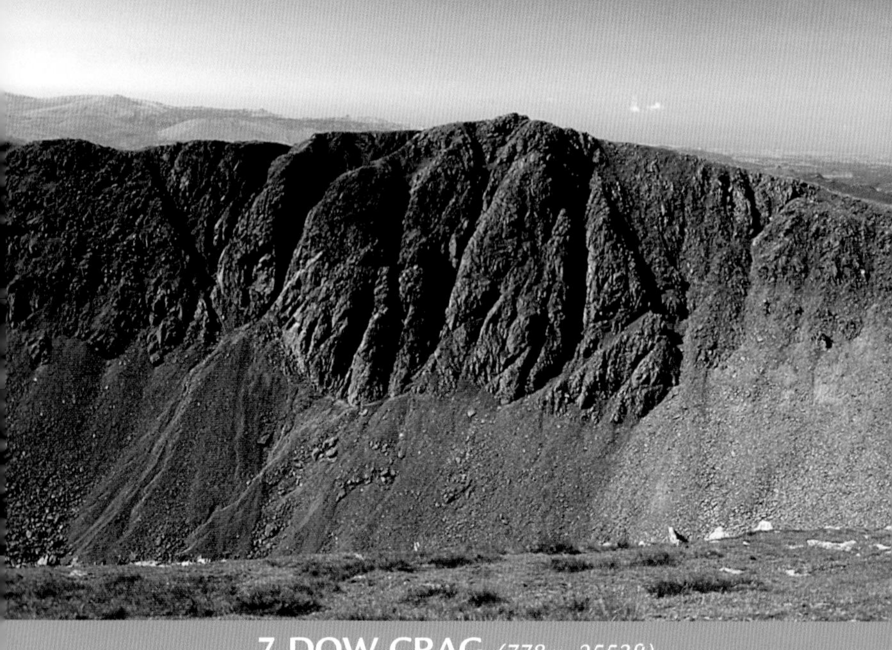

7 DOW CRAG *(778m, 2553ft)*

Dow Crag is one of the finest fells in the Lake District, revered by rock climbers and fellwalkers alike – good to look at, good to stand on, good to wander over and a superb climb whatever your capacity or approach. From the Duddon Valley all it offers is bulk, a tantalising peaked summit with no obvious line of direct ascent, but from the east it's a different matter. Whether you are on the Old Man, approaching up The Cove or looking up from Coniston Water, you see a real mountain, dominated by one absolutely massive crag. Its buttresses and gullies, on a par with Scafell, humble the bold and strike awe into the timid.

The South Rake, the simplest of scambles, gives fellwalkers their most intimate view of the cliff; otherwise walkers must be content to admire the wild precipice from a safe distance along its fearsome edge. The Crag is most commonly approached either across Goats Hawse or from the summit of the Walna Scar Road. The latter, northbound ridge, makes two impressive steps, over Brown and Buck Pikes, on the way. Cradled beneath the two is Blind Tarn, as lovely a crystal pool as you could imagine, while, further north, Goat's Water has an altogether darker feel, with crags and scree pressing down upon its steely waters.

 ↑ Dow Crag from the summit of the Old Man

ASCENT FROM THE WALNA SCAR ROAD FELL-GATE (28)

Via Goats Hawse 550m/1800ft 5.7 km/3½ miles

The approach from 'off the Walna Scar Road' via The Cove, entering the great amphitheatre beneath the famous crag, is one of great drama and excitement, hidden and unsuspected at the start. A sense of the presence of climbers past lends this mountain arena a special reverence and respect. **1** Start from the fell-gate car parking, and follow the open track west, passing the tiny, rush-filled Boo Tarn. To the left

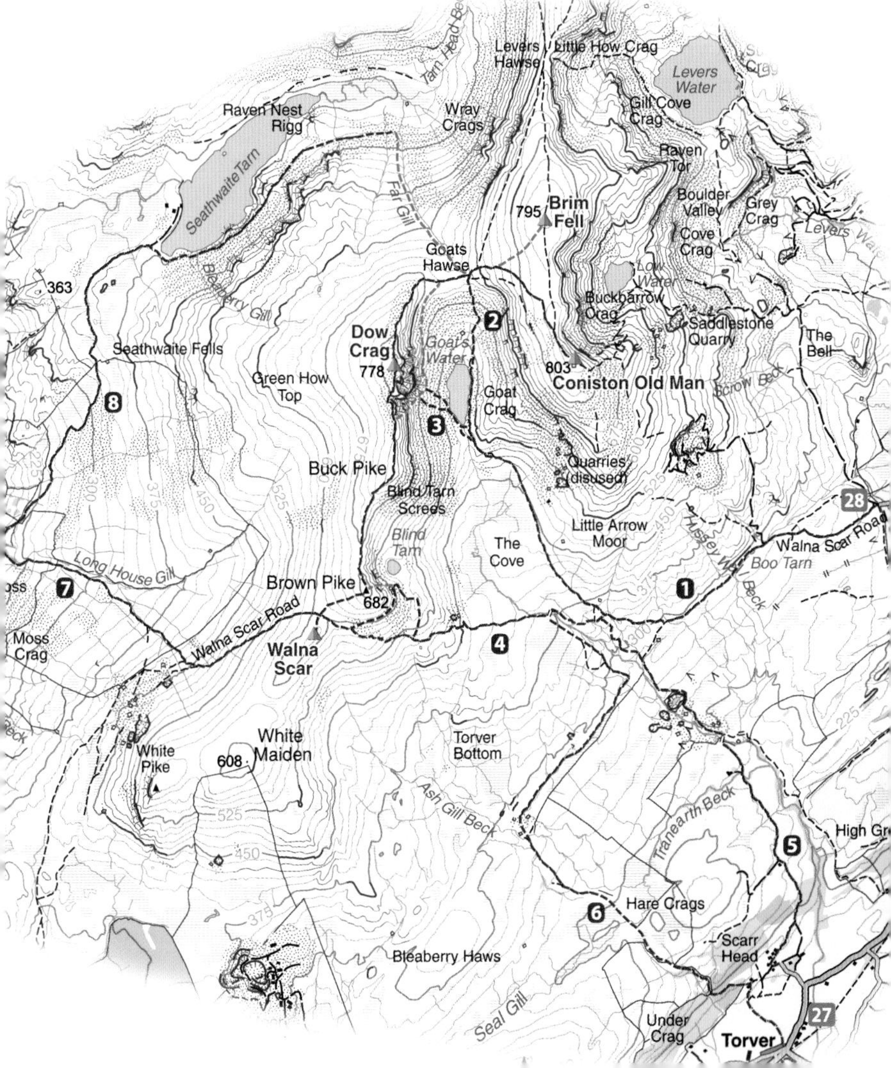

Dow Crag from the eastern shore of Goat's Water

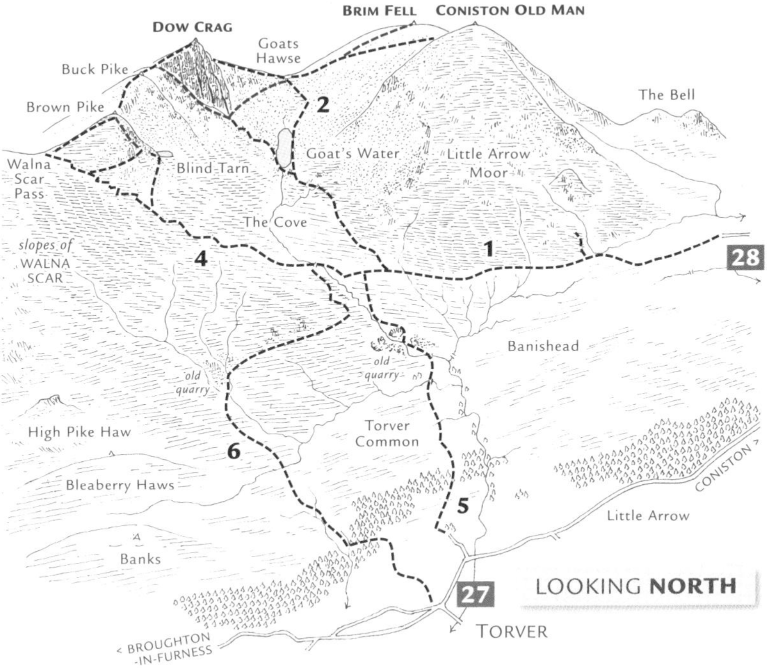

Blind Tarn and old slate quarry backed by Buck Pike

swathes of bracken shield the common, dotted with stones left by the Bronze Age farmers of this upland. The track begins to climb, winding through two rock cuttings, made by latter-day slate quarrymen. Travellers through the ages have seen no need to deviate from this ancient route-way. **2** Take the obvious pitched steps right, leading off the track 200m short of Cove Bridge (built to serve the Blind Tarn slate quarry). My lifelong friend Rodney Busby and I once spotted an adder coiled up on this path. They usually feel walkers' vibrations and scuttle off before you even see them but this one lingered long enough for me to down my rucksack and swiftly wield my

A rare encounter with an adder on the path in The Cove, unravelling for a quick exit

camera for a recording shot. Not only did I get the photo but it gave us the benefit of a passing hiss. The path mounts a rock-step beneath Goat Crag and advances to Goat's Water. The setting is wonderfully wild, not a tree or a shrub in sight, just boulders and coarse scree bearing down into the dark waters. To meet the demands of a regular clientele the path up to Goats Hawse has been pitched, drawing up to the saddle at the head of the combe. At the top, go left, turning from west to south as the worn ridge path climbs steadily to the final, triumphant summit.

Via the South Rake

5km/3 miles

3 If the weather is suitable and your energy levels up to it, serious consideration should be given to climbing South Rake. It is the fellwalker's one chance to get really close to Dow Crag. Ford the outflowing beck from Goat's Water passing giant boulders. The scree above is not at all pleasant, but there's no choice. The path climbs up to the foot of Great Gully, where there's a blue stretcher box down to the right. A contouring sheep trod can then be seen going right beneath the crag to Goats Hawse. Enter South Rake by bearing up left. Scramble by the entrance to Easy Gully, onto the rough ledges. The Rake is obvious. There is no sense of entering a deep cleft or forbidding gully, just a scrambly open weakness that does

View up Great Gully

Dow Crag from the top of South Rake – note the ewe and lamb on the perilous ledge!

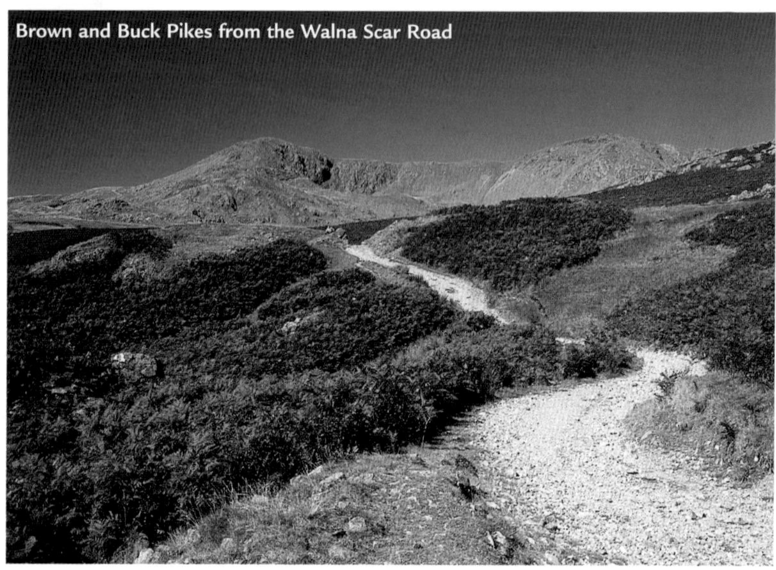
Brown and Buck Pikes from the Walna Scar Road

have loose stuff, but far more of the firm hand-holds that lend confidence and ensure steady progress. The outward views down to the tarn and across the blank side of the Old Man are fabulous, but most impressive are the near buttresses. Nonetheless, the Rake is no place for ordinary fellwalkers in bad weather. To enjoy it, do it on a sunny day, take your time and stop often – it is fun. The top comes sooner than you expect and, chuffed with yourself, you'll relish grappling with the summit when it arrives.

Via Walna Scar Pass 6km/3¾ miles

4 For the simplest ascent stick with the Walna Scar Road to the top of the pass, and bear right onto the rising ridge passing the cairns on Brown and Buck Pikes. On the way up, a visit to Blind Tarn is a delectable addition, using the old quarry greenway. The tarn is a little mysterious, there being only a soakaway pool and no sign of an escaping gill, not even tell-tale rushes. Explore the quarries and use a narrow trod traversing from the upper quarry back to the track close to the stone shelter, or scramble straight to the top of Brown Pike direct from the quarry ruins – the outcrops are mild-mannered stuff.

ASCENT FROM TORVER (27)

Via Banishead Quarry 670m/2200ft 6km/3¾ miles

There are two lines of approach to the Walna Scar Road from Torver.

5 The usual route, via Tranearth and Banishead Quarry starting from the Church Hall or road-end (see CONISTON OLD MAN Route 6 (page 85)).

Via Ashgill Quarry 6.7km/4¼ miles

6 Start from The Wilson Arms and follow the footpath lane rising via High Torver Park through woodland and up an old trackway onto the fell via gates and stiles leading to Ashgill Quarry. Traverse right to rise on an old path by Torver Beck to Cove Bridge.

ASCENT FROM SEATHWAITE (46)

Via Walna Scar Road 680m/2230ft 6km/3¾ miles

7 The Walna Scar Road climbs out of the Duddon Valley, tarmac quickly giving way to a rough track at the fell-gate. Popular with mountain bikers too, the 'road' provides a straightforward, efficient means of getting onto the Dow Crag ridge, turning off left onto Route 4 at the road summit. There is also the well-marked field-path route via Turner Hall and High Moss (Rucksack Club Hut), which takes a great slice out of road walking.

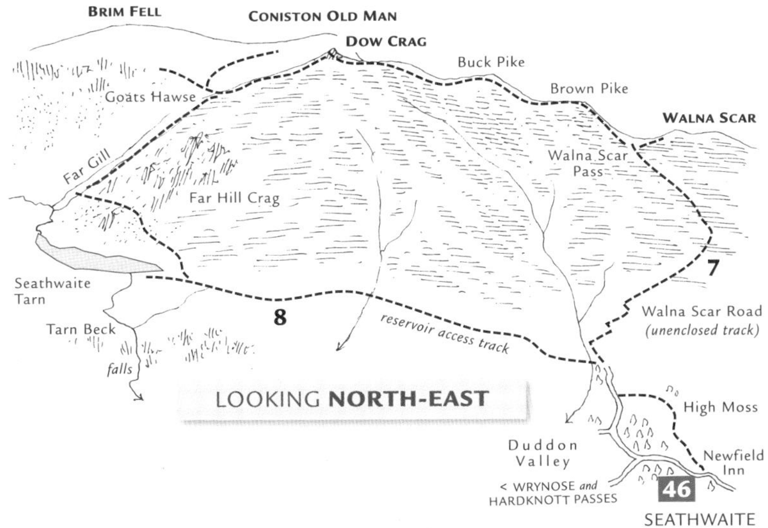

Via Seathwaite Tarn 8km/5 miles

8 Where the track begins, so too does the gated reservoir access track bound for Seathwaite Tarn, which supplies water to the lower Furness area. The track traverses the lower western slopes and branches right, just short of the dam, to join a path which draws across the fellside, passing a measuring gauge, beneath Near and Far Hill Crags. The path peters out opposite Blake Rigg Crag, at which point turn up hill to follow Far Gill to Goats Hawse and Route 2.

THE SUMMIT

There are summits and there are summits: Brim Fell needs a cairn, Dow Crag doesn't. There's no room for one thing. The irregular battlement of the summit bastion (see the photograph below), like a Roman altar, has a 'focus'. I count this among the best summits in the Lake District, an easy scramble on and off, north and south, but beware the east! The view down the cliff is utterly breathtaking. There are few summits with quite this sense of the precipitous. Southward along the edge are further glimpses down the face from the high brow. Peer down Easy and Great Gullies to marvel at the void (see opposite). The ridge path runs besides the remains of a wall, originally constructed to stop sheep from venturing onto the cliff. The lack of such protection today means you may see Herdwick standing goat-like on amazing ledges. I witnessed a ewe and lamb work their way down, stepping from ledge to ledge, engrossed in grazing. Sheep must get to a point where they either fall or successfully unravel their way back up the cliff. The names Goat's Water and Buck Pike here testify to their predecessors – a lost population of wild goats.

Swirl Hawse from the north ridge

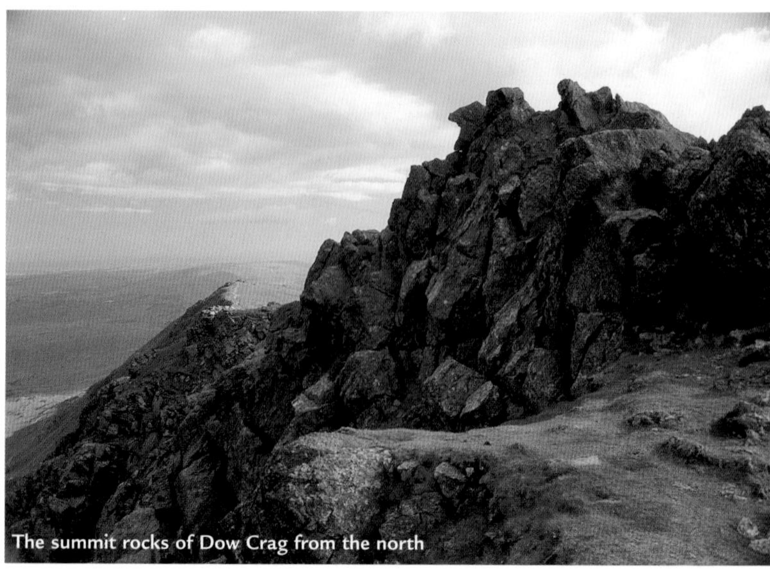

The summit rocks of Dow Crag from the north

SAFE DESCENTS

The Cove from the top of Great Gully

For all the eastern scarp threatens, especially with a stiff south-westerly blowing, the walker can find safe haven more readily from this top than many another. If you follow the ridge S, stepping down first from Buck Pike, then Brown Pike, the summit of the Walna Scar Road is sure to be found. Then either go right for Seathwaite in the Duddon Valley, 2¼ miles away, or left for Coniston, 3¼ miles away. It's a similar story should you trek N, for the ridge naturally declines to the broad saddle of Goats Hawse from where a pitched path leads S down by Goat's Water and on via a rock step at Goat Crag down The Cove, again to meet the Walna Scar Road. This time Coniston is 2 miles away and the Duddon Valley uphill and over the pass. The steeper slope N from Goats Hawse has no real dangers, but the terrain to the reservoir track is rougher and the distance to Seathwaite just that bit greater at 4¼ miles.

RIDGE ROUTES

BRIM FELL	↓130m/420ft	↑150m/480ft	1.2km/¾ mile
CONISTON OLD MAN	↓145m/465ft	↑150m/480ft	1.6km/1 mile

Dow Crag from Goats Hawse

Climb carefully down the N side of the summit outcrop, descend with the ridge path to the broad depression of Goats Hawse. The main continuing path curves up with a right-hand bias: for Brim Fell branch off at will up the predominantly grassy slope; for the Old Man stick with the trade route and, in mist, remember that the steepest ground lies to the east.

WALNA SCAR	↓180m/585ft	↑20m/70ft	1.6km/1 mile

Follow the ridge S, via Buck and Brown Pikes, down to the Walna Scar track. The modest summit and cairn lie at the top of the first rise beyond.

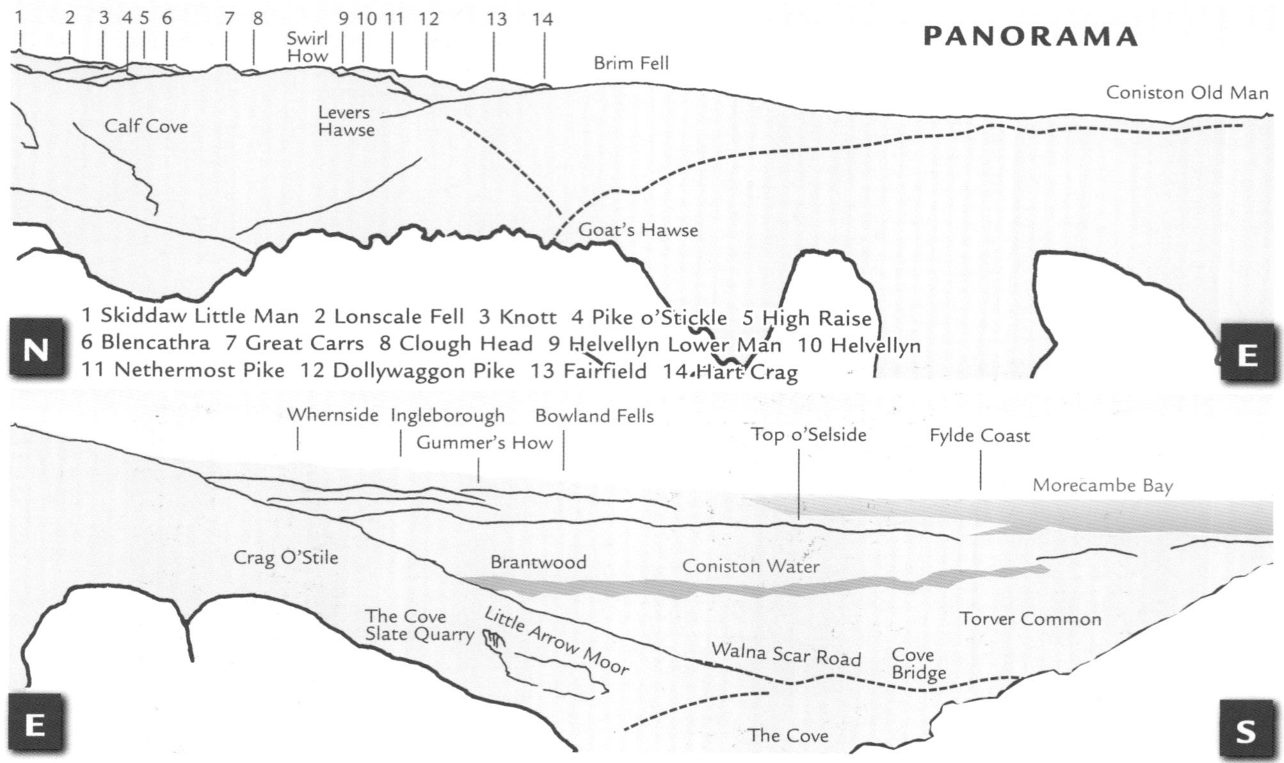
PANORAMA
1 2 3 4 5 6 7 8 9 10 11 12 13 14
Swirl How
Brim Fell
Coniston Old Man
Calf Cove
Levers Hawse
Goat's Hawse
1 Skiddaw Little Man 2 Lonscale Fell 3 Knott 4 Pike o'Stickle 5 High Raise
6 Blencathra 7 Great Carrs 8 Clough Head 9 Helvellyn Lower Man 10 Helvellyn
11 Nethermost Pike 12 Dollywaggon Pike 13 Fairfield 14 Hart Crag
N
E
Whernside
Ingleborough
Gummer's How
Bowland Fells
Top o'Selside
Fylde Coast
Morecambe Bay
Crag O'Stile
Brantwood
Coniston Water
Torver Common
The Cove Slate Quarry
Little Arrow Moor
Walna Scar Road
Cove Bridge
The Cove
E
S

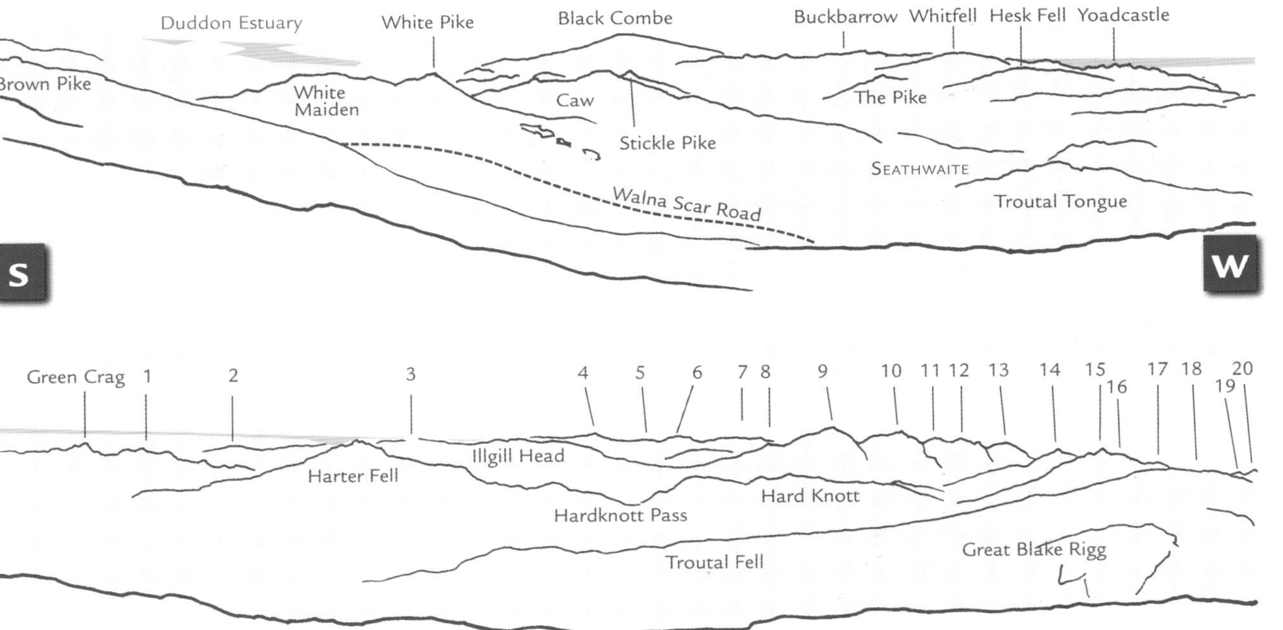

1 Crook Crag 2 Irton Pike 3 Whin Rigg 4 Seatallan 5 Caw Fell 6 Haycock 7 Scoat Fell 8 Slight Side 9 Scafell 10 Scafell Pike 11 Broad Crag 12 Ill Crag 13 Great End 14 Esk Pike 15 Bowfell 16 Crinkle Crags 17 Grey Friar 18 Glaramara 19 Carl Side 20 Skiddaw

8 GREAT CARRS *(788m, 2585ft)*

A curving crescendo of a ridge rises up from the meadows of Little Langdale and culminates on the peaks of Great Carrs and Swirl How. Forming the bridgehead with the Mid-Western Fells on Wrynose Pass, it steps purposefully up, with Rough Crags, Wet Side Edge and Little Carrs, the trajectory of most ascents. Walks begun from Wrynose Pass involve just 395m/1295ft of ascent but the saving is lost when any walk is extended and circular routes are limited, Swirl How and Grey Friar being simply out-and-back destinations from the summit. From Wrynose Bottom the fell is guarded by a high rim of crags dominated by Hellgill Pike, which can be climbed with a tough off-beat clamber up the west side of Hell Gill. The lonely upper reaches of the Greenburn Beck valley, a glacial hollow filled with boulders and marsh, afford the least attractive approach. Most walkers wisely settle for Swirl Hawse and Prison Band, rather than slog up the excessively steep grass slope of Broad Slack.

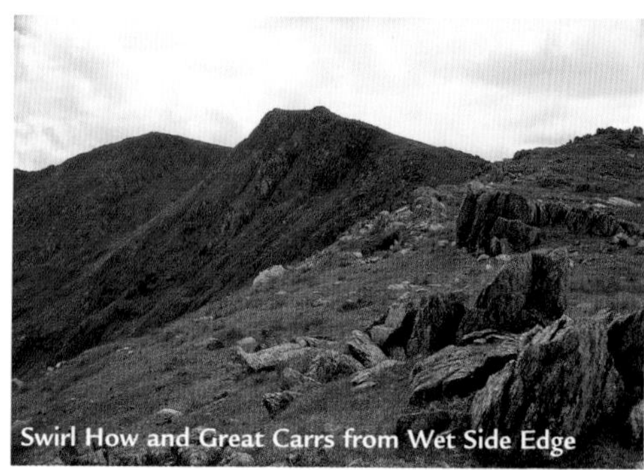
Swirl How and Great Carrs from Wet Side Edge

 ↑ Swirl How and Great Carrs forming the head of the Greenburn Beck valley from Rough Crags

ASCENT FROM LITTLE LANGDALE (37 – OFF MAP E & 39)

Via Wet Side Edge 670m/2200ft 6.5km/4 miles

There are two ways onto the Wet Side Edge ridge, the shorter of which begins from above Fellfoot Farm. **1** Immediately above Castle Howe find a recessed gate/stile on the left. Follow the track with a wall on your left, go through the next gate and slip over the facing bank, past a guide cairn, to ford the infant River Brathay. Climb the steep bank ahead, between irregular walled enclosures, past the distinctive rocks on Hollin Crag and turn right, up the easy ridge.

2 This lowest section of the ridge can be gained from the old Greenburn Mine access track. The track can either be joined from Fellfoot via Bridge End or, more commonly, from the vicinity of Slater Bridge via the lane by Low Hall Garth climbing hut.

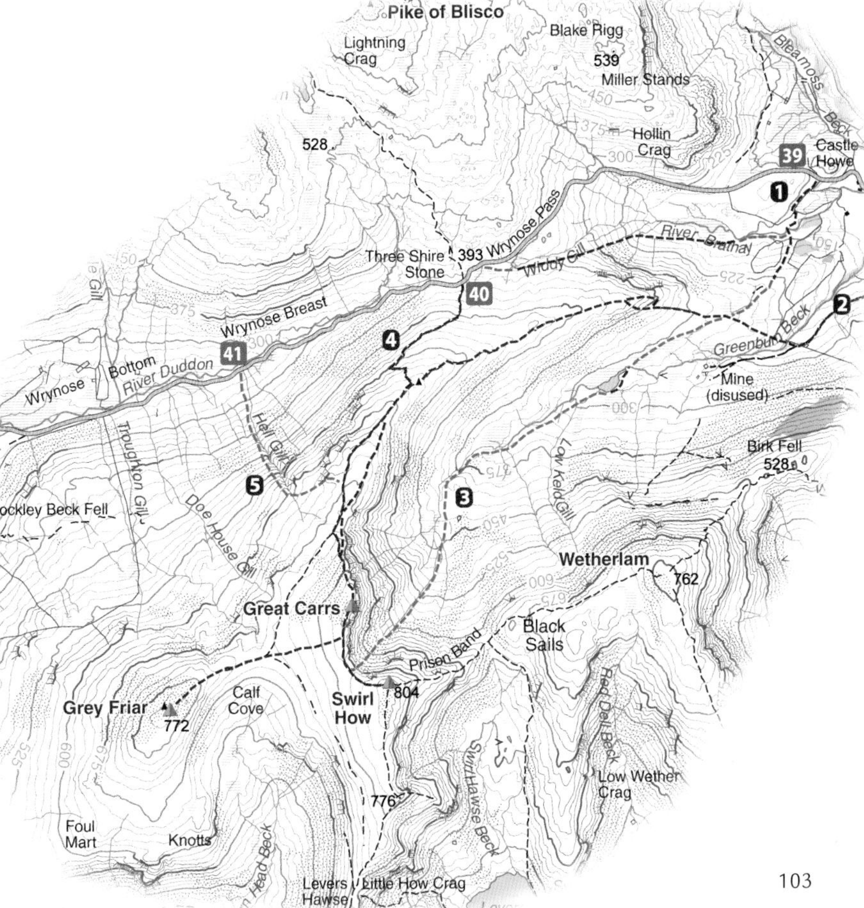

The Langdale Pikes from Hollin Crag

About 2km from Slater Bridge, cross a footbridge over Greenburn Beck, situated directly right after the intake wall gate at GR295023. The ridge path angles up the left side of Rough Crags above Greenburn Tarn progressing steadily by Wet Side Edge (a misnomer). The path from Wrynose enters from the right at a prominent cairn. From here, either keep with the main path or slant left to follow the true ridge path climbing more steeply up to Little Carrs, crossing the traversing path for the Fairfield saddle and Grey Friar. Follow the exciting rocky scarp edge to the summit.

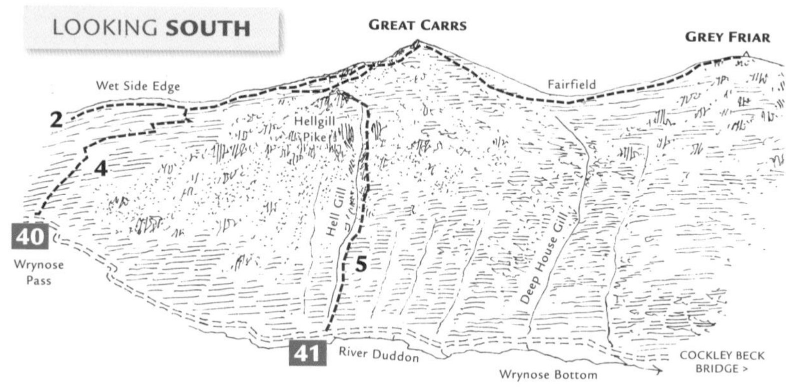

Greenburn Tarn dam causeway

Walkers consider the map from the ridge above Rough Crags, with Cold Pike, Crinkle Crags and Pike o'Blisco in the background

Via Greenburn Beck 6.5km/4 miles

3 The mine access track leads not only to the historically important remains of the old coppermine, but also along the dwindling trod into the wild corrie beyond Greenburn Tarn, aiming for the saddle between Swirl How and Great Carrs. Soggy ground culimates in a painfully steep grass slope, where the sad remains of a Halifax bomber litter the scree.

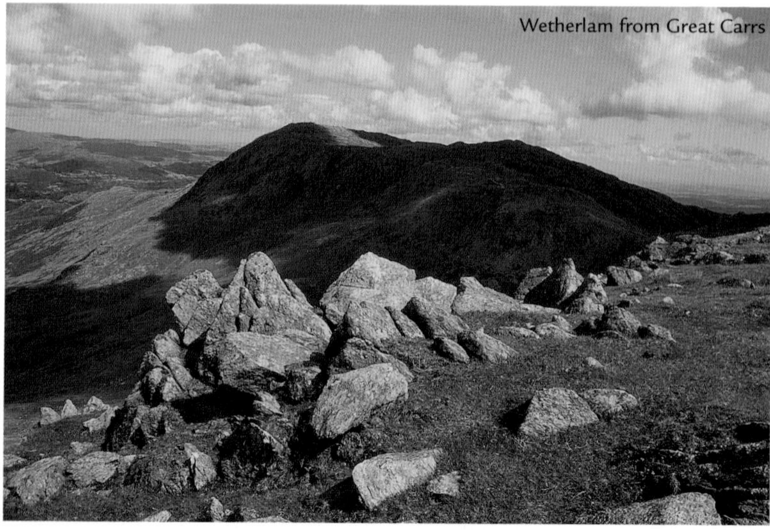
Wetherlam from Great Carrs

ASCENT FROM WRYNOSE PASS (40)

Via Wrynose Pass 395m/1295ft 2.2km/1½ miles

4 The Wrynose Pass ascent is oh, so tempting. A high-level walk that can start at 393m/1295ft and involve only the same height gain again on a simple ridge is hard to ignore. As a there-and-back route to the top of Great Carrs, it is just fine. There are two parking areas, although the only marked path onto the ridge begins from the higher one at the top of the pass. Note the huge specimen erratic close left as you climb just west of south towards the ridge. A large cairn marks the point of arrival on the ridge-top. Commit its characteristics to memory for your return. If mist descends with you, you'll not wish to drift down the ridge too far!

ASCENT FROM WRYNOSE BOTTOM (41)

Via Hell Gill 523m/1715ft 1.8km/1¼ miles

The serpentine road descends west from the pass into Wrynose Bottom. (The two short lengths of wall on the fellside are old shelter bields for sheep.) **5** This is one of those climbs that make sense both on the map and on the ground in fair weather, but strangely show little or no sign of use. Find room to pull off the open road just west

Little Stand from the head of Hell Gill

North-east to Little Langdale

of the footpath, signed on the north verge (GR266023). A cattle feed rack in the vicinity of the starting point confirms that cattle are being given their chance to graze the lower dale slopes, which is good news for plant life diversity. The striking cleft of Hell Gill is not a place to fear, unlike its namesake on Bowfell's Band. Keeping to the west side, ascend above the rowans and enter the upper half of the ravine as it slips through the rock band, passing a small pinnacle. Buzzards wheeled above me during my fell climb and the rare visit of *Homo sapiens* was greeted with disdain. From the higher realms of the gill the views across the valley are quite superb – with Little Stand, Cold Pike and, beyond, a grand array of fine fells including Scafell. As the slope eases you can comfortably drift half-left to climb Hell Gill Pike, sufficiently offset from the main ridge path to enjoy exclusivity for high-level camps, and then cross to join Route 2.

THE SUMMIT

Great Carrs boasts a narrow grassy summit ridge, above a fine craggy escarpment, culminating in a small rocky top and its bedraggled cairn. It's an impressive spot to rest, peering straight down into the wild hollow of Greenburn. Ahead is Wetherlam and right Swirl How, and to the north, beyond Little Stand, are the mighty Scafells.

A memorial cross and cairn is located a few metres down the west slope from the lip of Broad Slack at GR270007. Beside it is the undercarriage of the Halifax bomber, a reminder of a tragic accident on a training flight in 1944. The remains of the fuselage lie in the scree over the edge, while the Merlin engine stands outside the Ruskin Museum in Coniston, where a more thorough explanation of the sad event is given.

SAFE DESCENTS

The main descending ridge, trending from north to east, offers safe ground towards the Wrynose Pass in 1¼ miles and, later, taking care over Rough Crags, Little Langdale (Slater Bridge) in 4 miles.

RIDGE ROUTE

GREY FRIAR ↓130m/425ft ↑145m/480ft 1.2km/¾ mile

Descend due W, grassy all the way, crossing the Fairfield saddle.

SWIRL HOW ↓20m/65ft ↑40m/130ft 0.5km/¼ mile

Follow the curving ridge S to E.

The summit looking to Coniston Old Man, Brim Fell and the peak of Dow Crag

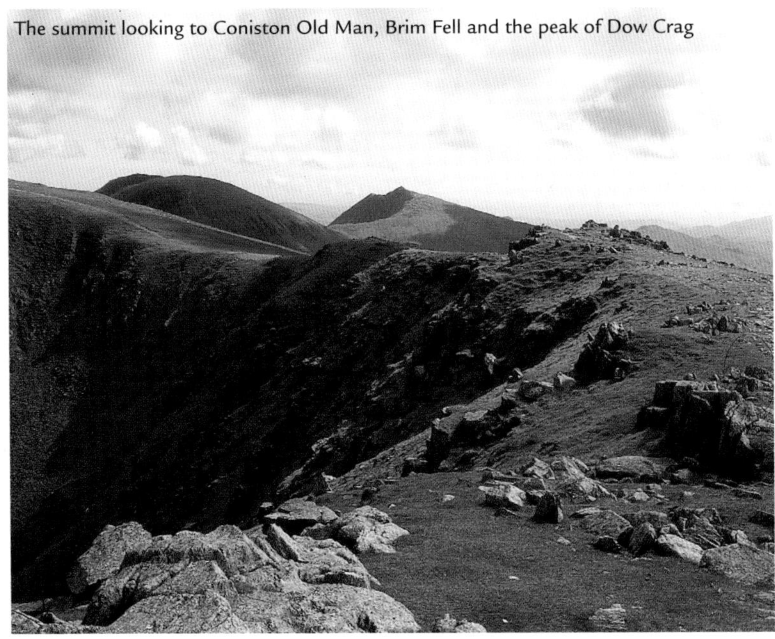

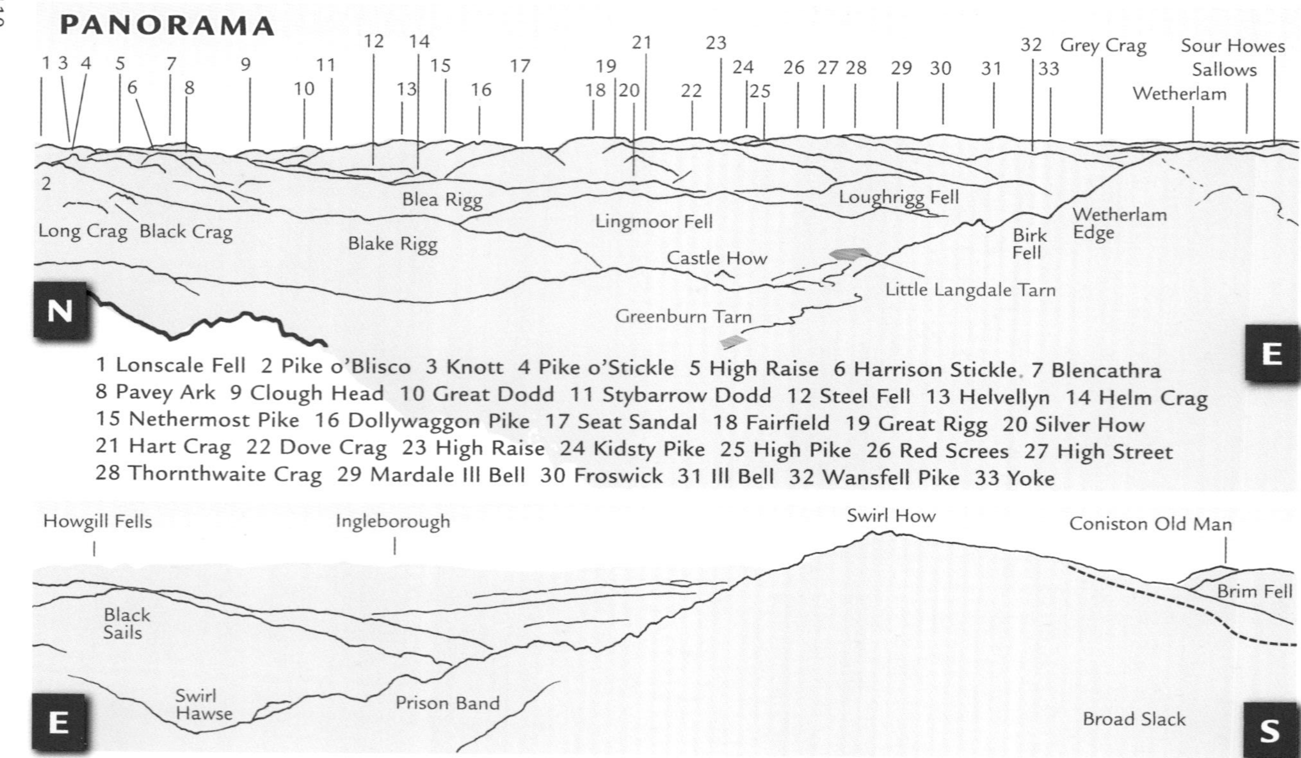
PANORAMA
Grey Crag
Sour Howes
Sallows
Wetherlam
Blea Rigg
Loughrigg Fell
Long Crag
Black Crag
Lingmoor Fell
Wetherlam Edge
Blake Rigg
Birk Fell
Castle How
Little Langdale Tarn
Greenburn Tarn
N
E
1 Lonscale Fell 2 Pike o'Blisco 3 Knott 4 Pike o'Stickle 5 High Raise 6 Harrison Stickle 7 Blencathra
8 Pavey Ark 9 Clough Head 10 Great Dodd 11 Stybarrow Dodd 12 Steel Fell 13 Helvellyn 14 Helm Crag
15 Nethermost Pike 16 Dollywaggon Pike 17 Seat Sandal 18 Fairfield 19 Great Rigg 20 Silver How
21 Hart Crag 22 Dove Crag 23 High Raise 24 Kidsty Pike 25 High Pike 26 Red Screes 27 High Street
28 Thornthwaite Crag 29 Mardale Ill Bell 30 Froswick 31 Ill Bell 32 Wansfell Pike 33 Yoke
Howgill Fells
Ingleborough
Swirl How
Coniston Old Man
Brim Fell
Black Sails
Swirl Hawse
Prison Band
Broad Slack
E
S

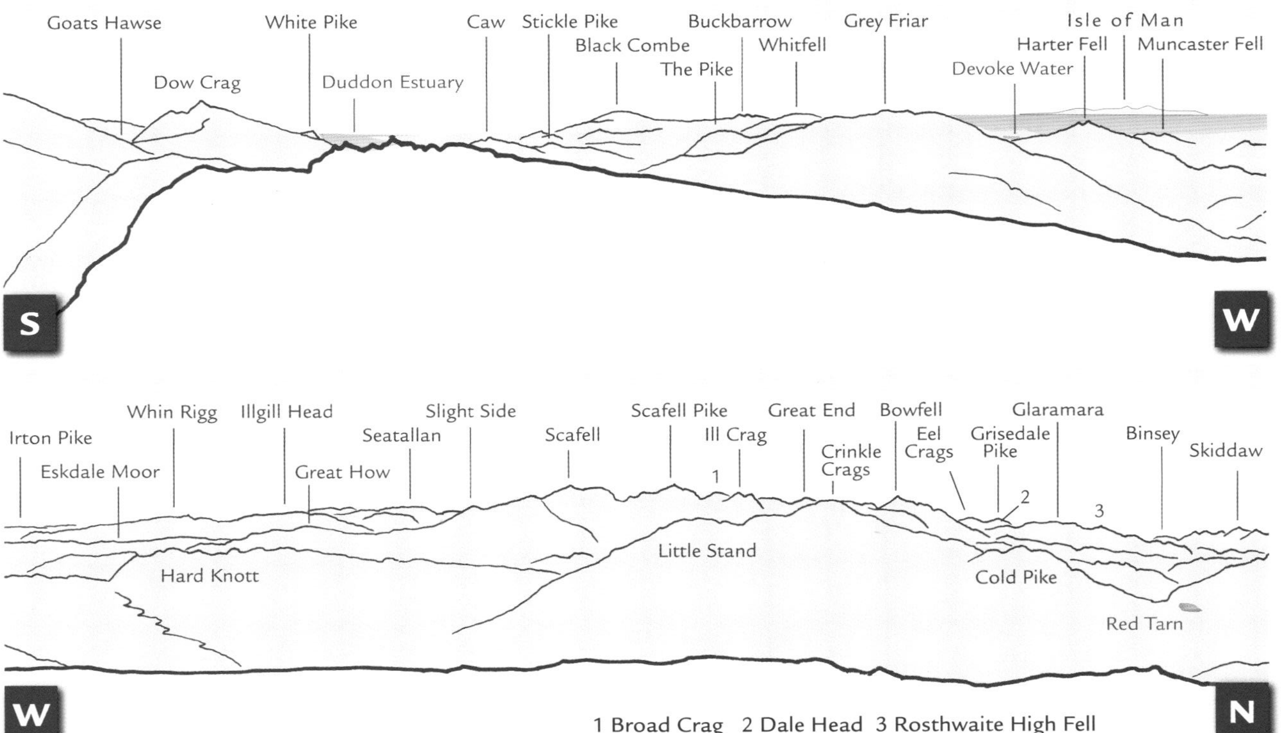
Goats Hawse
Dow Crag
White Pike
Duddon Estuary
Caw
Stickle Pike
Black Combe
Buckbarrow
The Pike
Whitfell
Grey Friar
Isle of Man
Harter Fell
Muncaster Fell
Devoke Water
S
W
Irton Pike
Eskdale Moor
Whin Rigg
Illgill Head
Great How
Seatallan
Slight Side
Scafell
Scafell Pike
Ill Crag
1
Great End
Crinkle Crags
Bowfell
Eel Crags
Grisedale Pike
2
Glaramara
3
Binsey
Skiddaw
Hard Knott
Little Stand
Cold Pike
Red Tarn
W
N
1 Broad Crag 2 Dale Head 3 Rosthwaite High Fell

9 GREAT WORM CRAG *(427m, 1401ft)*

Divided into long walled enclosures, spreading their tendrils above the meadows and woods of Hall Dunnerdale, the ground swells to the gentle scarp of Great Worm Crag. It is clearly a distinct summit, but for many fellwalkers it is nothing more than an intermediate halt, a means to an end, on the approach march to Green Crag from off the Birkerfell Road. However, there are enough who appreciate its situation as an end in itself. They know a good view when they see one and, most of all, value the ease with which it may be achieved.

ASCENT FROM BIRKERFELL ROAD – DEVOKE WATER (5)

Via Freeze Beck 197m/645ft 1.2km/¾ mile

There are three natural routes to the top. **1** From the point where Freeze Beck flows under the open road a path ascends. After a positive start it falters over marshy ground then resumes more confidently, past a large heap of anciently gathered stones and rising to the skyline summit cairn, a far more modest assemblage. **2** From the cattle grid, where the road emerges onto the open fell, ascend to the left of the wall. As the ridge becomes more apparent trend left away from the wall, passing above a sheepfold with a fine view towards Caw, and angle across the shallow combe to the summit cairn.

 ↑ Great Worm Crag from Caw

ASCENT FROM BIRKERFELL ROAD – WOODEND BRIDGE (6)

Via Birkerthwaite 217m/712ft 3km/1¾ miles

3 Follow GREEN CRAG Route 5 (page 122) onto Great Crag and thereafter make a beeline south-east up to the summit.

SUMMIT

A small cairn on a grassy rise marks an otherwise bland summit. The outlook is spacious. Attention is inevitably drawn north towards Green Crag. Either side of this rocky eminence are the distant Pillar and the Scafells to its left and Bowfell over its immediate right-hand shoulder.

Summit of Great Worm Crag

RIDGE ROUTE

GREEN CRAG ↓90m/290ft ↑40m/130ft 2.4km/1½ miles

Follow a good path ENE skirting marsh to the top of White How and then bear NNW following an intermittent path up the broad ridge to the rocky top.

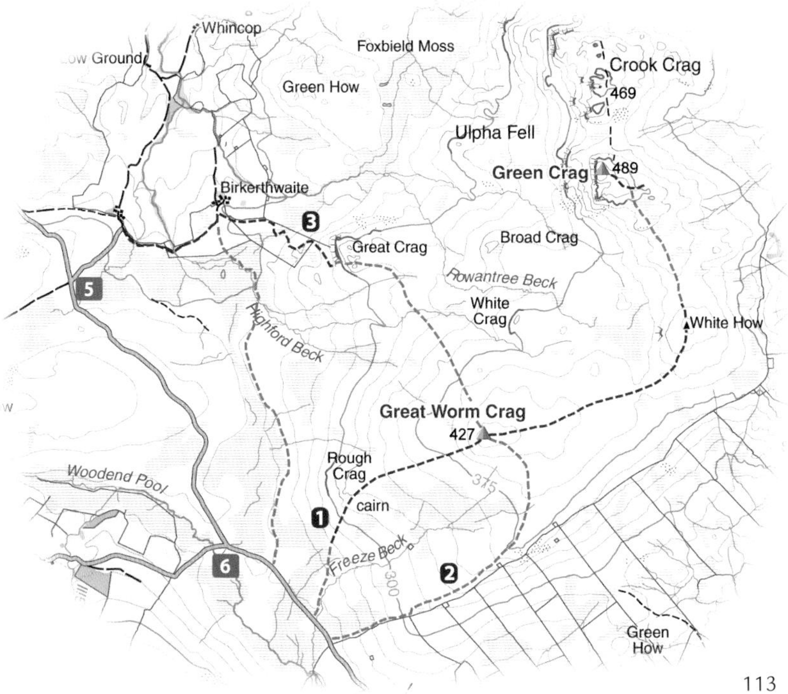

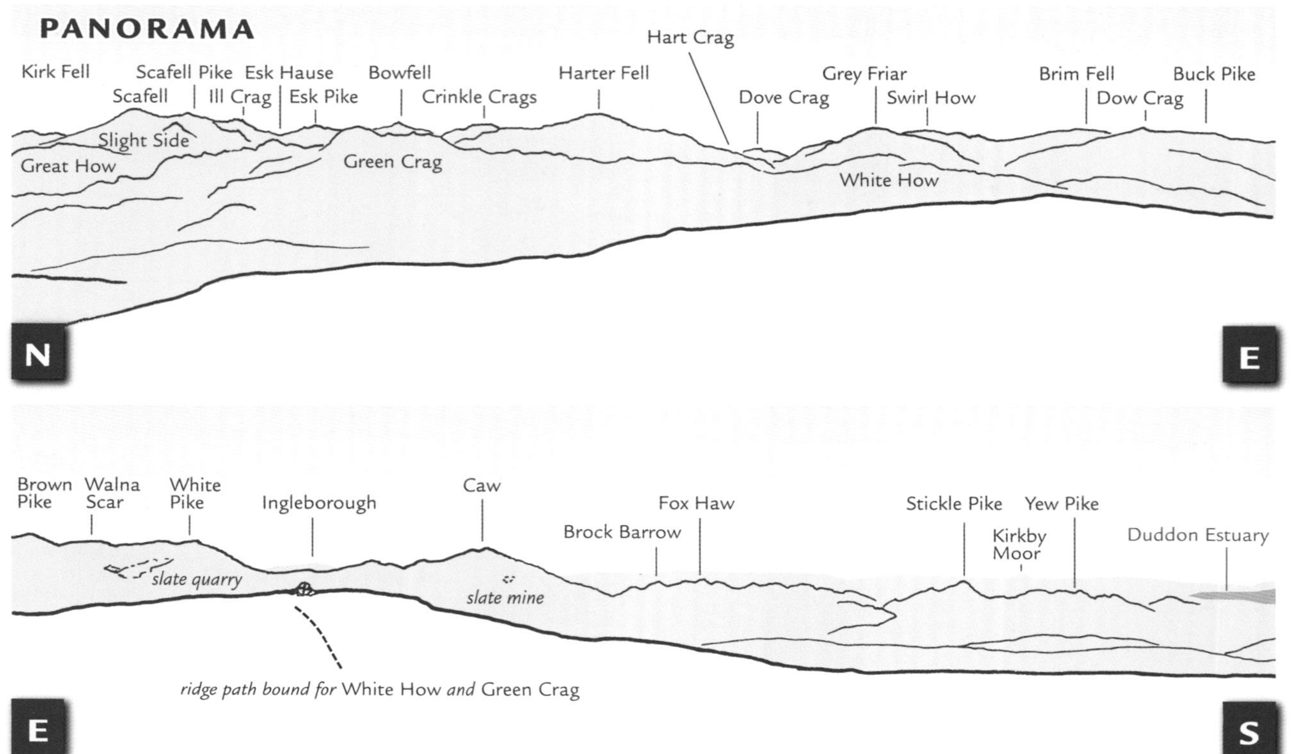
PANORAMA
Kirk Fell
Scafell
Scafell Pike
Ill Crag
Esk Hause
Esk Pike
Bowfell
Crinkle Crags
Harter Fell
Hart Crag
Dove Crag
Grey Friar
Swirl How
Brim Fell
Dow Crag
Buck Pike
Slight Side
Great How
Green Crag
White How
N
E
Brown Pike
Walna Scar
White Pike
Ingleborough
Caw
Brock Barrow
Fox Haw
Stickle Pike
Kirkby Moor
Yew Pike
Duddon Estuary
slate quarry
slate mine
ridge path bound for White How and Green Crag
E
S

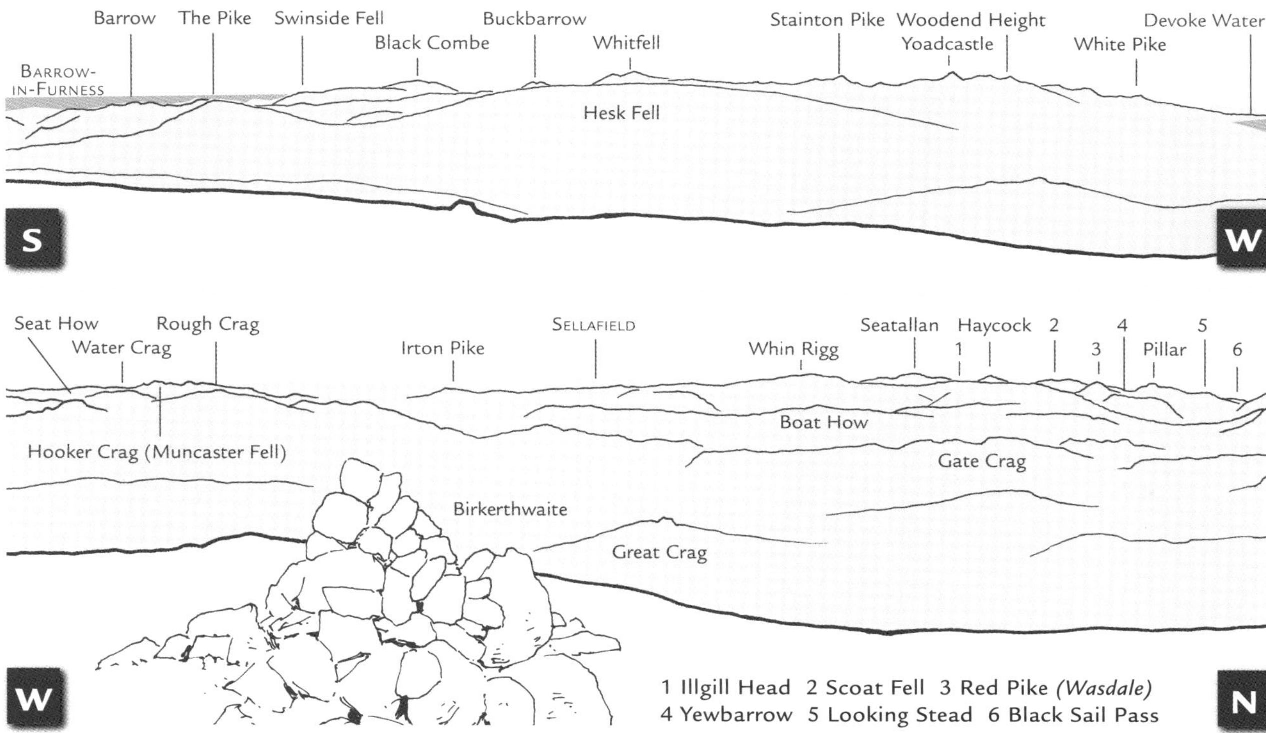
Barrow
The Pike
Swinside Fell
Black Combe
Buckbarrow
Whitfell
Stainton Pike
Woodend Height
Yoadcastle
White Pike
Devoke Water
Barrow-in-Furness
Hesk Fell
S
W
Seat How
Water Crag
Rough Crag
Irton Pike
Sellafield
Whin Rigg
Seatallan
Haycock
1
2
3
4
Pillar
5
6
Boat How
Hooker Crag (Muncaster Fell)
Gate Crag
Birkerthwaite
Great Crag
W
N
1 Illgill Head 2 Scoat Fell 3 Red Pike (Wasdale)
4 Yewbarrow 5 Looking Stead 6 Black Sail Pass

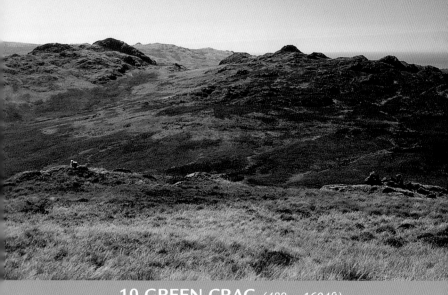

10 GREEN CRAG *(489m, 1604ft)*

Wainwright took the view that this was the last bit of decent fellwalking south of Eskdale. The many excursions in this guide prove him wrong but there is no denying the extra special qualities of Green Crag. It has something of the Northern Highlands about it: shapely craggy knots elevated from a bleak, boggy moorland. But what makes it different and so superb is dear, wooded, Eskdale. Only a surly soul could deny that Eskdale is the most exquisite of valleys and, coupled with Green Crag as the high point of a day's walk from the valley bottom, life can offer little better.

While many are content to stroll up Stanley Ghyll by graded paths and stout footbridges to stand before the plunge pool of shady Stanley Force, the fellwalker will revel in the savage beauty of Birker Force, spilling from a rim of craggy ground fringing the upland pastures. It is worth wrenching yourself away from the verdant tracks and paths of the Duddon and Esk to gain the solitude of lesser-known paths. The approach from Birkerthwaite over Great Crag best conveys the fell's qualities and character, and may be made part of a circular expedition including Great Worm Crag for some lovely, lonely fellwandering.

Cairn on White How looking south to Caw and Stickle Pike

 ↑ Green Crag from the western slopes of Harter Fell

ASCENT FROM THE WOOLPACK INN (3)

Via Low Birker 410m/1345ft 4km/2½ miles

Whether starting from the youth hostel or the Woolpack Inn, start by walking west along the valley road to the lane signed to Penny Hill Farm. Cross the picturesque River Esk at Doctor's Bridge. There are now two options. **1** This is the more direct route. Go right following the lane and track

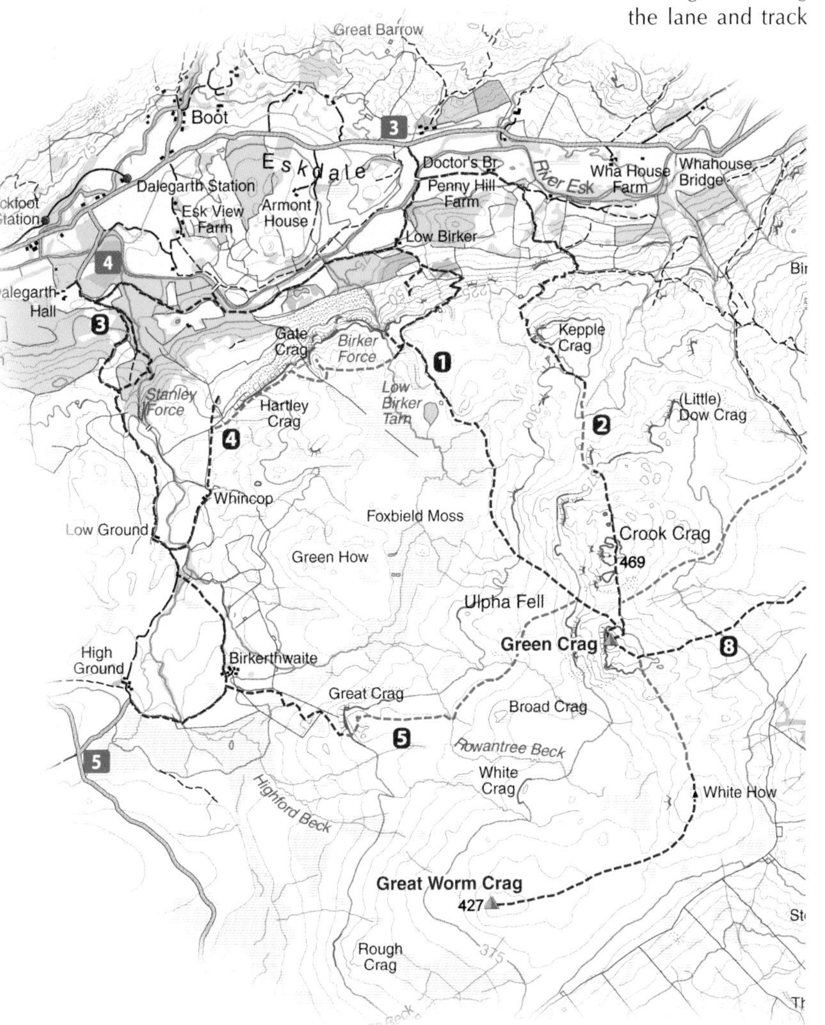

Map continues p118

to Low Birker. Immediately past the house bear up left on the path climbing through the bracken. An early fork right, through a hand-gate, gives access to a rough fellside and view of the cascading Birker Gill from below, but this is not a sane route to the scarp top. Keep with the main path, which higher up passes through dense juniper, to a hand-gate in the enclosure corner. The peat road now begins a quick sequence of zig-zags and then levels to pass a roofless peat store (potentially a splendid camping barn). The track then broaches the moor missing the best view of Birker Force, so make a point of bearing right to have a proper look – also a good place for a refreshment break. Your route now becomes altogether bleaker, skirting marshy ground and rising across the shoulder of a knoll above Low Birker Tarn. A brief descent leads to a long southward slanting traverse. Look out for the solitary thorn with its crow's nest promising firmer ground up ahead.

Birker Force

Map continued from p117

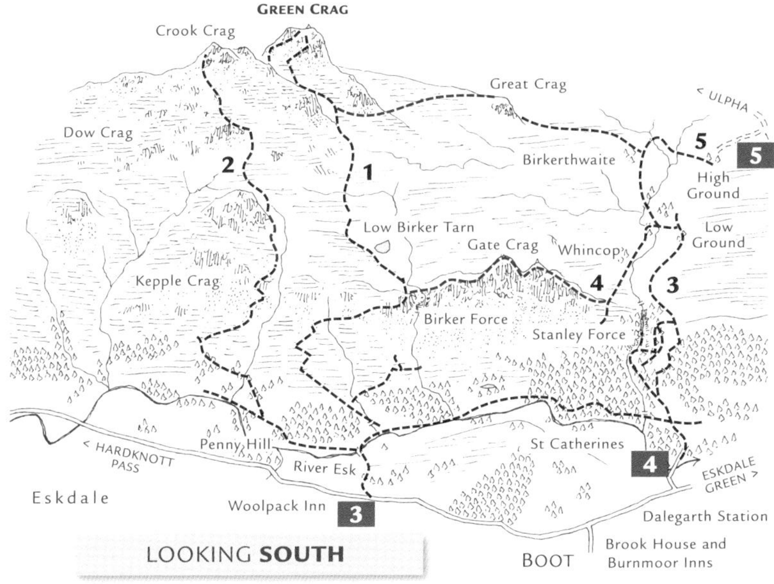

Keep on the path all the way through the light bracken, making for the damp slope that rises to the saddle between Crook Crag and Green Crag.

Low Birker peat hut

Green Crag from Crook Crag

2 Follow the hedged lane ahead towards Penny Hill Farm. A permissive path has been created to avoid unnecessary disturbance to the farmyard so you are ushered right and left through gates, rejoining the open track leading to another gate and a lonesome pine. The track then forks. Keep right, rising to a gate, then slant left up to a wall and go right to a gate by an old pen. Rising with the wall on your left, ignore the 'Harter Fell' sign directing left and keep right on the winding track, passing three ruined peat stores as you round Kepple Crag. Then slipping over a low saddle between damp combes, head straight up the fell south without a path. Keep to the right of the prominent outcrops to find a fresh path which glances by the lateral ridge top of Crook Crag, en route for the main saddle past a unique boundary stone, and carries on straight up to the summit.

ASCENT FROM DALEGARTH HALL (4)

Low Ground via Stanley Force 120m/395ft 2km/1¼ miles

3 From the car park a lane leads south from the river, crossing the line of the Eskdale Trail – recommended as a means of completing circular walks at scenic dale-floor level. There are two options: either remain with the rising gated lane and subsequent track; or visit the luxuriant environs of Stanley Ghyll, linking back to the open track above the woodland. To visit the waterfall, enter the wooded National Park Access Area through a gate. The popular path leads upstream crossing three footbridges in the darkly shaded ravine en route to the 40ft plunge pool of Stanley Force, the spray making paths and woodwork slippery. Visitors are warned not to venture beyond, as there is no route through to the open fell. (During my visit a walker ignored the advice and returned shamefacedly admitting that the notice was spot on – some seem to believe that such notices are put up for disinformation!) Having enjoyed the waterfall, backtrack and take the stepped path beside a tiny gill from between the second and third footbridges. The path bends right to descend, with a lovely view ahead of Scafell framed by the foreground woodland, but at this point take the path left to emerge from the wood at a gate and rejoin your original track. Go left, shortly passing through a gate and keep on the green track to the lonely retreat of Low Ground. Cross the stile beside the white-washed cottage and turn left down its access lane to a fork.

Via Gate Crag 350m/1150ft 4.5km/2¾ miles

From the end of Route 3, Route 4 leads off on the left fork to Whincop, but there are two other tracks leading off from the right fork, each useful links to Route 5. The main track leads to High Ground, still a working farm, and eventually meets the road but turning left on a footpath at the conifer spinney leads you directly to and through Birkerthwaite. **4** Take the left fork and at the first gate left in a dip, enter an enclosure containing young deciduous trees. Cross the stone bridge and follow the track to Whincop. Pass through the environs of this old steading, whose name means 'gorse viewpoint'. Go left of the house down a short lane to a ladder-stile and flag bridge, keeping the wall to the left amid bracken. Ignore the next ladder-stile, defended by a damp patch of ground and instead skirt right intent on the prominent rising scarp ridge. Ford the tiny gill and make up the rock spine on an evident path. The immediate views into Eskdale are charming and warrant frequent contemplative pauses, with

Cairn on Gate Crag

Upper Eskdale from above Birker Force

the backdrop of Scafell and the fells at the head of Eskdale equally inspiring. The ridge culminates at the cairned top of Hartley Crag. Continue, dipping to cross the broken wall short of Gate Crag, the next rise in the ridge. Another cairn marks the top of this higher crest, which also offers much for the eyes and camera. There is no path to the head of Birker Force from here, but the terrain, although damp, is simple and your course is due east.

ASCENT FROM BIRKERFELL ROAD – DEVOKE WATER (5)

Via Great Crag 285m/935ft 4km/2½ miles

5 If you press me I'll admit that my favourite route to the top begins from the Birkerfell Road at the point where the Devoke Water access track departs west. Go east, down the open road to High Ground. Bear right, with the wall on your left, on the gated track signposted to Birkerthwaite. At the white-walled Ganny House Cottage branch off right to the gate in the paddock corner. Pass through the sheep pen, now with a wall on your left. Ignore the wall-stile by the next gate and rise gently to a broken stile/gate at the fence top. A grass path slants on below Great Crag towards the modest saddle. Where the remains of an old wall abut the crag you can scramble up a steep ramp, or skirt round the crag altogether and climb the summit from the east. There are two cairned tops, both excellent viewpoints. From here there is no path across rough fell, but your route is in a north-easterly direction bound for the saddle north-west of the Green Crag stack. Turn right on Route 1 and find a ramp, high on the north side, which gives access to the summit.

ASCENT FROM THE DUDDON VALLEY (46 & 45)

From Birks Bridge down through the Wallowbarrow Gorge the River Duddon is at its most impressive for walkers. The circuit from The Newfield Inn up the gorge from the memorial footbridge to Fickle Steps, rising to Grassguards and turning back south on the track to High Wallowbarrow is one of Lakeland's most cherished dale walks. If

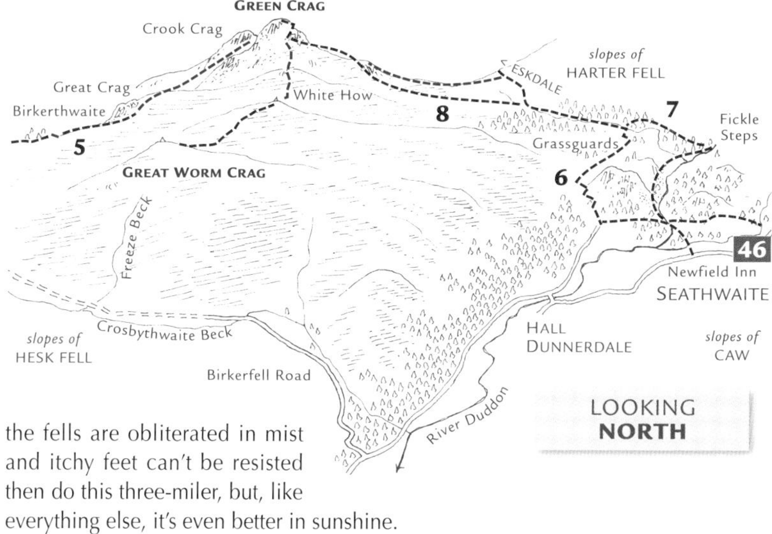

the fells are obliterated in mist and itchy feet can't be resisted then do this three-miler, but, like everything else, it's even better in sunshine.

Via Wallowbarrow Crag 380m/1250ft 5.2km/3¼ miles

6 Two paths converge on the memorial footbridge. One begins opposite The Newfield Inn, while the second begins at the school house, both crossing Tarn Beck

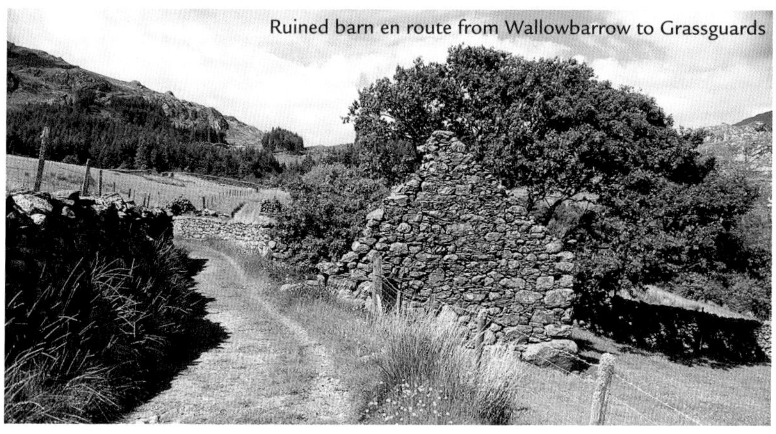

Ruined barn en route from Wallowbarrow to Grassguards

on footbridges. From the memorial footbridge, follow the path ahead into pasture, through gates to reach High Wallowbarrow Farm. Turn right before the house, climbing through more gates up to the saddle beside Wallowbarrow Crag. This is a popular venue for climbers, being south-facing and low the routes are usually dry and quickly reached. An open track pursues a northerly course through deer gates in the tall fence and enters a lane flanked by massive drystone walls. The views hereabouts are quite delightful. Approaching Grassguards itself, use the permissive path avoiding the farmyard and skirt around the garden hedge through hand-gates to reach Grassguards Gill and Route 7.

Via Wallowbarrow Gorge 390m/1280ft 5.5km/3½ miles

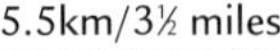

7 Grassguards can also be reached on a footpath ascending the gill from Fickle Steps. The stepping stones are fickle indeed, other than in drought conditions, and difficult to cross, despite the metal cable. The better approach is up the gorge from the memorial footbridge, the large boulder scree a startling feature and the river tightly hemmed in with trees. **8** From Grassguards the path is clearly marked by gates and planks. Watch for the left turn at the top, as the footpath to Eskdale veers through the broken wall right but your path bears left. Cross a ladder-stile over the wall onto the open fell, a narrow sheep track pursuing a rather serpentine course west-south-west towards Green Crag. The summit is attained by rounding an outcrop, right then left.

Old boundary stone beneath Green Crag

THE SUMMIT

The greatest crags on Green Crag face west. The summit is ringed by rock walls, which can be efficiently penetrated either via a ramp from the north or a small step from the east. Being a fell-top frequented only by the more discerning walker the small summit cairn is not much disturbed and looks old. The views are long – the string of tops to Black Combe outshone by the major summits of the Western and Mid-Western groups and the Coniston fells to the right of the nearby peaked summit of Harter Fell.

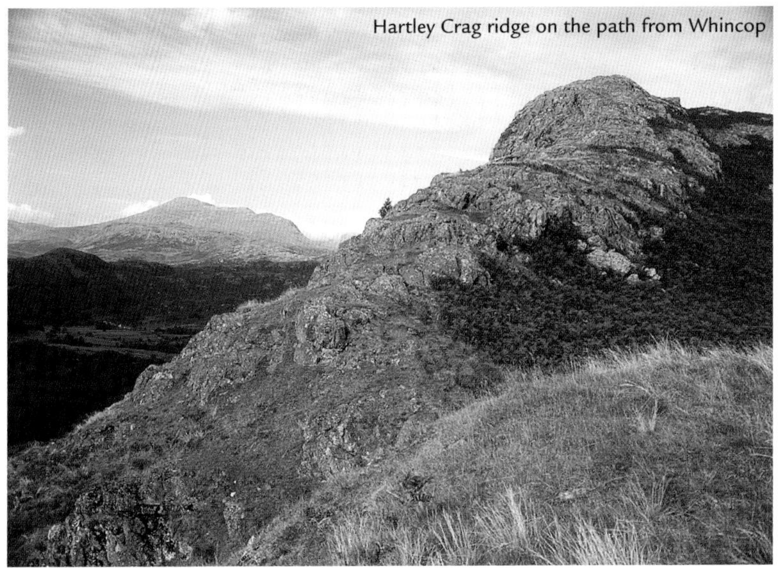
Hartley Crag ridge on the path from Whincop

SAFE DESCENTS

Care is needed right from the start, particularly in mist. Backtrack by whichever of the two routes you arrived by, so that you are retracing familiar ground. Then aim north down to the broad grassy saddle. Find the embedded stone boundary marker in the midst of the saddle and take a bearing NE, crossing the featureless peaty, tussocky moor. Cross a fence stile at the corner of forestry and join the Eskdale–Duddon path.

RIDGE ROUTES

GREAT WORM CRAG ↓40m/130ft ↑90m/290ft 2.4km/1½ miles

An intermittent path holds to the broad ridge, with some marsh to skirt and one nice top to stand on, White How, at which point the ridge changes orientation from SSE to SW.

HARTER FELL ↓145m/465ft ↑310m/990ft 3.2km/2 miles

Head down to the broad saddle N of the summit. Locate the boundary stone, take a bearing NE across the moor. Cross the fence stile at the NW end of the largely felled forestry. A clear path climbs, initially with a tall fence on the right, continuing ENE to the summit.

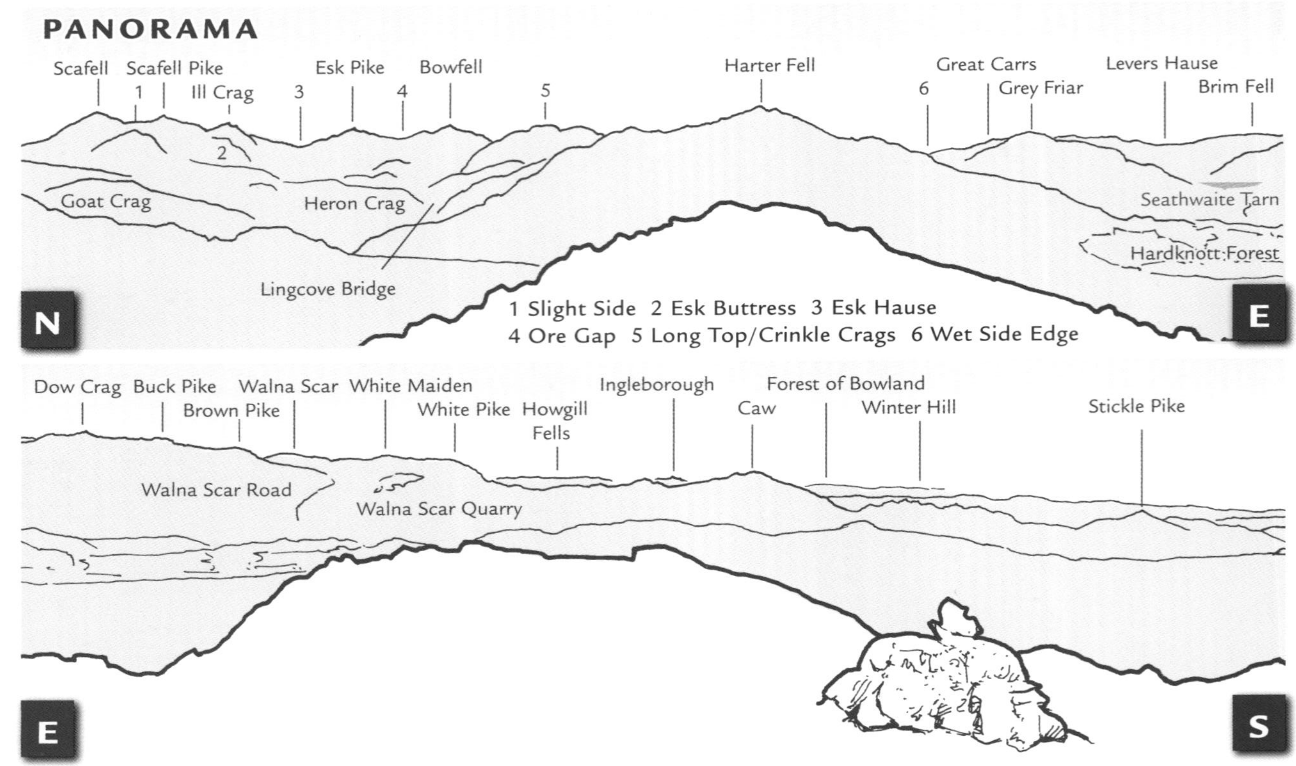
PANORAMA
Scafell
Scafell Pike
1
Ill Crag
3
Esk Pike
4
Bowfell
5
Harter Fell
6
Great Carrs
Grey Friar
Levers Hause
Brim Fell
2
Goat Crag
Heron Crag
Seathwaite Tarn
Hardknott Forest
Lingcove Bridge
N
E
1 Slight Side 2 Esk Buttress 3 Esk Hause
4 Ore Gap 5 Long Top/Crinkle Crags 6 Wet Side Edge
Dow Crag
Buck Pike
Brown Pike
Walna Scar
White Maiden
White Pike
Howgill Fells
Ingleborough
Caw
Forest of Bowland
Winter Hill
Stickle Pike
Walna Scar Road
Walna Scar Quarry
E
S

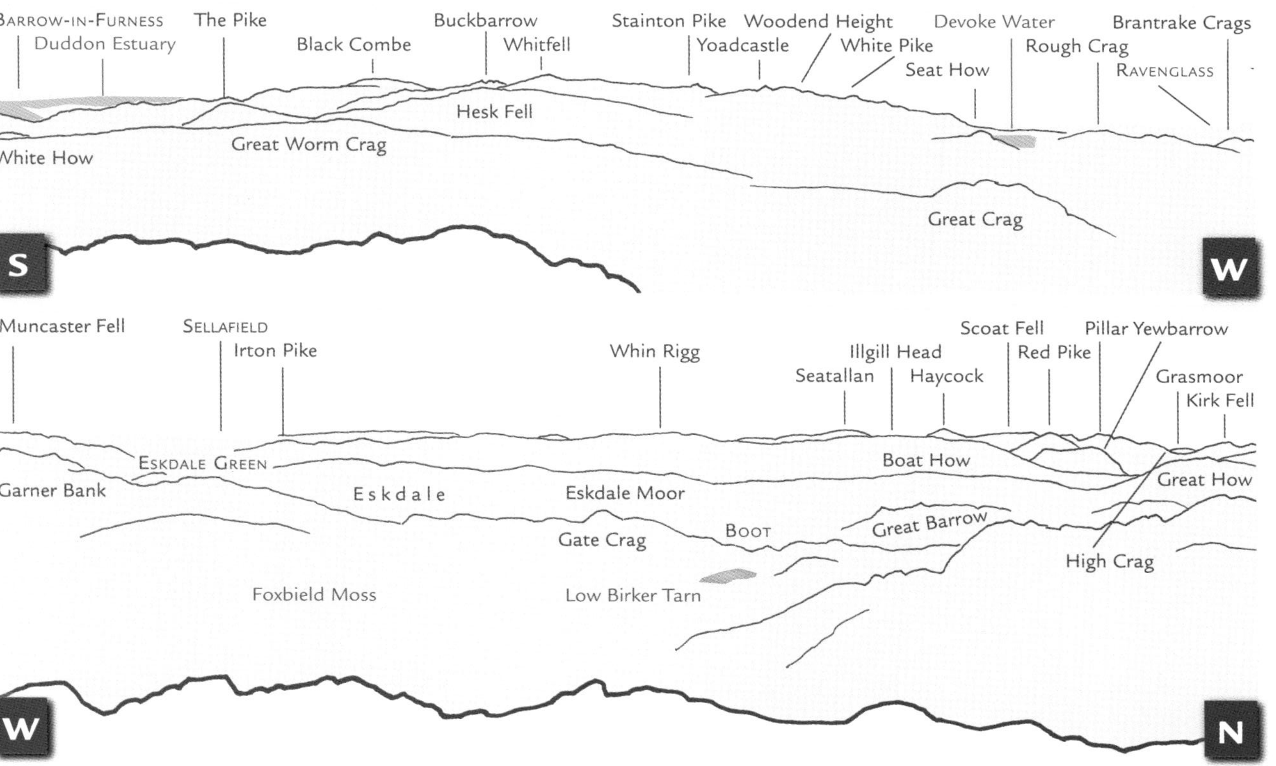
Barrow-in-Furness
Duddon Estuary
The Pike
Black Combe
Buckbarrow
Whitfell
Stainton Pike
Yoadcastle
Woodend Height
White Pike
Seat How
Devoke Water
Rough Crag
Ravenglass
Brantrake Crags
Hesk Fell
Great Worm Crag
White How
Great Crag
S
W
Muncaster Fell
Sellafield
Irton Pike
Whin Rigg
Seatallan
Illgill Head
Haycock
Scoat Fell
Red Pike
Pillar Yewbarrow
Grasmoor
Kirk Fell
Eskdale Green
Boat How
Great How
Garner Bank
Eskdale
Eskdale Moor
Gate Crag
Boot
Great Barrow
High Crag
Foxbield Moss
Low Birker Tarn
W
N

11 GREY FRIAR *(772m, 2533ft)*

The Franciscan Grey Friars, like the famous north Lakes huntsman John Peel, were renowned for their grey attire. Perhaps Grey Friar has some lost connection with itinerant monks because this fell is no more grey than any other Lakeland peak. In fact from a distance it seems to lack any distinction. Even from Hardnott Pass it looks bulky, featureless and none too inviting.

Whatever the long view, as a climb it is pleasurable, especially for its northern outlook, which shows the Scafells in true proportion for once. Another attraction is that, being west of the main Coniston ridge, it does not gather many wandering visitors, but only those who make the extra effort to cross the hause and rest beside either of the twin summit cairns.

The map shows how nature has bequeathed an apparently dour fell a curious long, low toe-hold in verdant Seathwaite and the dramatic Wallowbarrow Gorge. Of the watercourses most closely identified with the fell, that of Tarn Beck needs special mention as it tumbles west from the hanging valley cradling Seathwaite Tarn, bounding excitedly over

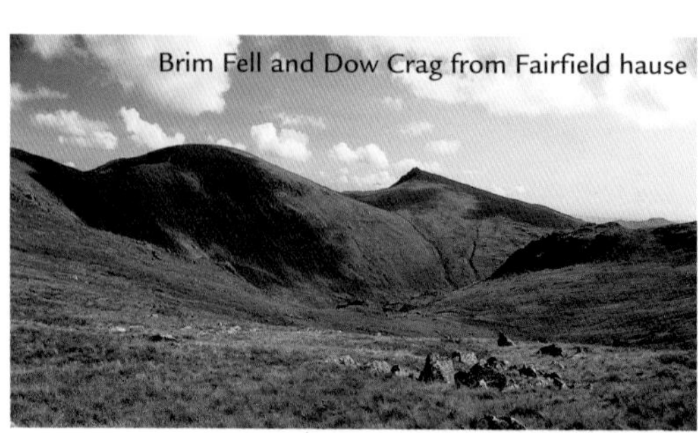

Brim Fell and Dow Crag from Fairfield hause

↑ Grey Friar from Goats Hawse

great boulders. Seathwaite Tarn, an austere reservoir, may lack the more obvious charm of many a Lakeland corrie tarn but the craggy slopes give it a wild dignity.

Despite extensive rocky ground, only Great and Little Blake Riggs have climbing potential. Beneath Great Blake Rigg, a little further up the combe, are ruins and spoil from three small-scale coppermine levels. The head-stream, leading into Calf Cove, has several easily observed waterfalls.

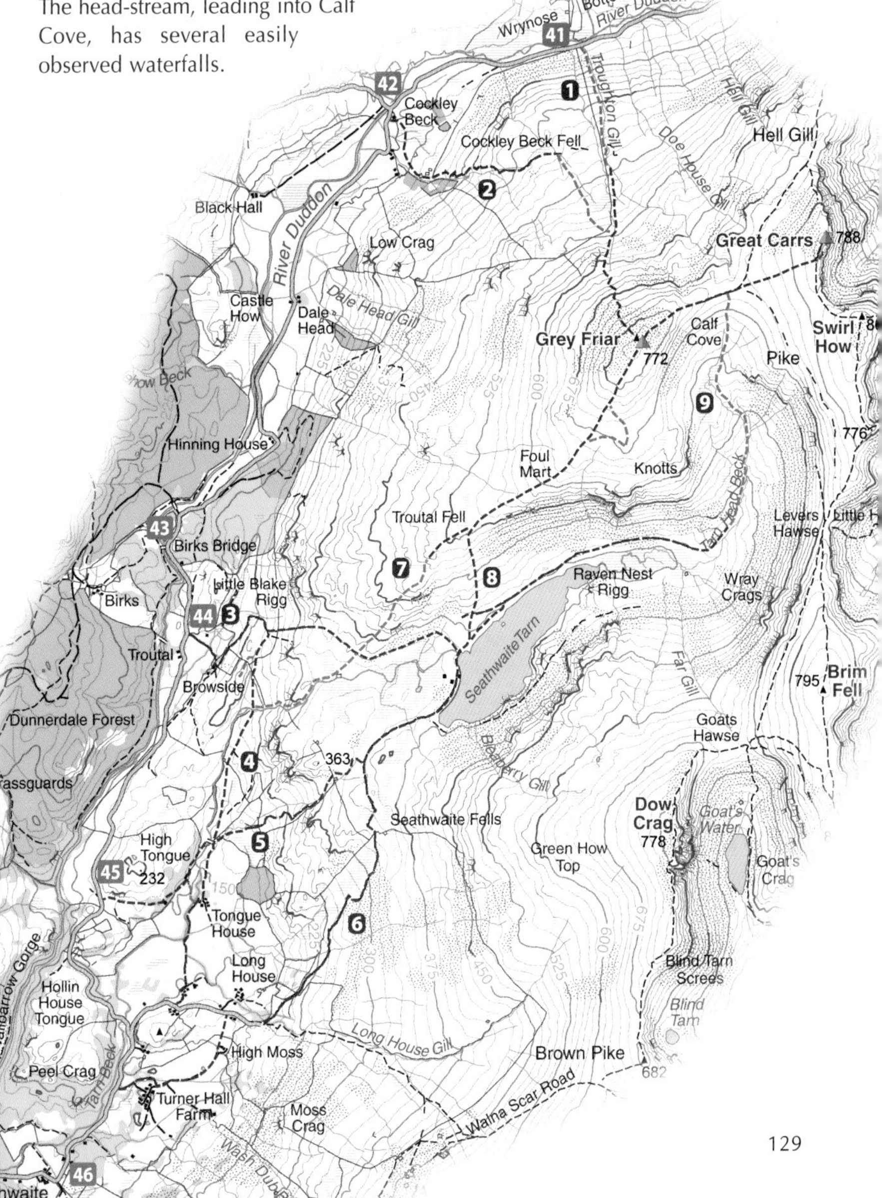

Grey Friar from Hellgill Pike

ASCENT FROM WRYNOSE BOTTOM (41) AND COCKLEY BECK BRIDGE (42)

Via Troughton Beck 520m/1710ft 2km/1¼ miles

The open road running down-dale from Wrynose Pass crosses a cattle grid at GR257019. **1** Immediately before this, you can start a direct ascent of Grey Friar. Climb the initially steep grass and boulder slope between Troughton Gill and the fence (no path). Rise to the top of the fenced (broken wall) enclosure on your right.

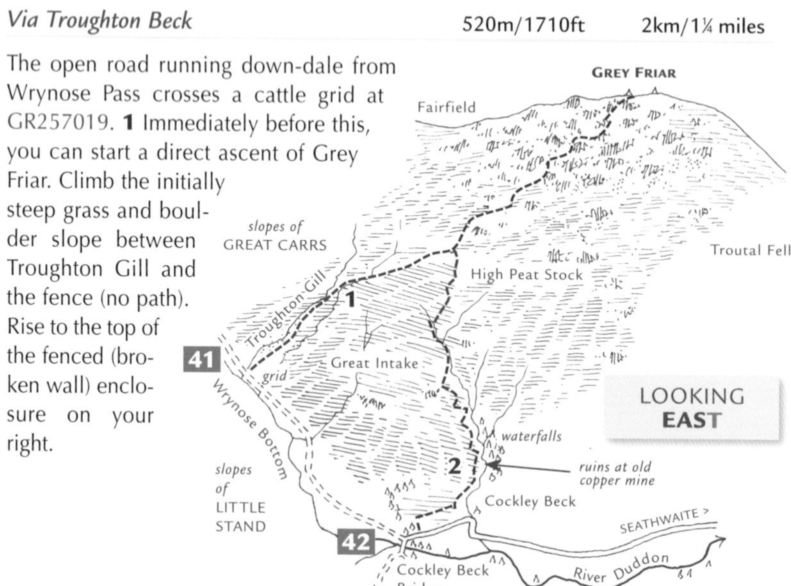

Via Great Intake 550m/1800ft 2.5km/1½ miles

2 This point may also be reached from Cockley Beck Bridge, where there is better casual car parking available and a cottage tea room. Immediately south of the house find a stile guiding a footpath along the edge of a paddock to a wall-stile. Go right, over damp ground to join a track emerging from behind the farm buildings. Follow this, winding uphill past the remains of an old coppermine (right) to a stile/gate. The track ventures onto the broad marshy shoulder. Bear south-south-east, rising to a stile in the fence to meet the direct ascent.

Go round to the left of the outcrop, following small cairns, and climb quite steeply on a southerly course, dodging intermittent outcrops, to reach the north top on the skyline.

ASCENT FROM THE DUDDON VALLEY (44, 45 & 46)

Via Troutal Fell 580m/1910ft 4.2km/2¾ miles

Lower down the valley a cluster of attractive approach routes begin, Seathwaite Tarn dam the principal mid-point objective. **3** An efficient path starts from Troutal, following the gated approach track to Browside. Go left from the gate near the isolated house on a track through a further gate soon switching back uphill to a gateway in the top wall. Three paths could be followed from this point, but the best, a nice turf trod, is signposted right. This curves around the right side of an outcrop and comes back left. Watch for waymark posts guiding round marshy ground as you head on towards the dam.

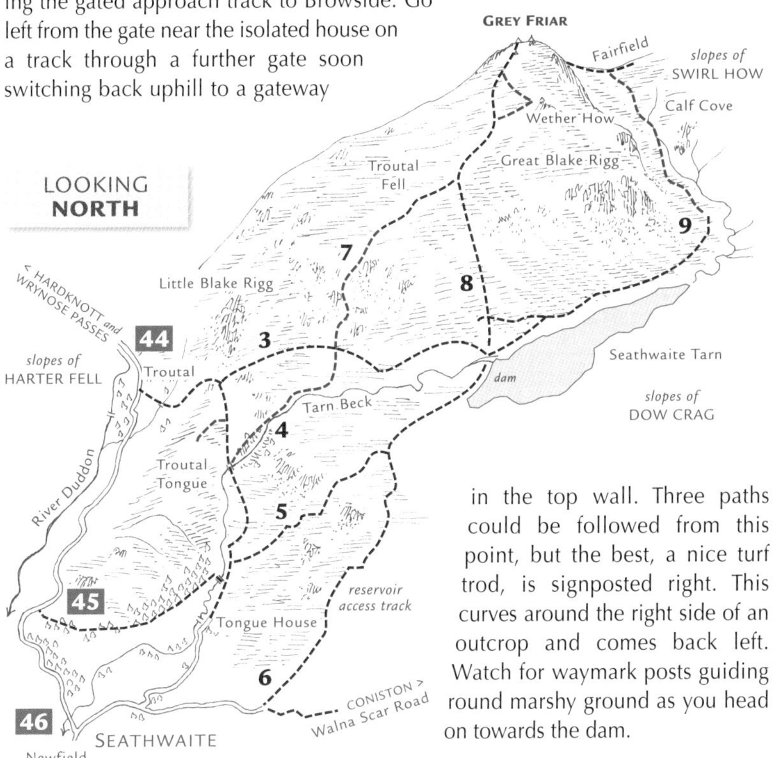

Troutal from the path above Browside

Via Tarn Beck **620m/2040ft 5.5km/3½ miles**

4 A superb second option homing in on this tract of fell explores the delights of the Tarn Beck valley either from Seathwaite (road walk via Hollin House to Tongue House) or the common above Fickle Steps. From the common, trace the footpath east down through bracken and woodland behind a barn into pasture at a stile and then either continue to Tongue House or go left by Thrang Cottage and on to a hand-gate to cross a small footbridge over Tarn Beck. A footpath now accompanies the beck upstream, avoiding wet ground as best it can and heading for a wooden footbridge at the bottom of the Tarn Beck cascades. (While walkers will be grateful for the standard footbridge, many may consider the setting deserved a more scenic model.) The footpath continues over a ladder-stile and through a gate to link up with Route 3. (On the way you can visit the top of Troutal Tongue (troutal = 'trout hall', tongue = 'a low jutting ridge'), to your left, over a stile at the ridge-end – a superb viewpoint for Harter Fell.) But the really exciting choice branches off up the rough north bank through the bracken climbing through the breach where the wall meets the falls, scrambling easily up the sequence of great boulder steps beside the amazing fuming falls. Once on the level wet moor bear left from the old sheepfold to join the contouring path (Route 3), or **7** climb straight on up the fellside, aiming for the notch in the skyline, onto Troutal Fell, a narrow path emerging as you reach the ridge. **5** A well-used footpath also winds up the rough pastures from Tongue House to meet the reservoir access track.

Footbridge at the foot of the Tarn Beck cascades

Via Calf Cove **660m/2170ft 9.2km/5¾ miles**

6 For greatest ease, follow the Walna Scar Road up from Seathwaite. There is also the well-marked path through the fields via Turner Hall and High Moss (the Manchester-based Rucksack Club Hut), which takes a significant slice out of road walking. As the road turns into a track at a gate, take the left branch through another gate, this being the access track to the dam. Cross the dam wall footway. **8** From this point a direct ascent heads straight ahead up the obvious rigg slightly east of north onto Troutal Fell, with a clear path underfoot. This is a very pleasant approach. The summit dome seems distant for much of the way. In the closing stages, a brief deviation right will take in the cairn on the prominent pike of Wether How, high above Great Blake Rigg. Returning to the path, the summit plateau is shortly reached at a guide cairn. **9** The path that leads along the northern shore of Seathwaite Tarn is rather more likely to be used as a return leg, but venturing into the headstream via Calf Cove is an interesting expedition. Beyond the reservoir the path passes an area of coppermining activity, crossing a spoil apron – a good pitch for a wild camp. Pass ruined miners' dens vacated in the early 19th century, on a dwindling path which contours by two further blocked mine levels with associated spoil tongues and ruined stone huts. Follow the western and then the eastern bank of Tarn Head Beck climbing steadily into Calf Cove, passing successive perched erratics, fine subjects for the camera, and climb without a path to Fairfield hause. Go left (west), now with the clear ridge path.

THE SUMMIT

A gentle dome informally interspersed with low outcrops and two parallel ribs, some 40m apart, each surmounted by a cairn, define the highest ground. The summit faces the less flattering aspect of Brim Fell, Coniston Old Man and Dow Crag but the view

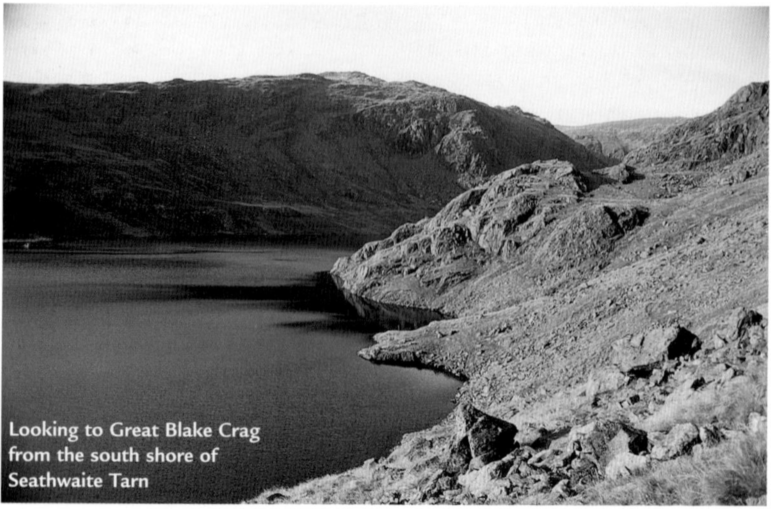

Looking to Great Blake Crag from the south shore of Seathwaite Tarn

Matterhorn Rock near the summit of Grey Friar

to the north is excellent. Watching fellow fell-top visitors is an interesting pastime in itself. So often walkers casually miss the best prospects by assuming the summit is the only place to halt. I have been to this spot three times this season and seen walkers ignore the northern cairn on each visit.

SAFE DESCENTS

In mist a plateau top like this can be troublesome, especially with craggy slopes tucked imminently under the broad SE and NW edges, the SE being the more treacherous. Cautious walkers can thread down through the broken north-western slopes en route to Cockley Beck Bridge in low cloud. However, it is far better to take a bearing SW onto Troutal Fell and seek the easier slopes leading to the Seathwaite Tarn dam. Although more long-winded, the slopes leading into Calf Cove from Fairfield hause are also quite benign. Walk ENE to the grassy col and then slip pathless into the hollow keeping with Tarn Head Beck and avoiding the valley marshes by traversing above Seathwaite Tarn. The two routes converge at the dam. You can then either follow the open path to the N of the outflowing beck to reach Troutal via Browside, or, having crossed the dam, join the assured track to the metalled Walna Scar road leading to Seathwaite... and an inn!

RIDGE ROUTE

GREAT CARRS ↓145m/480ft ↑130m/425ft 1.2km/¾ mile

If only all ridge routes were this simple... but guidance may be necessary in mist. From the summit cairn aim NE, pass the Matterhorn Rock (see photograph above) and descend with the ridge path to arrive at a three-way fork on Fairfield hause. Take the middle course ENE, up the largely grassy slope to the summit.

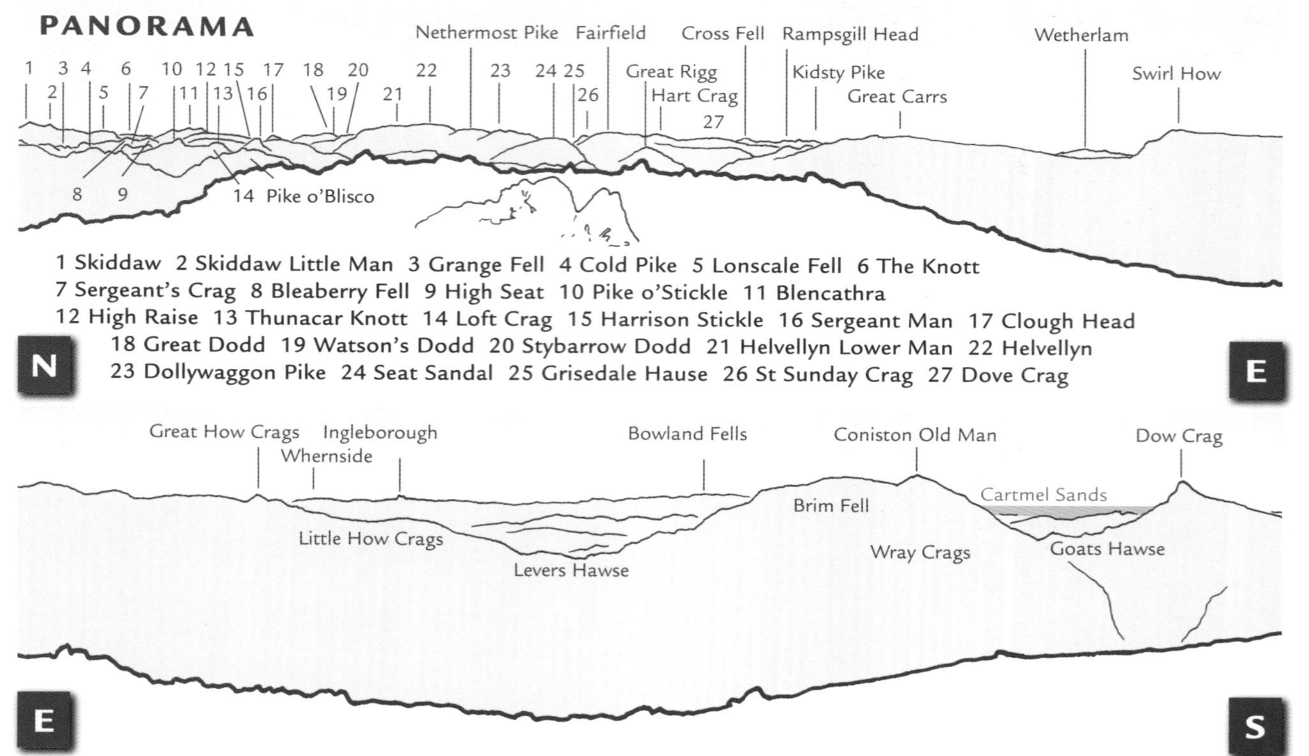
PANORAMA
Nethermost Pike
Fairfield
Cross Fell
Rampsgill Head
Wetherlam
Great Rigg
Hart Crag
Kidsty Pike
Great Carrs
Swirl How
14 Pike o'Blisco
1 Skiddaw 2 Skiddaw Little Man 3 Grange Fell 4 Cold Pike 5 Lonscale Fell 6 The Knott
7 Sergeant's Crag 8 Bleaberry Fell 9 High Seat 10 Pike o'Stickle 11 Blencathra
12 High Raise 13 Thunacar Knott 14 Loft Crag 15 Harrison Stickle 16 Sergeant Man 17 Clough Head
18 Great Dodd 19 Watson's Dodd 20 Stybarrow Dodd 21 Helvellyn Lower Man 22 Helvellyn
23 Dollywaggon Pike 24 Seat Sandal 25 Grisedale Hause 26 St Sunday Crag 27 Dove Crag
N
E
Great How Crags
Ingleborough
Whernside
Bowland Fells
Coniston Old Man
Dow Crag
Cartmel Sands
Brim Fell
Little How Crags
Levers Hawse
Wray Crags
Goats Hawse
E
S

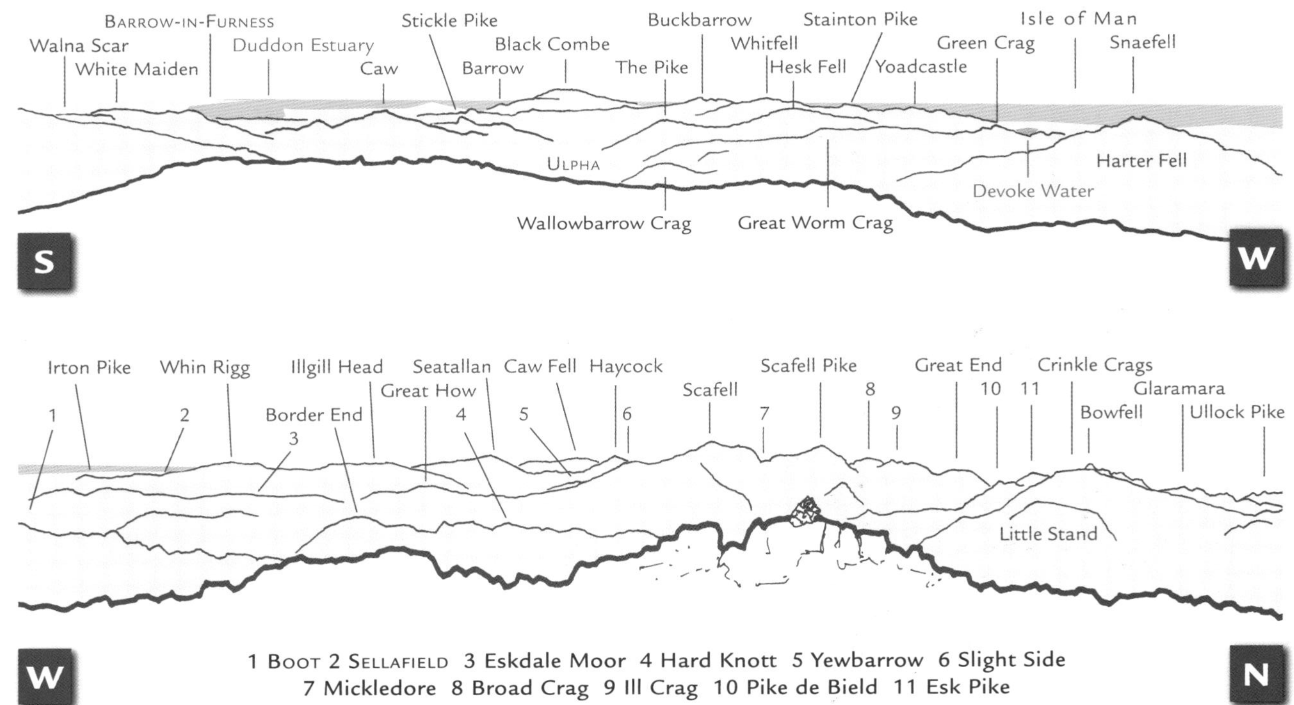
Barrow-in-Furness
Walna Scar
White Maiden
Duddon Estuary
Caw
Stickle Pike
Black Combe
Barrow
Buckbarrow
The Pike
Whitfell
Hesk Fell
Stainton Pike
Yoadcastle
Green Crag
Isle of Man
Snaefell
Ulpha
Harter Fell
Devoke Water
Wallowbarrow Crag
Great Worm Crag
S
W
Irton Pike
1
Whin Rigg
2
Illgill Head
Border End
3
Great How
Seatallan
4
Caw Fell
5
Haycock
6
Scafell
7
Scafell Pike
8
9
Great End
10
11
Crinkle Crags
Glaramara
Bowfell
Ullock Pike
Little Stand
W
N
1 Boot 2 Sellafield 3 Eskdale Moor 4 Hard Knott 5 Yewbarrow 6 Slight Side
7 Mickledore 8 Broad Crag 9 Ill Crag 10 Pike de Bield 11 Esk Pike

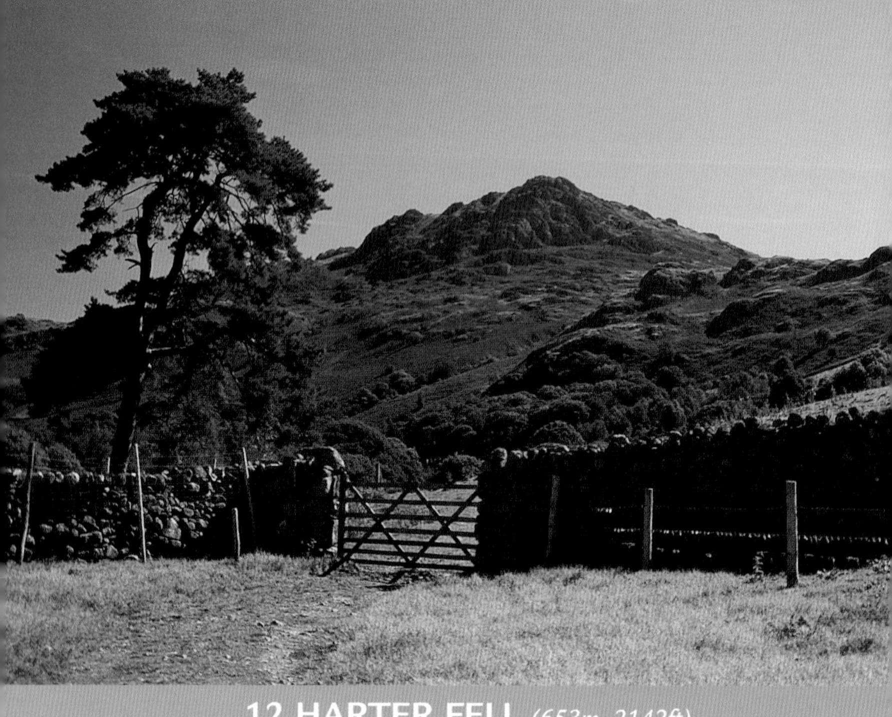

12 HARTER FELL *(653m, 2142ft)*

Harter Fell is every inch a fellwalker's fell. There are no climbs here, despite the abundance of rock, especially on the summit. And what a summit it is – a playground for scramblers and a viewpoint for dreamers. Its craggy top catches the traveller's eye from the Duddon at Cockley Beck Bridge and from Hardknott Pass, where its heather-tiered northern slopes can be clearly seen, but the best view of all is from Eskdale, where it rises from the woods and meadows to a majestic peak. It is a fell of great individuality and no little beauty which marks the real beginning of the high fells from the south-west. Even better, the conifers of Hardknott Forest that have dominated the fell's lower slopes have now come of age and great swathes have been felled with plans afoot for more diverse woodland to grace the Duddon Valley. Climb Harter from Eskdale and sense for yourself the wonderful setting.

 ↑ Harter Fell from Penny Hill

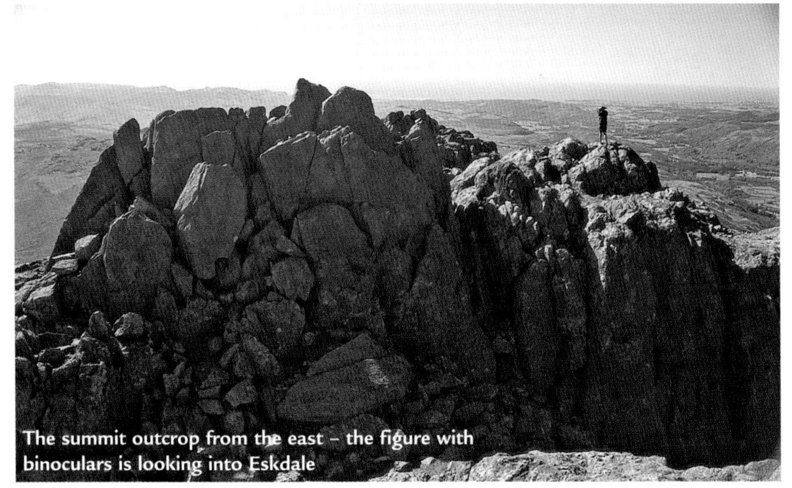

The summit outcrop from the east – the figure with binoculars is looking into Eskdale

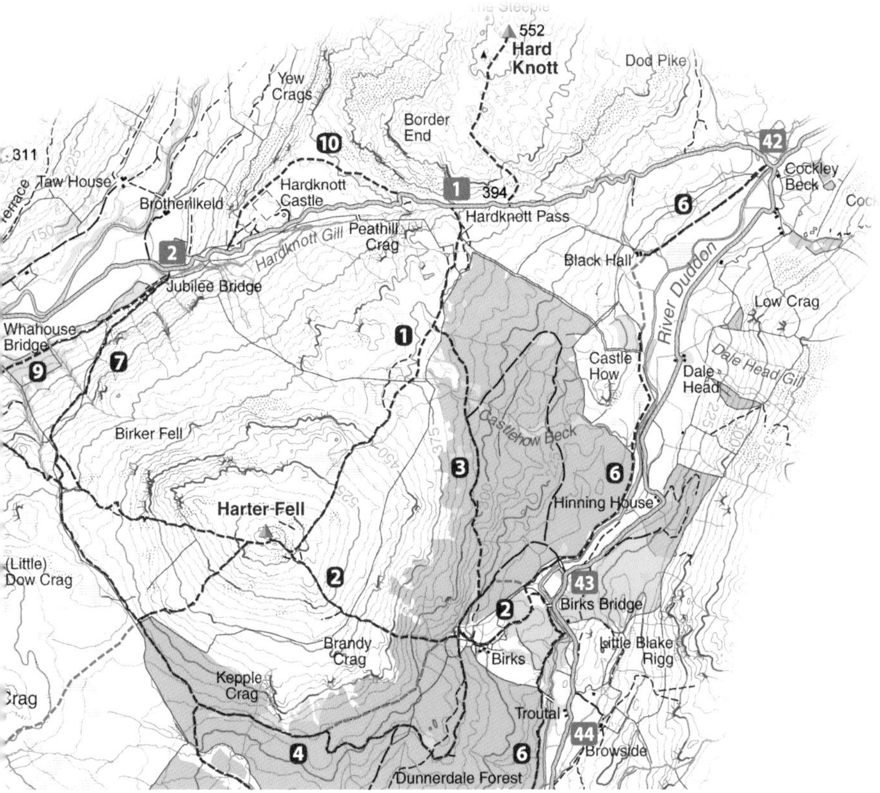

Map continues p140

Map continued from p139

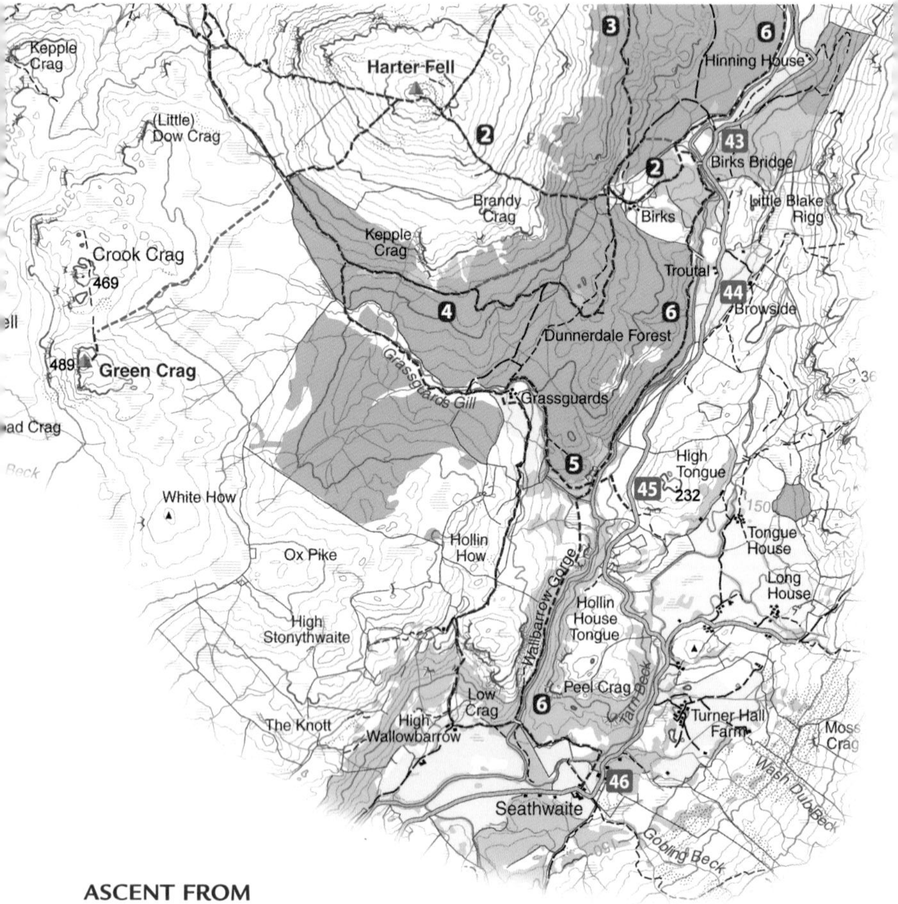

ASCENT FROM HARDKNOTT PASS (1)

Via Demming Crag 262m/860ft 2.5km/1½ miles

1 From the top of the pass cross the cattle grid and descend with the road on the west side to where a bridleway is signposted left. Follow this path south. Ignore the electric fence stile and cross another fence stile to the right of the broken wall corner. The continuing path traverses an undulating marshy tract of fell. With the upper fringe of forestry close left, drift right to cross a further fence stile. A clear path climbs steadily over heathery ground pitching through a gully, home to the headstream of Castlehow Beck, and rising to join the path from Birks Bridge as the summit tors are met. Approach the summit from the east through a natural breach.

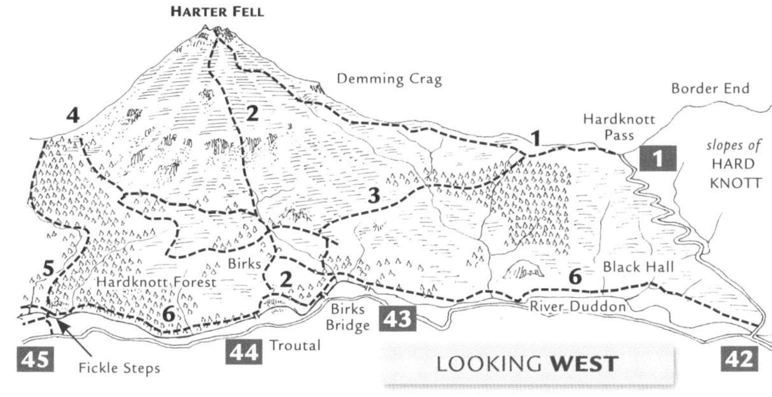

ASCENT FROM BIRKS BRIDGE (43)

Direct 466m/1530ft 2km/1¼ miles

2 From the picturesque environs of Birks Bridge follow a waymarked bridleway up through the oaks of Great Wood and by the Shropshire outdoor centre at Birks onto a track leading to an east–west forest track. Follow the low waymark posts defining a path up beside old walled enclosures, past a felled hollow and up the steep bank due west, climbing beside the stony gill onto the heather banks until you reach a fence-stile. Cross the stile and pass an outcrop with the romantic name Maiden Castle. Soon grass replaces ling as the summit rock bluffs draw near. **3** A seldom-trod footpath runs across the fellside almost due north from the forest track from the outdoor centre. This crosses a further forest track to complete the climb through the residual conifers and reach a hand-gate onto the open fell, joining the path from Hardknott Pass (Route 1).

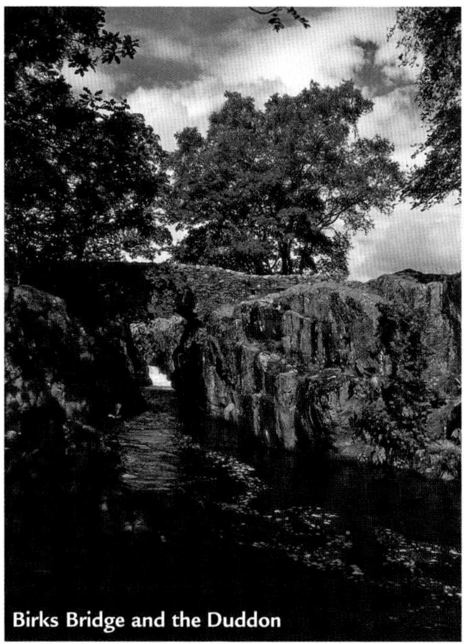
Birks Bridge and the Duddon

ASCENT FROM THE DUDDON VALLEY (45 & 46)

Via Grassguards 470m/1545ft 4km/2½ miles

4 Forest tracks, either from Birks or Grassguards, converge to rise across the southern slopes of Harter Fell, and follow the ancient pedestrian pass leading into Eskdale.

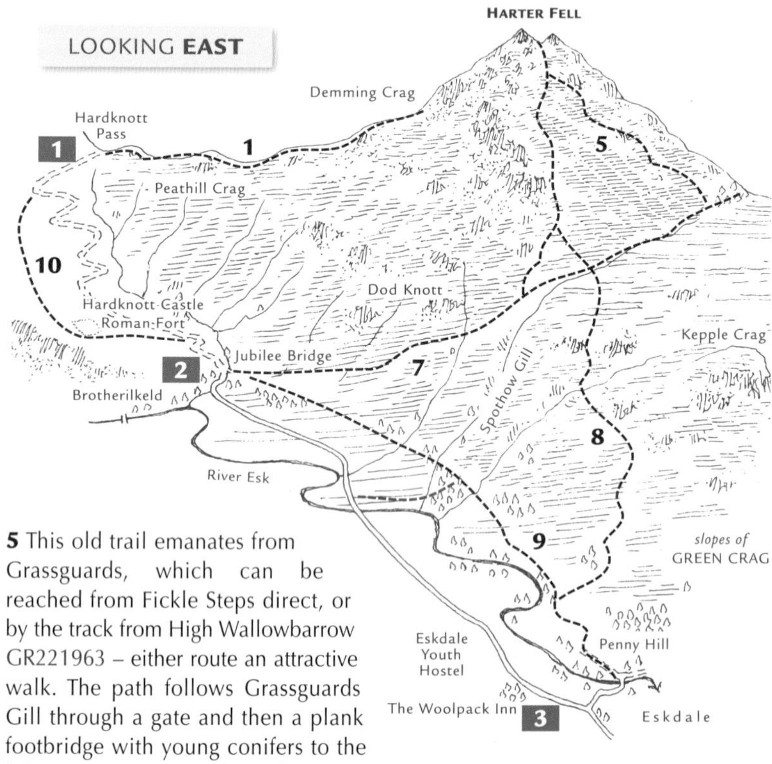

5 This old trail emanates from Grassguards, which can be reached from Fickle Steps direct, or by the track from High Wallowbarrow GR221963 – either route an attractive walk. The path follows Grassguards Gill through a gate and then a plank footbridge with young conifers to the left, mature ones to the right, in an open tract, crossing through a broken wall to the right as the Green Crag path branches left and then exiting the forest at a hand-gate in the fence. Once out of the forest turn sharp right, climbing first with the tall fence, then on open fell, on a good path to the top.

DUDDON VALLEY PATH

Cockley Beck Bridge to High Wallowbarrow via Fickle Steps 4.75km/3 miles

6 A perfect walk for a wet or windy day, this valley path from Cockley Beck Bridge can be followed all the way down to High Wallowbarrow, keeping close to the river most of the way. It can also be used to link the ascents from Duddon for a circular route. A journey of great contrasts, the route begins on a farm track thought to lie on top of the Roman road which once switched up to Hardknott from Black Hall – a former youth hostel and now home to tetchy sheep dogs (the author got nipped for his pains). Still crossing meadows and bending south, the path joins the river beneath Castle How, and heads on by Birks Bridge, now enveloped in woodland and rising and falling on rocky bluffs behind Troutal. After a short densely forested stretch to Fickle Steps, you cross Grassguards Gill footbridge and, after a brief climb, reach the grand finale – the verdant confines of the Wallowbarrow Gorge, with its massive boulder scree. Quite superb.

ASCENT FROM ESKDALE (2 & 3)

Via Jubilee Bridge 562m/1840ft 3.2km/2 miles

7 Satisfying circular walks are to be prized. One such begins from Jubilee Bridge, situated at the foot of the Hardknott Pass. Combining this ascent of Harter Fell with a visit to the Roman Fort on the rigg overlooking the upper Eskdale gorge on the way down (via Routes 1 and 10) brings scenic moments galore. Begin by crossing the little stone

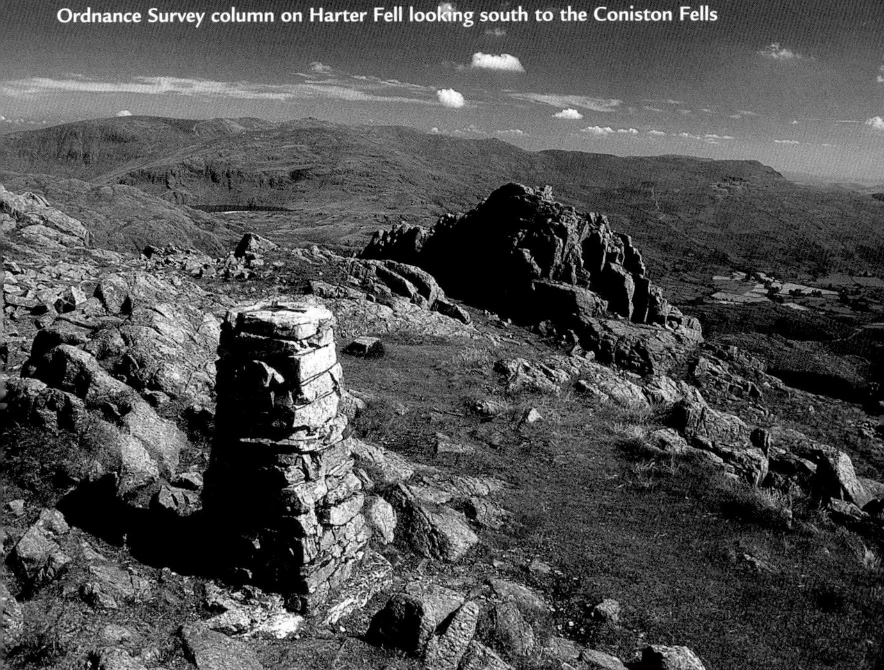

Ordnance Survey column on Harter Fell looking south to the Coniston Fells

Brotherilkeld from the path beneath Dod Knott

footbridge, built in 1977 to commemorate the silver jubilee of Queen Elizabeth II's accession to the throne in 1952. Pass through successive kissing-gates and be sure to take the peat road, the more obvious made-track, ahead. This green-way duly begins to rise and the view back into upper Eskdale is a scene to savour (see photograph opposite). A grand girdle of Lakeland's mightiest fells grace the horizon and in the green dale are scattered old farms with names such as Wha House, Taw House and Brotherilkeld, recalling the Scandinavian settlement of this area. Climb on through the bracken through two hand-gates. As the path from Boot (Route 8) merges from the right, bear away left from the notoriously marshy path that runs on beside the fence to Grassguards and take a clear ascending path. Climb with occasional pitched steps to join forces with the path from the forest edge, beneath a classic volcanic outcrop, and find the gap between the summit battlements.

Via Penny Hill 580m/1900ft 4km/2½ miles

8 From Boot either follow the Eskdale Trail to Doctor Bridge, or start from the Woolpack Inn following the road west to the lane signed 'Penny Hill', which leads over the bridge – a lovely spot to look into the cool clear waters of the Esk. (The river's name means 'source' – a variant of Exe in Devon and Axe in Staffordshire.) Go straight ahead along the hedged, then walled, lane towards Penny Hill Farm. A permissive path, through gates, ushers walkers right and then left avoiding the farmyard. Rejoin the track east of the farm, go through a gate and, as the track forks, go right, rising to a gate. Through the gate, the path veers up left to a wall. Angle right to a gate by old sheep pens and continue up the turf peat road. At the right-hand bend follow a wooden signpost pointing left to 'Harter Fell'. The path traverses with the intake wall to the left and below, slipping through a re-entrant gill aiming diagonally up the facing slope and a gap in the rocks to ford Spothow Gill and reach a stile in the fence. Join the path from Jubilee Bridge (Route 7).

Looking down on Hardknott Roman fort backed by the mighty Scafells at the head of Eskdale

ESKDALE VALLEY PATH

Jubilee Bridge to Doctor Bridge 2.5km/1½ miles

9 The Eskdale Trail crops up from time to time in this guide. A particularly choice passage leads down from Jubilee Bridge. It's largely a meadow-way which offers a pleasing end to a day's walk over Harter Fell.

Descent from Hardknott Pass via Hardknott Castle 2km/1¼ miles

10 A bridleway leaves the Hardknott Pass road at the top hairpin. This leads down past the Roman parade ground and along the scarp by the Roman fort, to rejoin the road just above Jubilee Bridge.

THE SUMMIT

The summit is unmistakable (see photographs below and facing) but whether you choose to clamber onto it is another matter!

The more modest situation of the Ordnance Survey column suffices for many visitors. The view is the real pleasure – a grand panorama with the Scafells and the head of Eskdale perfectly presented.

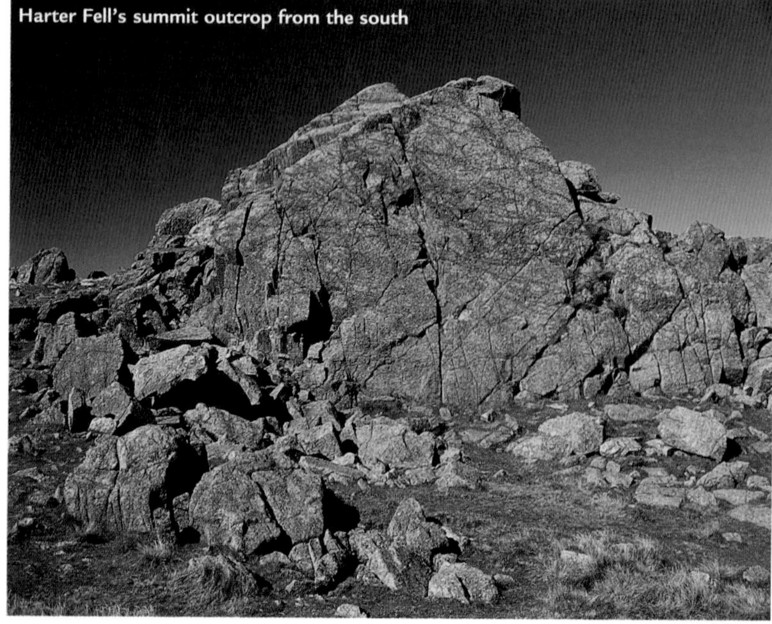

Harter Fell's summit outcrop from the south

...and from the west

SAFE DESCENTS

The first rule of thumb when leaving the summit of Harter Fell is that if there is a path underfoot, you can be confident that it takes you to safety – E to Birks, W to Boot and N to the top of Hardknott Pass.

RIDGE ROUTE

GREEN CRAG ↓310m/990ft ↑145m/465ft 3.2km/2 miles

Follow the regular path descending WSW. Take the left fork below the volcanic outcrop. This path leads down to the edge of the forestry. Glance by the tall fence and ignore the pass path which crosses the fence stile in the corner. Take a bearing SW across the rough peaty moor to reach the broad grassy saddle between Crook and Green Crags. Climb the bank S and gain the summit from the E.

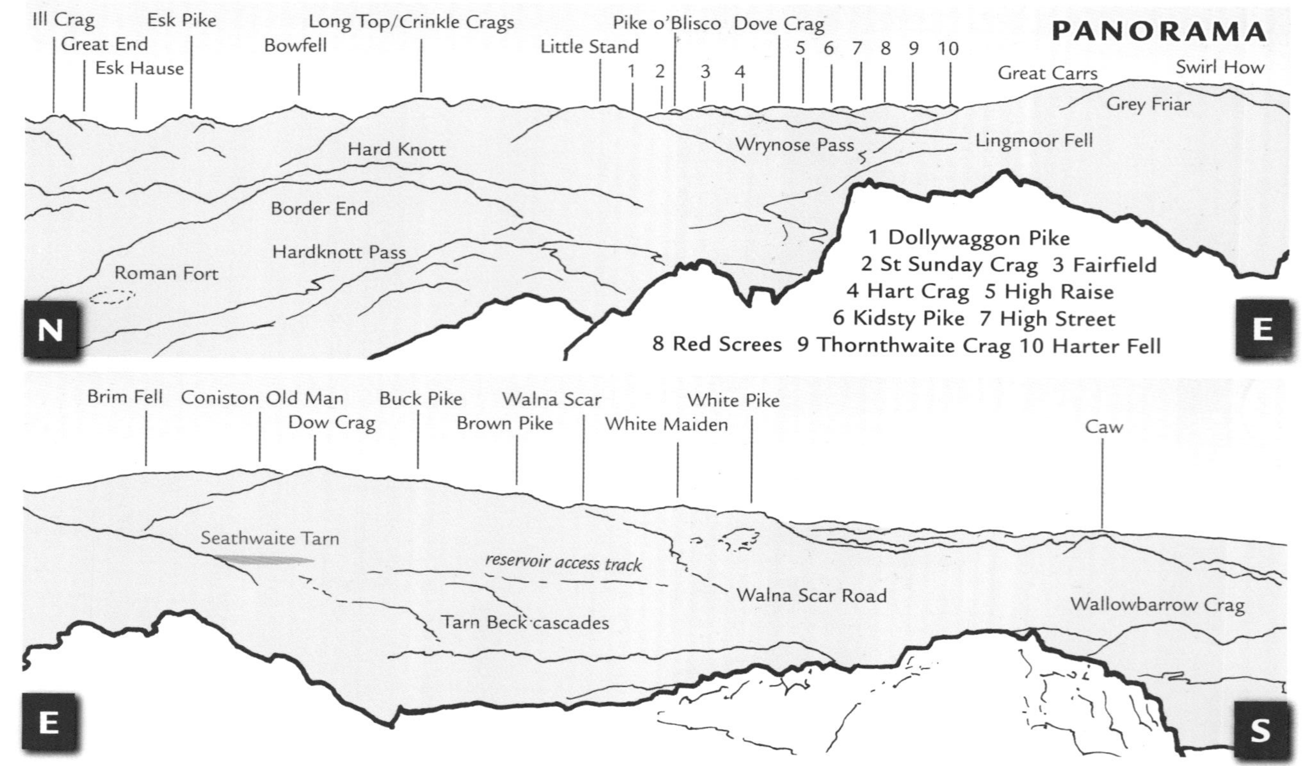
PANORAMA
Ill Crag
Great End
Esk Hause
Esk Pike
Bowfell
Long Top/Crinkle Crags
Little Stand
1
2
Pike o'Blisco
3
4
Dove Crag
5
6
7
8
9
10
Great Carrs
Swirl How
Grey Friar
Lingmoor Fell
Wrynose Pass
Hard Knott
Border End
Hardknott Pass
Roman Fort
1 Dollywaggon Pike
2 St Sunday Crag 3 Fairfield
4 Hart Crag 5 High Raise
6 Kidsty Pike 7 High Street
8 Red Screes 9 Thornthwaite Crag 10 Harter Fell
N
E
Brim Fell
Coniston Old Man
Dow Crag
Buck Pike
Brown Pike
Walna Scar
White Maiden
White Pike
Caw
Seathwaite Tarn
reservoir access track
Walna Scar Road
Tarn Beck cascades
Wallowbarrow Crag
E
S

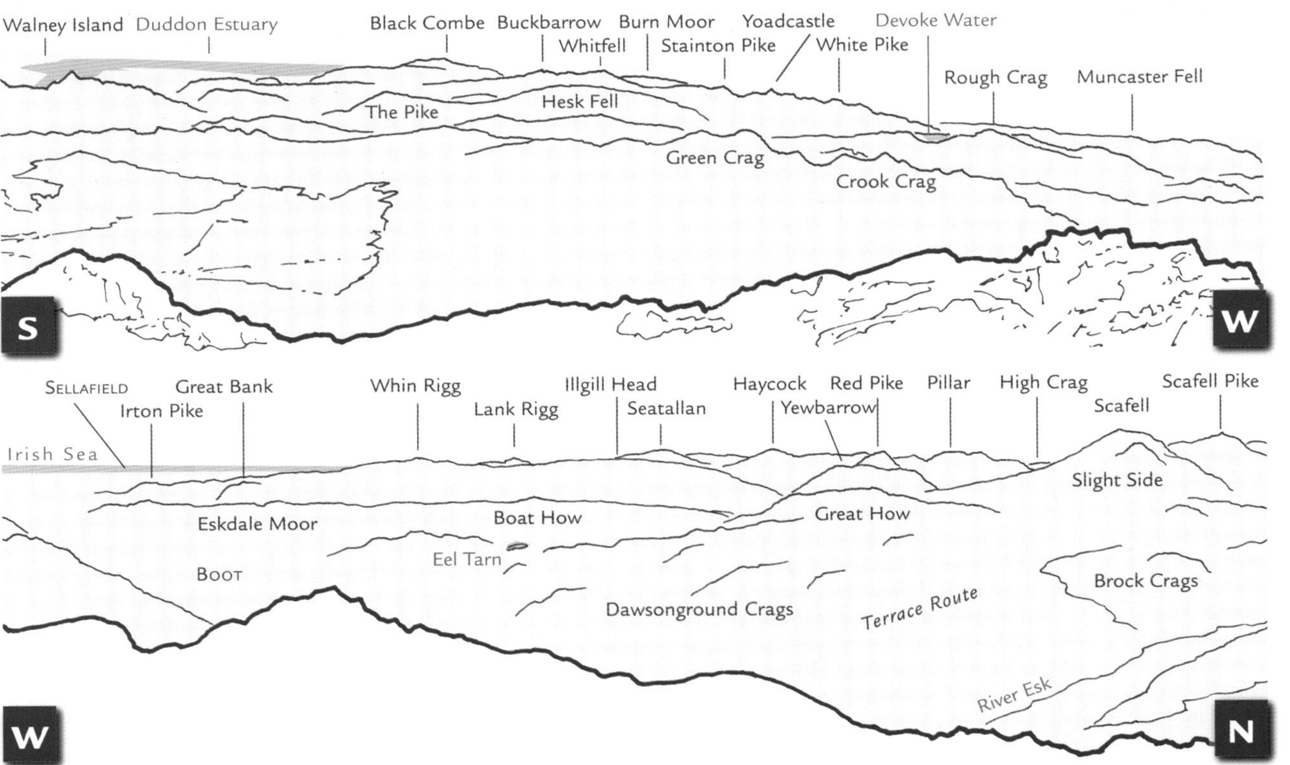
Walney Island
Duddon Estuary
Black Combe
Buckbarrow
Whitfell
Burn Moor
Stainton Pike
Yoadcastle
White Pike
Devoke Water
Rough Crag
Muncaster Fell
The Pike
Hesk Fell
Green Crag
Crook Crag
S
W
SELLAFIELD
Irton Pike
Great Bank
Irish Sea
Whin Rigg
Lank Rigg
Illgill Head
Seatallan
Haycock
Yewbarrow
Red Pike
Pillar
High Crag
Scafell
Scafell Pike
Slight Side
Eskdale Moor
Boat How
Great How
Eel Tarn
Boot
Brock Crags
Dawsonground Crags
Terrace Route
River Esk
W
N

13 HESK FELL *(476m, 1562ft)*

Let's not be too hasty. Puddings (and pudding-shaped fells) can be sweet. Hesk Fell may look like a Pennine outcast but it has interesting historic features to seek out, including the remains of a coppermine and a large Viking enclosure, and with The Pike it makes a striking connection with the Duddon.

Rainsborrow Wood, presently undergoing a programme to reinvigorate its deciduous diversity, hangs from the eastern scarp of The Pike, and enriches the look and feel of the Duddon Valley from Ulpha. Pike Side Farm adds to the scene with its Organic Farm Trail drawing attention to its rare sweet meadows unsullied by fertilizer and chemical treatments – this year's hay smelled sublime!

Remains of the Hesk Fell coppermine, with the shapely profile of The Pike beyond

↑ Hesk Fell from Whitfell

The farms along the Duddon base provide fleeces for Original Cumbrian Wool, a dynamic local venture which is turning the otherwise largely worthless fleeces of the Herdwick, and other traditional upland sheep breeds, into coveted, undyed and surprisingly soft fabric products.

The main body of the fell is presently partitioned by electric fencing, but the wanderer has been suitably acknowledged and accommodated with strategic stiles. To the west of the fell lies the vast upland bowl of Storthes, a wilderness wherein even the sheep may look lonely.

The Pike from the north-west

ASCENT FROM WOODEND BRIDGE (6)

Direct 240m/790ft 2.4km/1½ miles

1 Woodend Bridge, off the Birkerfell Road, is a common starting point for this fell, despite the fact that it lacks an attractive return route. Walk to the road-gate, which gives access into the walled enclosures leading to Woodend Farm, but turn left before it and follow up the pasture left, keeping the wall to the right until confronted by the electric fencing. Cross the stile. Ascend the featureless ridge, coming alongside a second fence that almost traverses the fell-top. A few stones have been gathered to form a summit cairn on the south side of the fence, necessitating a nifty step-over.

2 About a mile down the road from Woodend Bridge a bridleway leaves the Birkerfell Road south of the entrance to Crosbythwaite Farm. After a series of gates it reaches the ridge wall, passing close to the remnants of a D-shaped Viking stock enclosure, over an acre in size. It's a rare survival. For the summit, leave the bridleway right, following the wall up to and over a ladder-stile and climb the facing slope. Note several small stone alcoves higher up, created as modest bield shelters, replicating the scrapes that sheep naturally fashion for themselves.

6 To revel in the special view from The Pike, turn left at the Viking enclosure and keep the ridge wall close right, via a stile. Heed the notice on the summit. It's not worth even thinking about an eastward descent.

ASCENT FROM BOBBINMILL BRIDGE (21)

Via Rainsbarrow Wood and The Pike 377m/1235ft 5.2km/3¼ miles

3 From Bobbinmill Bridge take the rising footpath to the left, into partially felled woodland. Footpaths then diverge. The first goes through Rainsbarrow Wood, via kissing-gates and ladder-stiles, and then sharp left onto a permissive path at Pike Side Farm, going west and then north round The Pike to gain the ridge at the same point as the bridleway from Crosbythwaite. The second – the footpath through the top of Rainsbarrow – is a special treat. It swings round under the eastern scarp of The Pike anti-clockwise, and leads into a narrow lateral enclosure. At its end, it links to an old mine path climbing up left up to the same ridge junction from Baskell Farm. **4** Alternatively, following Holehouse Gill, ascend over stiles to join Pike Side Farm's unenclosed access track, waymarked towards the end as part of the Soil Association Farm Trail and bear round right to the junction. **5** An interesting variant path, a miners' trod, contours left from the ladder-stile on the final stretch up Hesk Fell (GR182943) to inspect the enigmatic remains of the early 19th-century copper-mine. Past the mine, climb up the open fellside north to gain the summit.

RIDGE ROUTE

YOADCASTLE ↓**100m/330ft** ↑**120m/390ft** **2.4km/1½ miles**

This is not an endeavour to relish on a misty day. The saving grace (while it remains) is the hefting fence which acts as a guide down to the head of the barren Storthes Gill basin. Leave the summit NW and descend to a stile over the electric fence. Follow on with the fence to the right and, where it bears right, continue W up the rough moor onto the broad and comparatively dry saddle, where a narrow path is gleefully joined. The summit bastion, like a frigate, is your obvious near target to the right.

Hesk Fell from Bigertmire Pasture

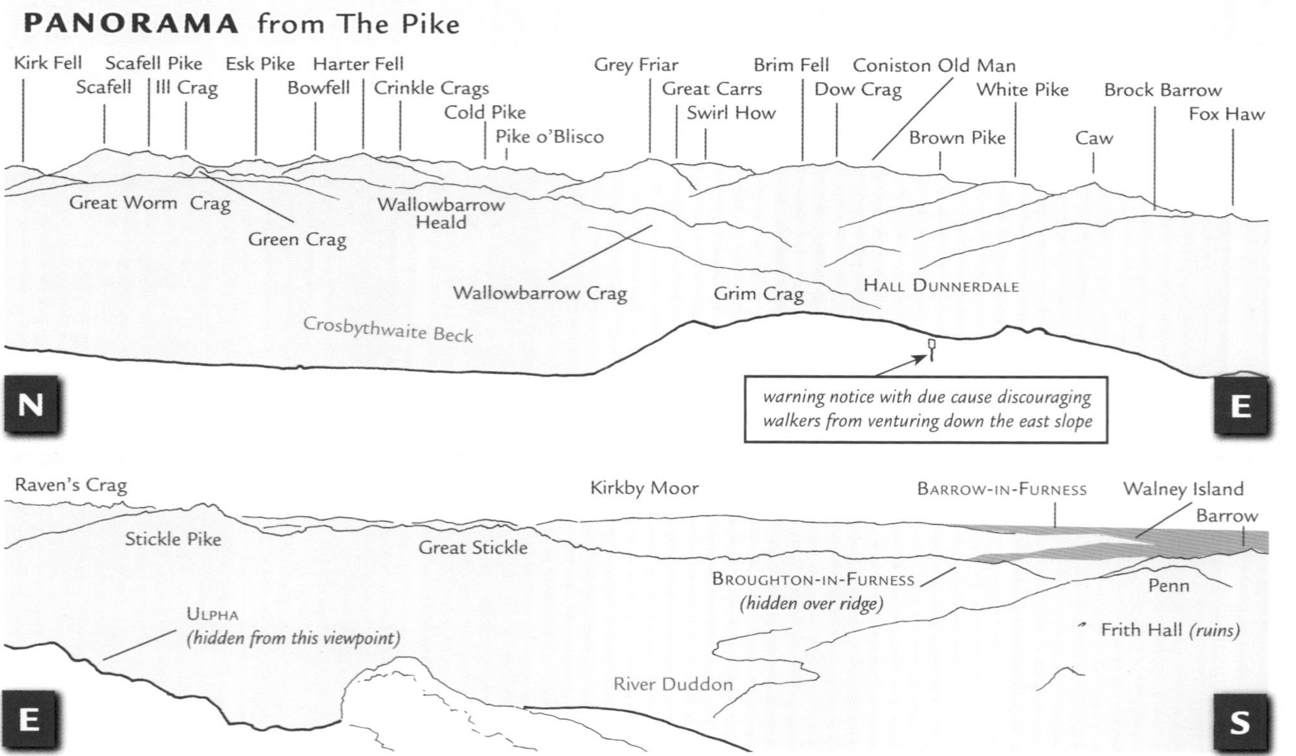
PANORAMA from The Pike
Kirk Fell
Scafell
Scafell Pike
Ill Crag
Esk Pike
Bowfell
Harter Fell
Crinkle Crags
Cold Pike
Pike o'Blisco
Grey Friar
Great Carrs
Swirl How
Brim Fell
Dow Crag
Coniston Old Man
Brown Pike
White Pike
Caw
Brock Barrow
Fox Haw
Great Worm Crag
Green Crag
Wallowbarrow Heald
Wallowbarrow Crag
Grim Crag
Hall Dunnerdale
Crosbythwaite Beck
warning notice with due cause discouraging walkers from venturing down the east slope
N
E
Raven's Crag
Stickle Pike
Great Stickle
Kirkby Moor
Barrow-in-Furness
Walney Island
Barrow
Broughton-in-Furness
(hidden over ridge)
Penn
Frith Hall (ruins)
Ulpha
(hidden from this viewpoint)
River Duddon
E
S

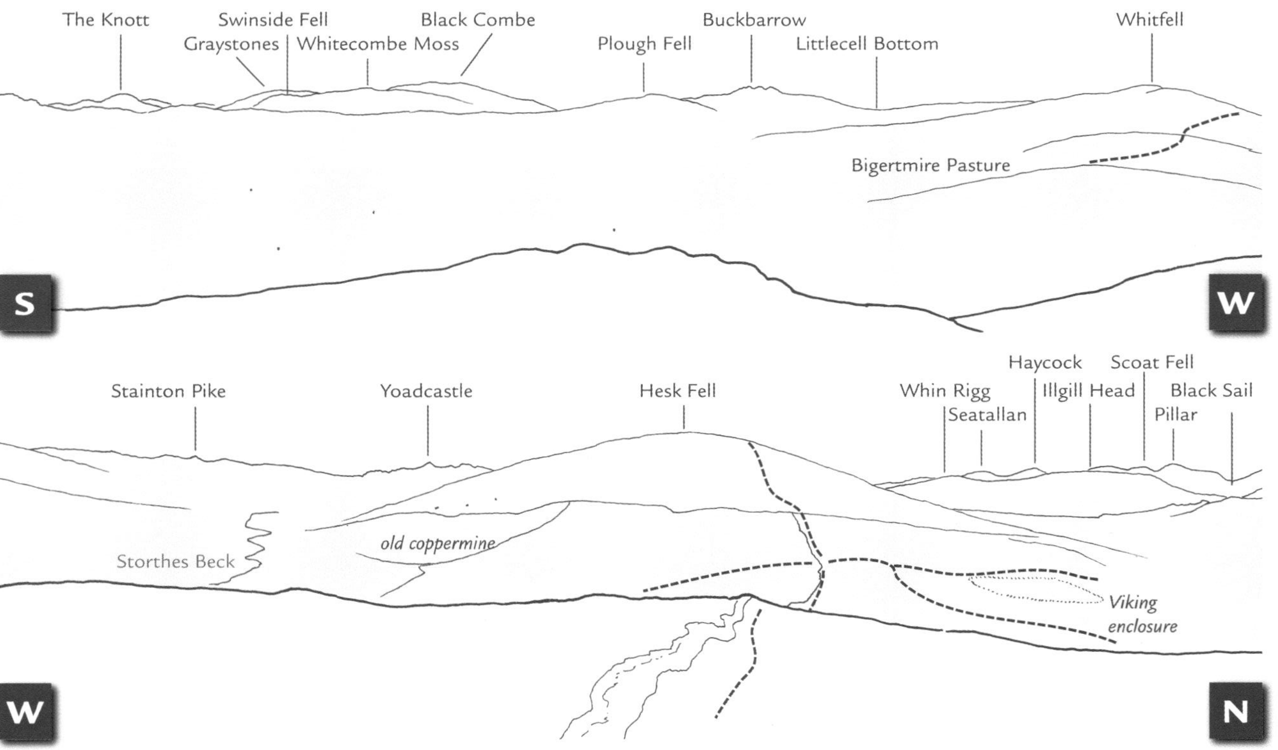
The Knott
Swinside Fell
Graystones
Whitecombe Moss
Black Combe
Plough Fell
Buckbarrow
Littlecell Bottom
Whitfell
Bigertmire Pasture
S
W
Stainton Pike
Yoadcastle
Hesk Fell
Whin Rigg
Seatallan
Haycock
Illgill Head
Scoat Fell
Pillar
Black Sail
old coppermine
Storthes Beck
Viking enclosure
W
N

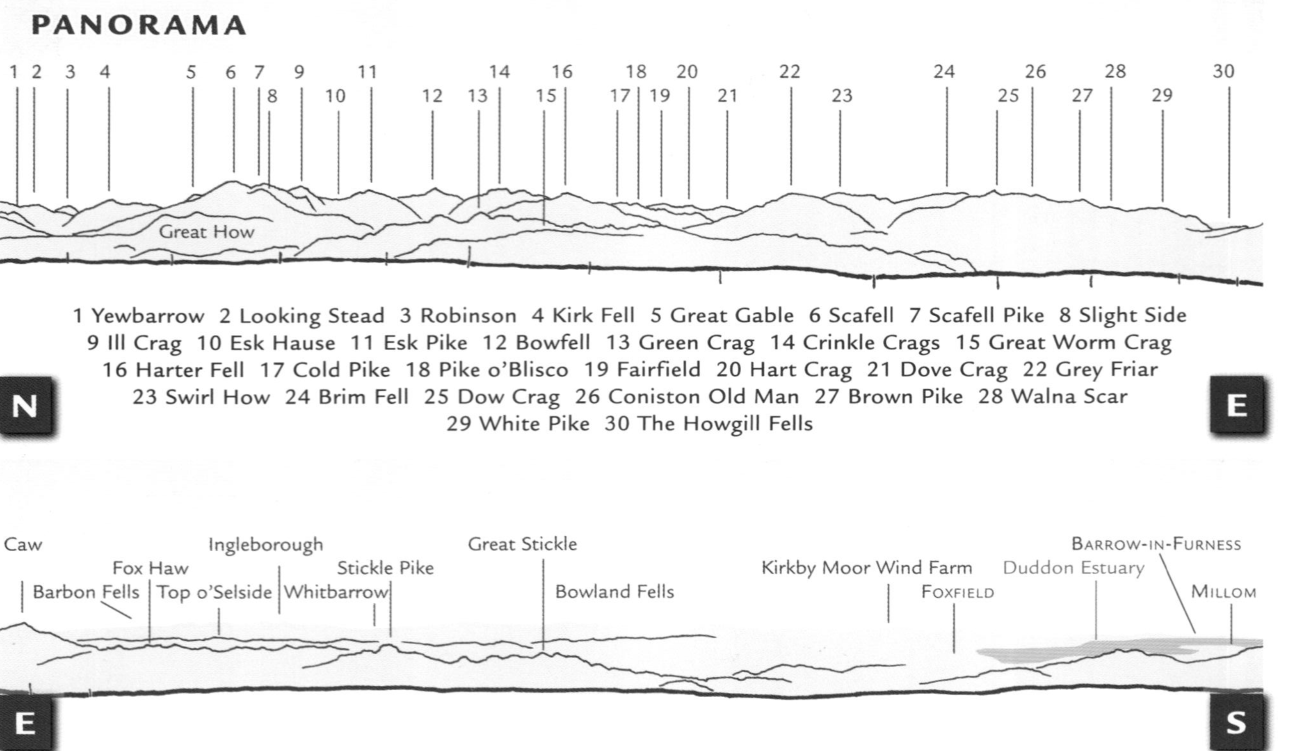
PANORAMA
1 2 3 4 5 6 7 8 9 10 11 12 13 14 15 16 17 18 19 20 21 22 23 24 25 26 27 28 29 30
Great How
1 Yewbarrow 2 Looking Stead 3 Robinson 4 Kirk Fell 5 Great Gable 6 Scafell 7 Scafell Pike 8 Slight Side 9 Ill Crag 10 Esk Hause 11 Esk Pike 12 Bowfell 13 Green Crag 14 Crinkle Crags 15 Great Worm Crag 16 Harter Fell 17 Cold Pike 18 Pike o'Blisco 19 Fairfield 20 Hart Crag 21 Dove Crag 22 Grey Friar 23 Swirl How 24 Brim Fell 25 Dow Crag 26 Coniston Old Man 27 Brown Pike 28 Walna Scar 29 White Pike 30 The Howgill Fells
N
E
Caw
Barbon Fells
Fox Haw
Top o'Selside
Ingleborough
Whitbarrow
Stickle Pike
Great Stickle
Bowland Fells
Kirkby Moor Wind Farm
Foxfield
Duddon Estuary
Barrow-in-Furness
Millom
E
S

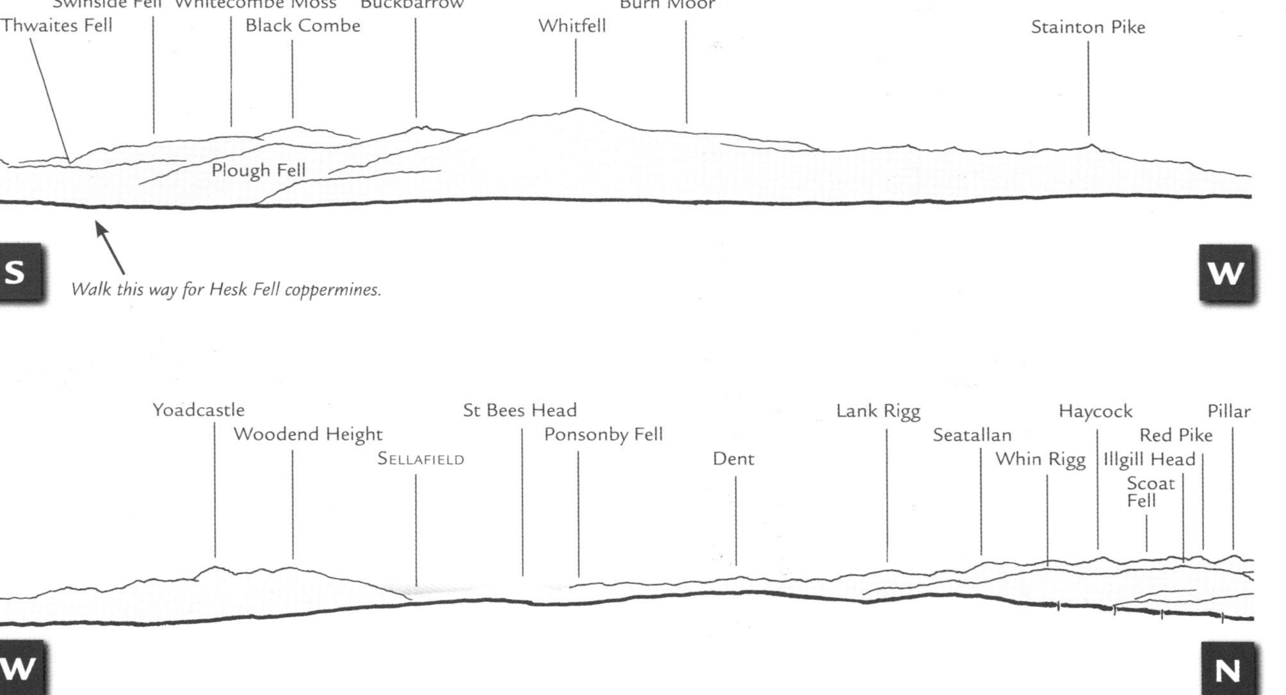
Swinside Fell
Whitecombe Moss
Buckbarrow
Burn Moor
Thwaites Fell
Black Combe
Whitfell
Stainton Pike
Plough Fell
S
Walk this way for Hesk Fell coppermines.
W
Yoadcastle
St Bees Head
Lank Rigg
Haycock
Pillar
Woodend Height
Ponsonby Fell
Seatallan
Red Pike
Sellafield
Dent
Whin Rigg
Illgill Head
Scoat Fell
W
N

14 HOLME FELL *(317m, 1040ft)*

Due south of the hamlet of Little Langdale rises a wooded ridge that reaches its full height above Yewdale's lovely parkland. One of the great little fells of Lakeland, Holme Fell boasts a southernmost facade of rocky ribs that jut through a dense cover of native trees to give it an air of impregnability. Within its woods and upland pastures lurks a wide variety of wildlife, of special note, before the bracken runs riot, being the swathes of bluebells amongst the birch trees. The dust and noise of slate quarrying has largely died away. Nature has carried out an exceedingly fine cover-up job, creating a sylvan place of peace where once men toiled. Some tell-tale signs remain, however, and the fell offers far more than a clutch of circular strolls through wooded glens and a good ridge walk, with Tilberthwaite and the extra-ordinary quarried hollows at Hodge Close making very worthwhile quests.

Tilberthwaite

 ↑ Holme Fell from Yewdale

APPROACHES TO HIGH OXEN FELL AND HODGE CLOSE FROM LITTLE LANGDALE (37 & 38)

Direct 220m/720ft 2.7km/1¾ miles

Hiding behind a mantle of trees Holme Fell is largely obscured from the Little Langdale valley, but from a choice of four routes one may begin to unravel its secrets. **1** The Cumbria Way climbs out of the woods, having casually inspected the thunderous Colwith Force, to emerge through hand-gates at High Park. Follow the road west to a footpath signed left, short of Stang End. This leads over a stile across the wet marsh of Little Fell close by Great How to enter woodland at a gate. It joins the Stang End/Hodge Close track

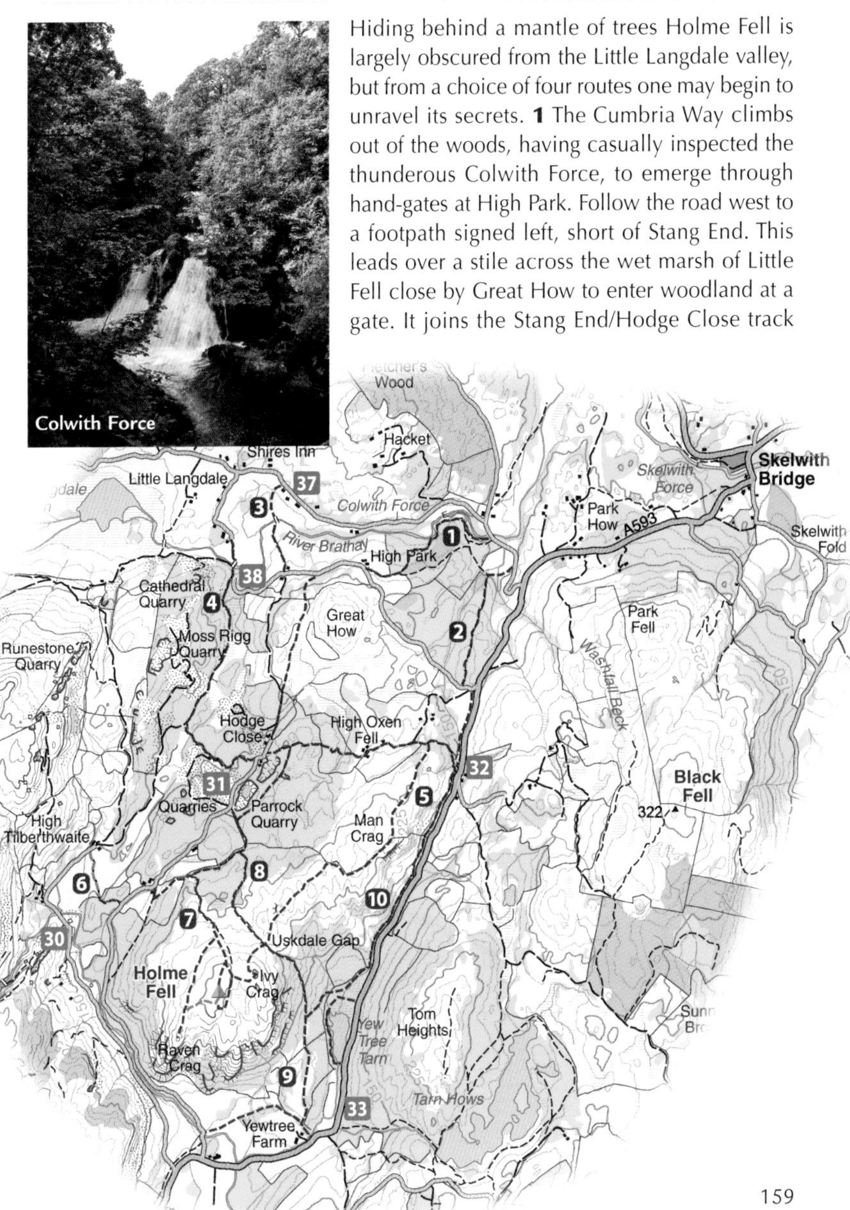

Colwith Force

and the route proceeds to the small community of Hodge Close. **2** Another woodland path, missing the falls, heads up due south to join the High Park road at its junction with the Coniston road. From here you can follow either a fenced roadside path leading to Oxen Fell High Cross, or a quiet byroad leading directly to High Oxen Fell Farm.

3 Directly from the community of Little Langdale a footpath leaves the road at a kissing-gate 300m east of Wilson Place at GR318033. Descending the pasture, cross a footbridge, a lovely spot to enjoy the sparkling beck, and walk on to a lane leading to Stang End. Follow the track south to get to Hodge Close. **4** From Three Shires Inn go 100m west to the minor road junction, take the descending lane winding down by several handsomely sited houses to the ford and raised footbridge. At this point there is a discreet car park accessed via the High Park lane off the Coniston road. Continue south along the track leading through a valley glade – ultimate destination High Tilberthwaite Farm – and after the high spoil of Moss Rigg Quarry watch for a leftward branching track in woodland, leading to Hodge Close.

ASCENT FROM OXEN FELL HIGH CROSS (32)

Direct 200m/655ft 2.5km/1½ miles

5 From Oxen Fell High Cross one may cheerfully follow the road to, and through, High Oxen Fell Farm to Hodge Close – a useful connection when orbiting the entire fell. To get directly onto the Holme Fell ridge walk up to the top of the first rise in this byroad where a recessed gate on the left gives access onto the fell beside power lines. A definite path passes a pool onto the emerging ridge. Young deciduous tree plantings

Holme Ground

Cairn in Uskdale Gap

here confirm that the landscape is proactively managed by the National Trust. The grazing is also moderated to suit regeneration of the native habitat. The path mounts a prominent knoll, then follows a metal fence, past an area of bluebells in season. Note an old cairn prominent well to the west of the ridge path. The path crosses a stile as the fence straddles the ridge and descends amongst the heather. As the fence bears right, ignore the carpet-wrapped stile and keep left to follow an undulating path through rocky knots and by a solitary larch and arrive at the Uskdale Gap cairn. Ivy Crag rises ahead, surmounted by the fell's largest cairn. Climb direct to this prominent shoulder, a very good viewpoint for Tom Heights and Black Fell. The summit is attained by skirting right, by a marsh, with a worn path stepping up the right-hand edge.

ASCENTS FROM YEWDALE

The saddle of Uskdale Gap is the focus of all, but one, of these ascents, accessed from the footpath which crosses the ridge from SE to NW.

From Low Tilberthwaite **(30)** 202m/665ft 3km/1¾ miles

6 From Low Tilberthwaite follow the road almost to High Tilberthwaite and take the gated footpath on the right through fields and woodland to the Hodge Close access road. Turn left on it to Holme Ground. **7** Pass through the facing gate on the right and rise to join the lateral bridleway. Turn left (north-east). After a fraction over 250m, a path branches right, up through the light birchwood, onto the open slope heading south-south-east direct to the summit. **8** Alternatively, continue with the bridleway a further 250m to a path, again right, passing up by evidence of small-scale slate quarrying which leads to a dam holding a charming stretch of water. The path passes to the right and climbs easily to reach Uskdale Gap. This approach can also begin from the car park adjacent to Hodge Close Quarry. Before you do this, take hold of your courage and inspect the two monumental quarry holes from

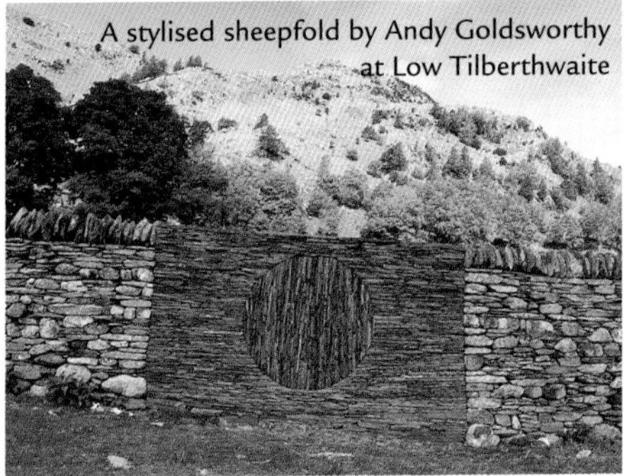
A stylised sheepfold by Andy Goldsworthy at Low Tilberthwaite

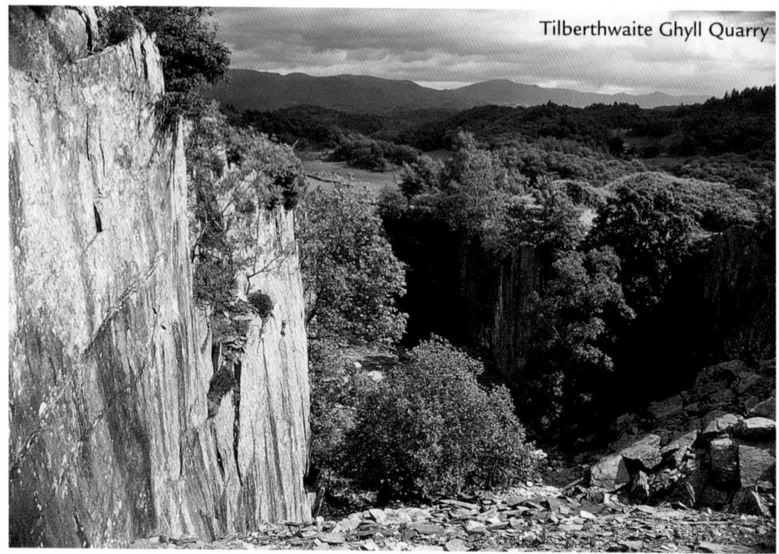

Tilberthwaite Ghyll Quarry

within. Follow the road north through the cluster of dwellings. After Hodge Close Cottage find a track on the right. This leads to High Oxenfell Farm, but, before you reach the gate, take the inviting path down into the tree-shaded quarry on your right. Clamber over a chaos of boulders into the quarry depths to the see an awe-inspiring cavern supported by a stout pillar and get a view into the 'blue lagoon' of Hodge Close Quarry. **9** If you want to walk right around the fell (10km/6¼ miles) on tracks and quiet roads, the gated meadow-way from Shepherd's Bridge to Yew Tree Farm is a useful link, as well as **10** the dale-floor path which tracks the Skelwith/Coniston road to High Oxen Fell Cross. (To make the natural link with neighbouring Black Fell follow the lovely Mountain Road east from here.)

THE SUMMIT

Holme Fell summit is a proud ridge with a short cliff to the east and cairns at either end, though the summit outcrop itself has no cairn. For the best view of Yewdale go a little further south to the cairn on the spur top of Raven Crag.

SAFE DESCENTS

Uskdale Gap is the answer. Refrain from rambling about on the rough plateau as there is no way down the E, S or W slopes. The nastiest trap lurks on the S with Calf and Raven Crags posing serious problems. Neither is there access into the valley pastures along these fronts. Retreat to Uskdale Gap, then either go right for Yew Tree Tarn or left for Low Tilberthwaite.

Bluebells east of Uskdale Gap looking to Tom Heights

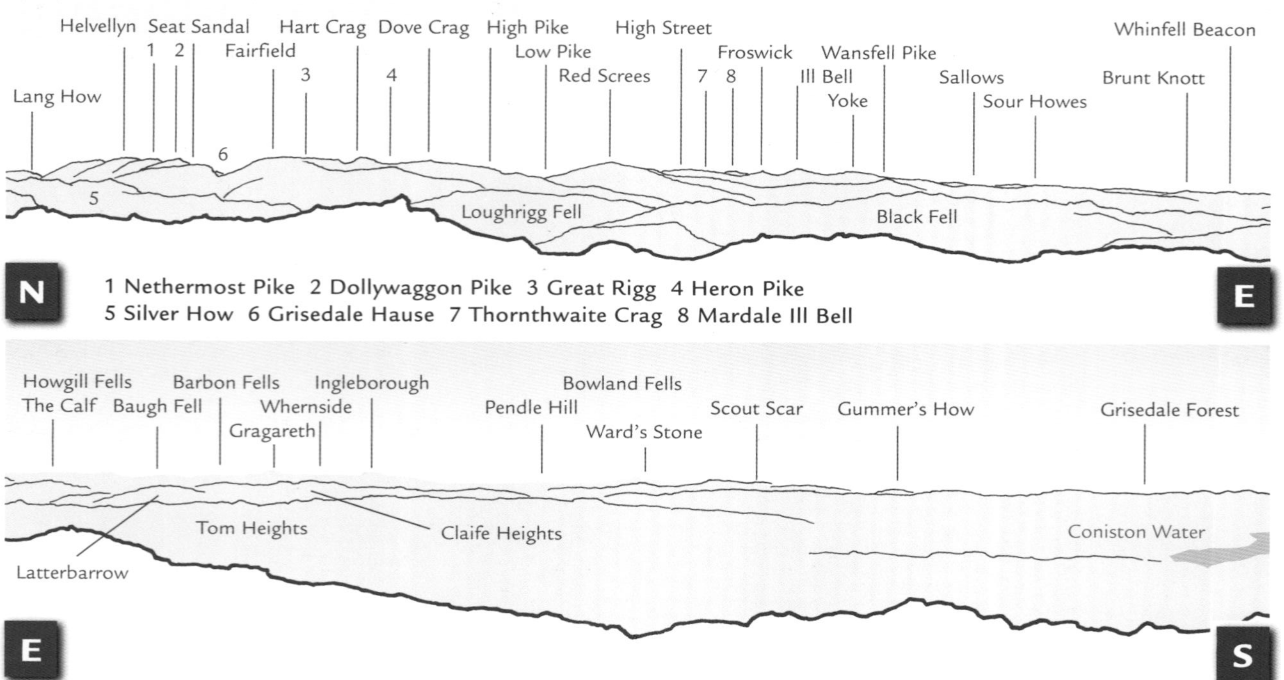
PANORAMA
Helvellyn
Seat Sandal
1
2
Hart Crag
Dove Crag
High Pike
High Street
Whinfell Beacon
Fairfield
Low Pike
Froswick
Wansfell Pike
3
4
Red Screes
7
8
Ill Bell
Sallows
Brunt Knott
Lang How
Yoke
Sour Howes
6
5
Loughrigg Fell
Black Fell
N
E
1 Nethermost Pike 2 Dollywaggon Pike 3 Great Rigg 4 Heron Pike
5 Silver How 6 Grisedale Hause 7 Thornthwaite Crag 8 Mardale Ill Bell
Howgill Fells
Barbon Fells
Ingleborough
Bowland Fells
The Calf
Baugh Fell
Whernside
Pendle Hill
Scout Scar
Gummer's How
Grisedale Forest
Gragareth
Ward's Stone
Tom Heights
Claife Heights
Coniston Water
Latterbarrow
E
S

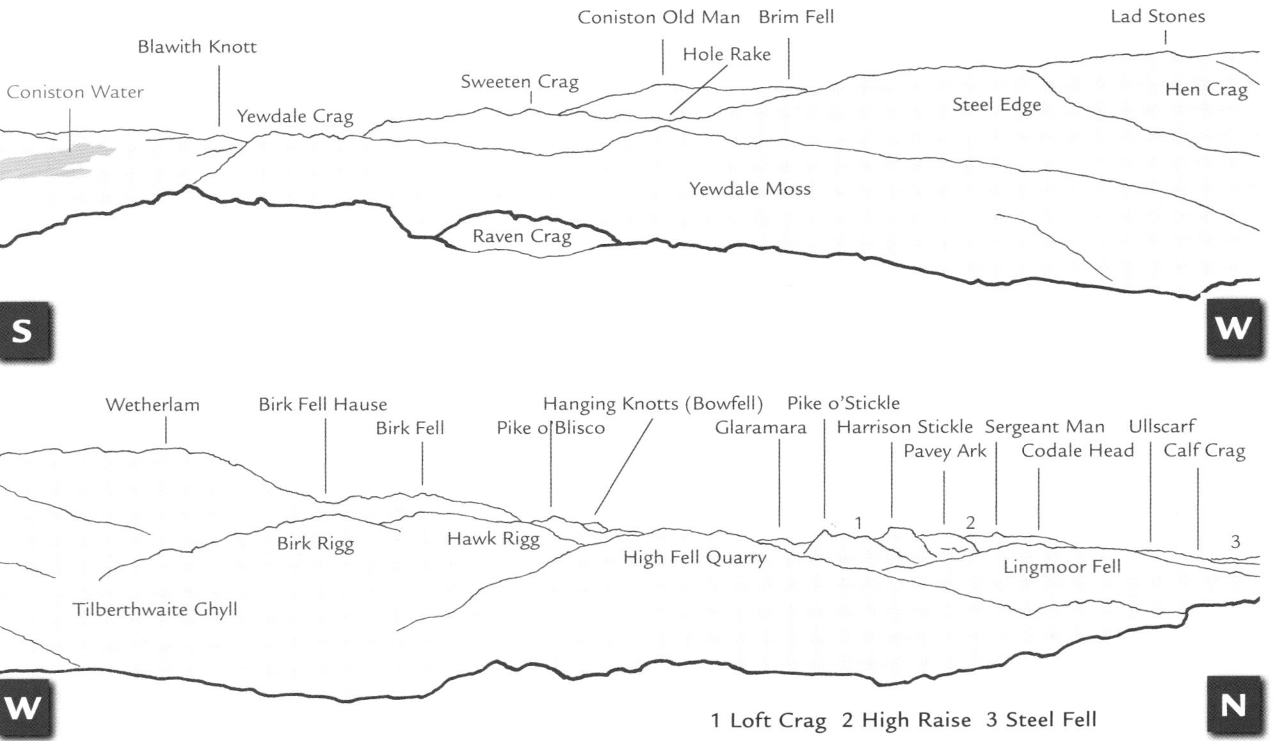
Coniston Old Man
Brim Fell
Lad Stones
Blawith Knott
Hole Rake
Sweeten Crag
Coniston Water
Hen Crag
Yewdale Crag
Steel Edge
Yewdale Moss
Raven Crag
S
W
Wetherlam
Birk Fell Hause
Hanging Knotts (Bowfell)
Pike o'Stickle
Birk Fell
Pike o'Blisco
Glaramara
Harrison Stickle
Sergeant Man
Ullscarf
Pavey Ark
Codale Head
Calf Crag
1
2
3
Birk Rigg
Hawk Rigg
High Fell Quarry
Lingmoor Fell
Tilberthwaite Ghyll
W
N
1 Loft Crag 2 High Raise 3 Steel Fell

↑ Eskdale from the eastern end of the ridge near Ross's Camp

15 MUNCASTER FELL *(231m, 758ft)*

While Black Combe is often considered the seaboard fell, no other fell in the Lake District better serves to show the link between land and sea than Muncaster Fell. The prevailing south-westerlies bring moist air giving 75mm of rain a year on the coastal fringe, allowing cereal crops to be grown. Further inland rainfall increases rapidly, first producing a succulent pastoral landscape where beef cattle predominate, and then rising up to the high fells, where 300mm of rain a year impose a regime where only the hardy Herdwick sheep can eke out an existence. This is typically British, but here the transitions are tightly compressed. The fell is so very evidently a marine bridgehead.

And this low, elongated ridge of wet moorland will have been a bridgehead of another kind. Whether marauding or colonising, over many millennia people have made their first footfall into the Cumbrian hinterland on this ridge, coming up from the ancient harbour at Ravenglass. Bronze Age and later

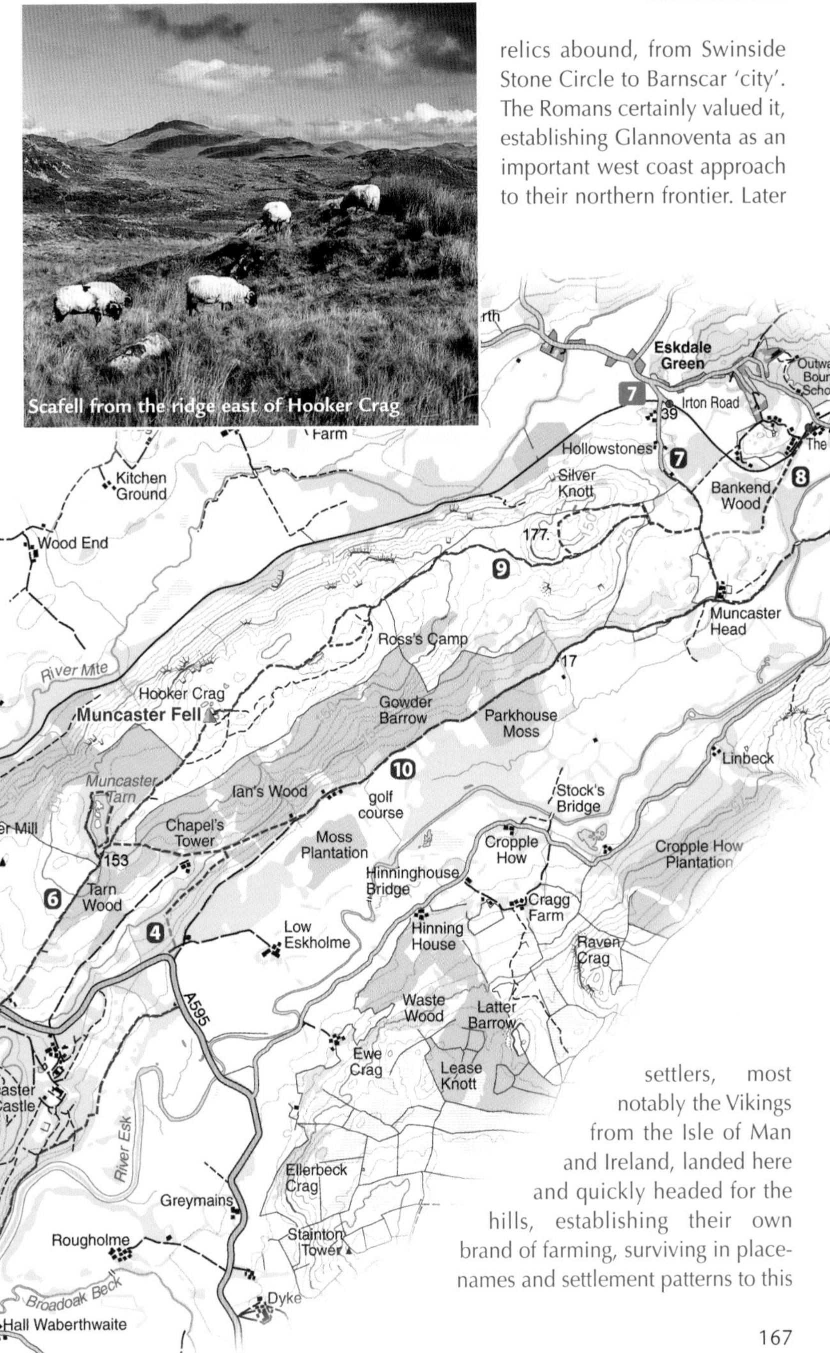

Scafell from the ridge east of Hooker Crag

relics abound, from Swinside Stone Circle to Barnscar 'city'. The Romans certainly valued it, establishing Glannoventa as an important west coast approach to their northern frontier. Later settlers, most notably the Vikings from the Isle of Man and Ireland, landed here and quickly headed for the hills, establishing their own brand of farming, surviving in place-names and settlement patterns to this

Substantial walls of Glannoventa Roman fort bath-house at Ravenglass, otherwise known as Walls Castle

day. So the walker, wandering alone on the wild and wet of Muncaster Fell, may sense an ancient footfall in every stride.

On either side of this narrow fell, from Ravenglass to Eskdale Green, are lush valleys drained by the rivers Esk and Mite, thus isolating the fell from any natural bond with any of the Western, Mid-Western or Southern Fells. These rivers, with the addition of the Irt (from Wasdale), recoil at the point of entry into the sea, halted by the

Black Combe from the triple-river confluence at Ravenglass

La'al Ratty at Muncaster Mill Station

massive sand bars at the fell's western tip. This quirky estuary ensures that almost all the rain from the high Scafells is brought together here before entry into the sea, making the most certain of harbours. The dune landscapes of Drigg and Eskmeals are also high-value wildlife habitats and unique in Cumbria.

Out to sea, the Isle of Man, composed of rocks akin to those of the Lakes, is at its closest to the mainland here, Douglas being just 38 miles from Ravenglass as the gull flies. Three man-made features make Muncaster Fell irresistible: Ravenglass village, a special conservation area, with its access to the estuary shore and Walls Castle; Muncaster Castle, with its magnificent gardens and links with Tom Fool; and La'al Ratty, the miniature railway which, with its distinctive dry hoot, brings back the joy of gentle travel through the loveliest of landscapes. A natural combination of ride and stride, travelling out with the train and walking back upon the fell, or vice versa, makes for the perfect summer's day outing. Indeed there are four fell-foot stations to choose from: Ravenglass, Muncaster Mill, Irton Road and The Green.

APPROACHES FROM RAVENGLASS (9)

Via Walls Castle and the Esk 230m/755ft 4.5km/2¾ miles

Use the generous village car park (GR085965). **1** Walkers in a hurry to reach the fell (or backtracking after the ridge route traverse from Eskdale Green) can follow a footway up from the village by the war memorial to the junction with the A595, continuing on, past the public entrance to Muncaster Castle grounds, to the sharp right-hand bend. Here the bridleway onto the ridge, Fell Lane, begins (Route 6).

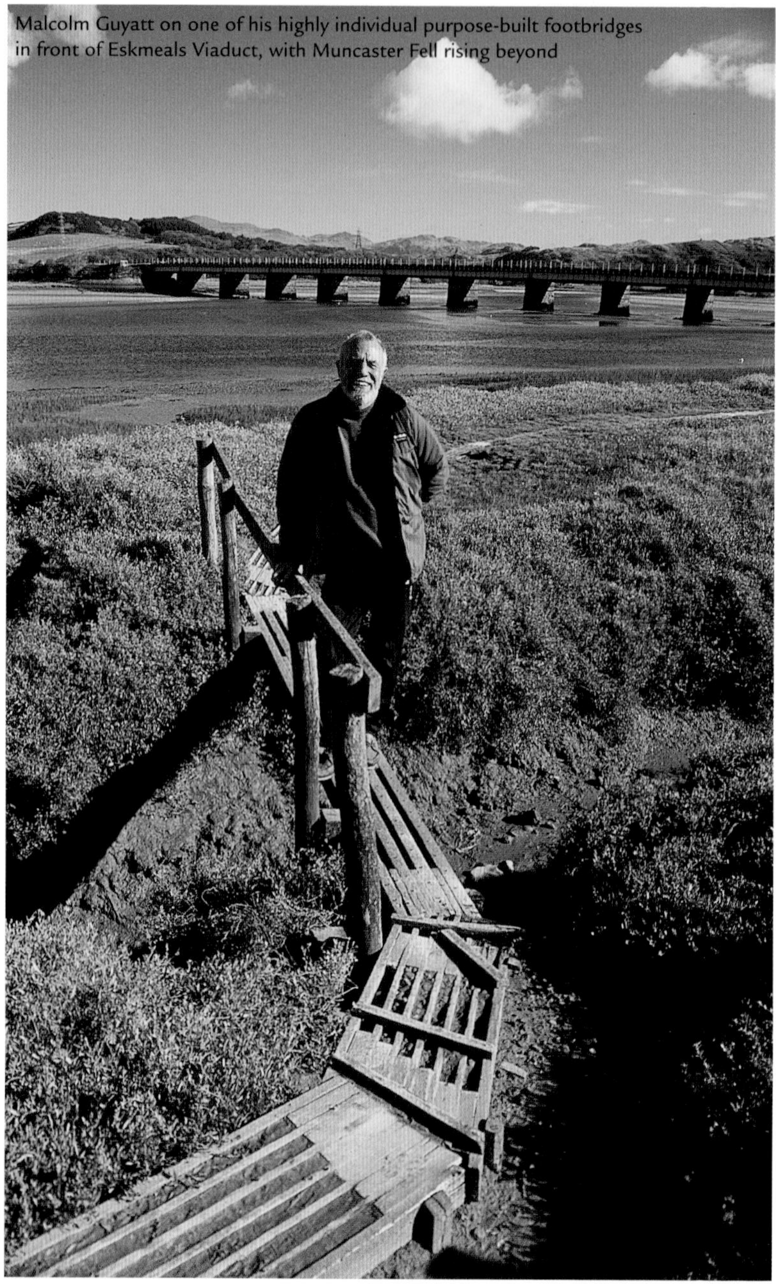

Malcolm Guyatt on one of his highly individual purpose-built footbridges in front of Eskmeals Viaduct, with Muncaster Fell rising beyond

Setting sun over Ravenglass haven

2 Cross the mainline footbridge south of the station to a hand-gate and the roadway by the Walls caravan park. Go right; a newly created footway weaves by woodland fringe beside the open Muncaster Estate road. Take a moment at the English Heritage enclosure to inspect the remarkable remains of Walls Castle. It claims to be the tallest, wholly Roman building in northern Britain. The regular stone coursing is authentic but the rendering may be later. The associated Roman harbour fort of Glannoventa is only visible now as a *vallum* feature (type of defensive palisade) in the enclosure across the roadway. The bath house contains a statue niche reminiscent of Chesters (Cilurnum) on Hadrian's Wall. Two rooms remain with a blocked hypocaust flue visible at the base of the south wall (at the figure's feet in the photograph). The building survives because it was used long after the Romans withdrew, probably set within a timber structure. It has legendary links with Avallach, the Celtic Lord of the Underworld.

Continue south, trees inhibiting any chance of a seaward view, although one may reach this point from the village at low tide along the shore. A 'Muncaster, Knotts End and Newtown' sign directs you left, along a drive. As you approach some buildings, a further left turn leads up a track by a recently instated pond. The fenced lane enters the trees. Here, either go left to Home Farm or continue into the Castle grounds beside the circular Muncaster Interactive building and the Sino-Himalayan Garden and turn left to leave through the crenellated gateway onto the A595 (locked at 5.30pm). In either case, go right along the roadside to the sharp right-hand bend to enter Fell Lane (Route 6).

3 An intriguing and pleasant alternative is to continue straight on on the footpath from Walls Castle, signed 'Cumbria Coastal Way', through Newtown Farm and then beneath Newtown Knott, surmounted by an old navigation tower. Crossing pasture enter woodland at a hand-gate, coming close to the bridleway along the Esk shore, almost opposite the Hall Waberthwaite ford. Go left upstream on a permissive path

Hall Waberthwaite across the Esk

to enter Croft Coppice, and beneath the tree-screened Muncaster Castle, ancient home of the Penningtons, onto the drive across Hirst Park to Hirst Lodge and the road. The family inheritance has long been handed down by the female line, leading to the impressive triple-barrelled surname Gordon-Duff-Pennington when Patrick Gordon-Duff married into the family! It is likely that the castle rests on the site of a Roman mansion residence – the name 'caster' implies no less and the situation is perfect, sheltered from the Irish Sea (Celtic Sea).

Chapel's Tower

4 Turning left at Hirst Lodge, follow the A595 and take the second right (bridleway sign), at the tight left-hand bend and, after 40m, come to decking on your left. A permissive path, up the wooded bank, reaches a lateral woodland track near a grand old spreading oak. Go right. (This track is prone to dampness.) Pass beneath Chapel's Tower. As a wall gateway nears, the path is ushered left to a ladder-stile into the rising path from Eskholme to Muncaster Tarn. Piercing the woodland like a rocket, Chapel's Tower is a folly built on the site of an ancient tree where King Henry VI was discovered hiding after defeat at the battle of Towton, near Hexham. Having enjoyed a few days' hospitality, the grateful monarch presented his host with a decorated green glass bowl adorned with gold and enamel, offering a blessing that family fortunes would be secure as long as the bowl remained intact. Needless to say only a replica is held in the castle. The vaunted original is kept cradled in cotton wool! The pepperpot tower was built to mark the continuance of this 'Luck of Muncaster'.

5 A delightful bridleway ascends from the Muncaster Mill Station within woodland, joining the access track from Branken Wall Farm to meet the main road at the foot of Fell Lane.

ASCENT FROM RAVENGLASS

Fell Lane (Route 6) is the focus of all ascents from the west. Routes 1, 2 and 5 all lead to its start and Routes 4 and 10 draw up to join forces with it at Muncaster Tarn.

Direct via Fell Lane **4km/2½ miles**

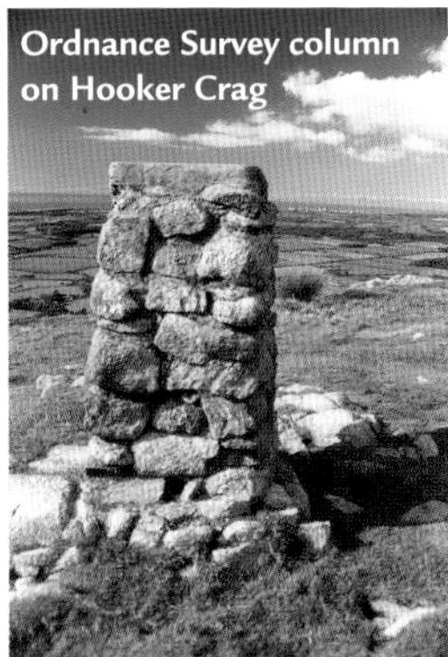
Ordnance Survey column on Hooker Crag

6 There is a gate halfway up, but otherwise it's plain sailing to the rhododendron canopy close to the tarn. Make a point of visiting this secret pool and indulge yourself upon the circuit path to sample its 'far from the madding crowd' tranquillity. Lilies grow in the south-western corner and in a wet season the tarn overflows at both ends. The track heads up by a gate onto the undulating fell, passing gorse bushes. It forks at the forest corner. The right hand path avoids the summit altogether, and much of the damper ground for that matter, but the summit is irresistible. The stronger path steps up the short bank to the left and heads for Hooker Crag (the fell summit).

Water lilies in Muncaster Tarn

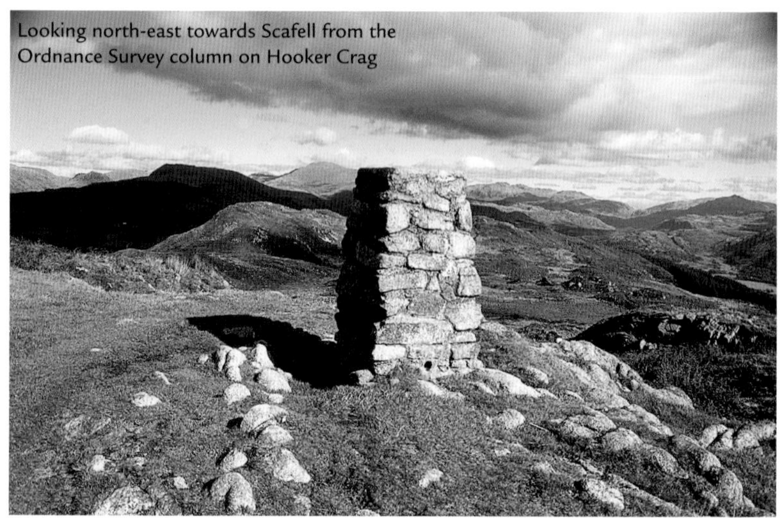
Looking north-east towards Scafell from the Ordnance Survey column on Hooker Crag

ASCENT FROM ESKDALE GREEN (7)

Via Irton Road and The Green Stations 150m/490ft 3.5km/2¼ miles

A smart move for summer Ratty riders is to park in Ravenglass, enjoy the ride all the way to Dalegarth, perhaps taking lunch there, and, returning, alight at either The Green or Irton Road Stations for a fine traverse of the scenic Muncaster Fell ridge. **7** The ridge path is most easily and swiftly gained from Irton Road Station (GR137000). Cross the railway bridge and follow the no-through road with its pleasing views into Eskdale, to end at Forest How. The green bridleway skirts the garden hedge to the right to slip through a gate onto a track with dense gorse to the right. The ridge path branches right from here, just short of a stile/gate. **8** The Green Station (GR145998) makes a neat country-walk approach. A narrow path leads west directly from the platform to a stile in a ford, with stepping stones. Rise on a firm path holding to the wall beside woodland. From its right-hand corner, which can be muddied by cattle, traverse the pasture with the short bank close left to meet up with the bridleway from Muncaster Head at the stile/gate, mentioned above. **9** The ridge walk begins here, with the path hugging the gorse (not as painful as it sounds) to reach a kissing-gate. A few paces further the path swings left on a steady stone-edged rise, with something like an outmoded television aerial prominent on the headland up to the right. To take fullest benefit of the ravishing eastern view into Eskdale stay on the lesser path straight up through the bracken keeping close to the ridge wall. At the top the briefest of breaches in this fell wall permits access to the Silver Knott bluff – the name might allude to silver birch, which makes quite an appearance on this quarter of the fell. A sheep trod leads south, away from the wall, just missing the highest ground. Descend the bracken bank by a large holly tree to join the incline ridge path. The main path heads west round the headland and dips down an incline to traverse a birch-dappled hollow before rising to come close to the ridge wall, over much damp ground. The gateway in the wall corner does not spell an end of soggy going, sadly. The path is immediately forced to make an exaggerated leftward sweep around a marsh. Some walkers head on (bound for the summit), climbing the prominent bank, while others angle on left to come past the collapsing stable stone inscribed 'Ross's Camp 1883', installed to mark the favourite viewpoint of John Ross, agent of the Muncaster Estate. The situation is splendid – a feast for the eyes. The continuing path is firm but has one drawback – it misses the summit completely! However, the path that mounts the bank, passing a large prominent boulder, snakes irresistibly along the ridge and skirts the few knolls flanking Hooker Moss to climb solidly onto Hooker Crag. The name actually means 'hollow marsh' (from 'hol' and 'kerr'); indeed locals always call Holker Hall, 'Hooker Hall'.

Valley path via High Eskholme 3.7km/2½ miles

10 After the elation of the ridge path, many walkers will value the opportunity to complete their walk in circular fashion, on foot rather than by train. At present there is no continuous path along the shady scarp base beside La'al Ratty, but a bridleway leading along the sunny southern foot of the fell via Muncaster Head and High Eskholme (golf club grounds) provides the perfect contrast to the moorland traverse. It is wooded for much of the way and interrupted by just one gate at High Eskholme itself. Walkers can roam in the woodlands, although few do. Immediately west of High Eskholme the right-of-way splits, forsaking the metalled roadway. The more useful option draws up right by some sheds, a steady well-graded path mounting to be joined at a ladder stile by the permissive path out of Chapel Wood (Route 4). Passing within sight of Chapel's Tower and going through a hand-gate en route, it meets the top of Fell Lane at the dam of Muncaster Tarn, a place of reflections.

THE SUMMIT

A fine stone-built OS pillar, constructed in the distinctive Eskdale granite, graces the top of Hooker Crag. There is ample scope to sit and glory in a wonderful panorama, a heady cocktail of mountain and maritime. This is the nearest Lakeland fell summit to the Isle of Man. If two parties meet on the top, they could lay claim to their own section of the summit knoll and remain oblivious of each other.

SAFE DESCENTS

There is no way to north or south off the ridge from the open fell. Steep pathless scarp, most richly wooded on the south side, offers no appropriate links with recognised paths on either hand. There are, in effect, two ridge paths. That from the summit is obvious enough, but the eastward trail weaves more laboriously towards the valley base of Eskdale Green. The westbound path quickly leads to the shelter and security of woodland by Muncaster Tarn and Fell Lane, en route for the village of Ravenglass, only 2½ miles distant from the summit.

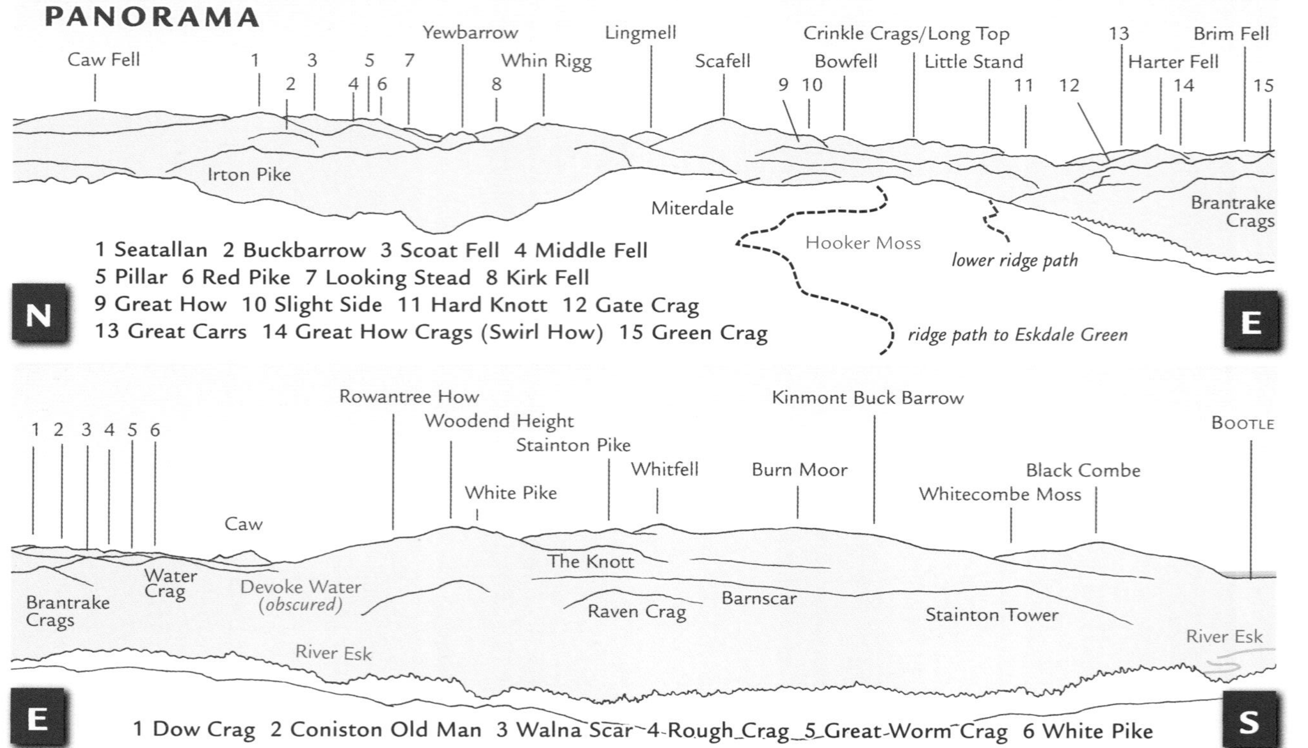
PANORAMA
Caw Fell
Yewbarrow
Whin Rigg
Lingmell
Scafell
Crinkle Crags/Long Top
Bowfell
Little Stand
Harter Fell
Brim Fell
Irton Pike
Miterdale
Hooker Moss
lower ridge path
ridge path to Eskdale Green
Brantrake Crags
1 Seatallan 2 Buckbarrow 3 Scoat Fell 4 Middle Fell
5 Pillar 6 Red Pike 7 Looking Stead 8 Kirk Fell
9 Great How 10 Slight Side 11 Hard Knott 12 Gate Crag
13 Great Carrs 14 Great How Crags (Swirl How) 15 Green Crag
N
E
Rowantree How
Woodend Height
Stainton Pike
White Pike
Whitfell
Burn Moor
Kinmont Buck Barrow
Whitecombe Moss
Black Combe
BOOTLE
Caw
Water Crag
Brantrake Crags
Devoke Water (obscured)
The Knott
Raven Crag
Barnscar
Stainton Tower
River Esk
River Esk
E
S
1 Dow Crag 2 Coniston Old Man 3 Walna Scar 4 Rough Crag 5 Great-Worm Crag 6 White Pike

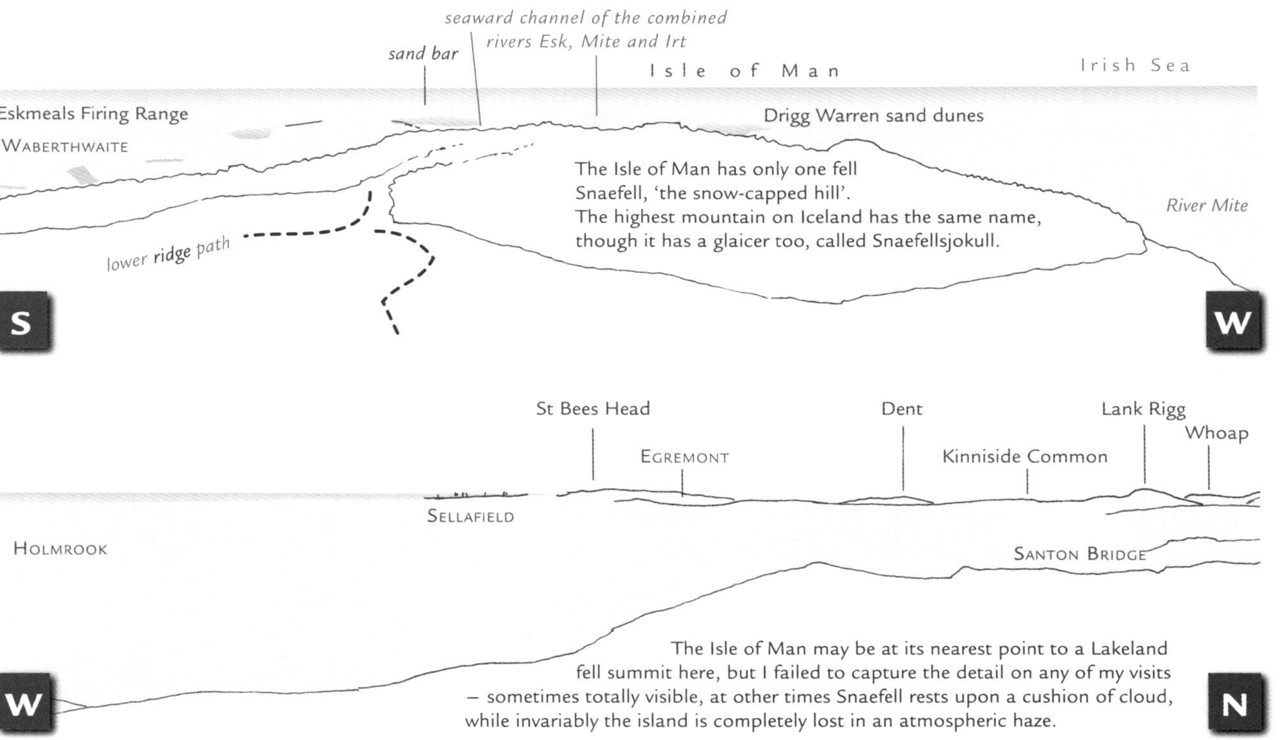
seaward channel of the combined rivers Esk, Mite and Irt
sand bar
Isle of Man
Irish Sea
Eskmeals Firing Range
WABERTHWAITE
Drigg Warren sand dunes
The Isle of Man has only one fell Snaefell, 'the snow-capped hill'.
The highest mountain on Iceland has the same name, though it has a glaicer too, called Snaefellsjokull.
River Mite
lower ridge path
S
W
St Bees Head
Dent
Lank Rigg
Whoap
EGREMONT
Kinniside Common
SELLAFIELD
HOLMROOK
SANTON BRIDGE
The Isle of Man may be at its nearest point to a Lakeland fell summit here, but I failed to capture the detail on any of my visits – sometimes totally visible, at other times Snaefell rests upon a cushion of cloud, while invariably the island is completely lost in an atmospheric haze.
W
N

16 STAINTON PIKE *(498m, 1634ft)*

Stainton Pike nestles into the eastern skyline of the south-western fells alongside Yoadcastle; from the A595 you sense the two summits as one fell mass, with each top a player on the stage of a modest fell drama. To pick out the Pike as a solitary objective, you need to view it from Corney Fell Road, above the junction with the A595 at Millgate. The Whitrow Beck approach shows the fell's cleanest profile, emphasised still further during the walk in by the homestead site. But from most other vantage points it has little distinctive form, merging into the vast moorland bowl of Storthes to the east. Apart from the summit, interest lies in the fragmentary remains of early settlement encountered on a roving ramble, the impressive gorge of Rowantree Force and the shining fell-top level of Holehouse Tarn. (Hole House itself lies at the foot of Storthes, on the Duddon side of the fell.) To judge by the ridge path, walkers traversing from Whitfell to Woodend Height tend to ignore Stainton Pike, most remiss!

 ↑ Stainton Pike from Fell Lane

ASCENT FROM WABERTHWAITE OR BROAD OAK (11)

Via Rowantree Force 393m/1290ft 4.2km/2½ miles

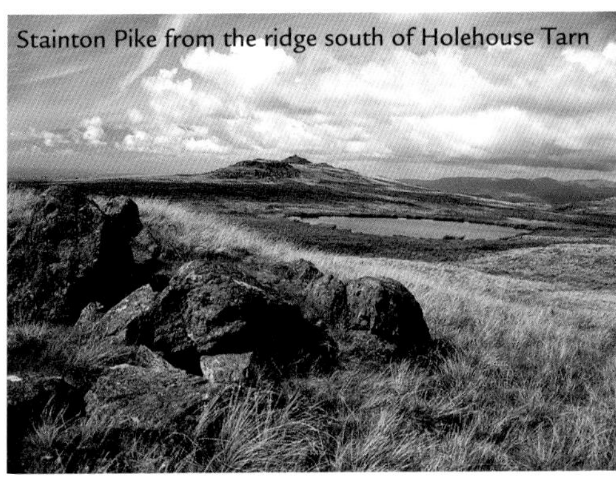
Stainton Pike from the ridge south of Holehouse Tarn

Park on the verge of the A595 just beyond the entrance to Fell Lane, south of Broad Oak. **1** Follow the lane, ignoring the cattle grid and passing through the facing gate. The bridle track embarks on a winding course across a rough pasture of rushes and gorse, no more than an intermittent path after the ford, sometimes in doubt, but continuing eastward between Samgarth and Whitrow Becks. Finding drier ground, draw alongside Whitrow Beck and wander through the intriguing homestead enclosure. A more certain path now angles right following up the gullies at the foot of Red Gill. A cairn then indicates the start of a grooved path left, partially lined with boulders,

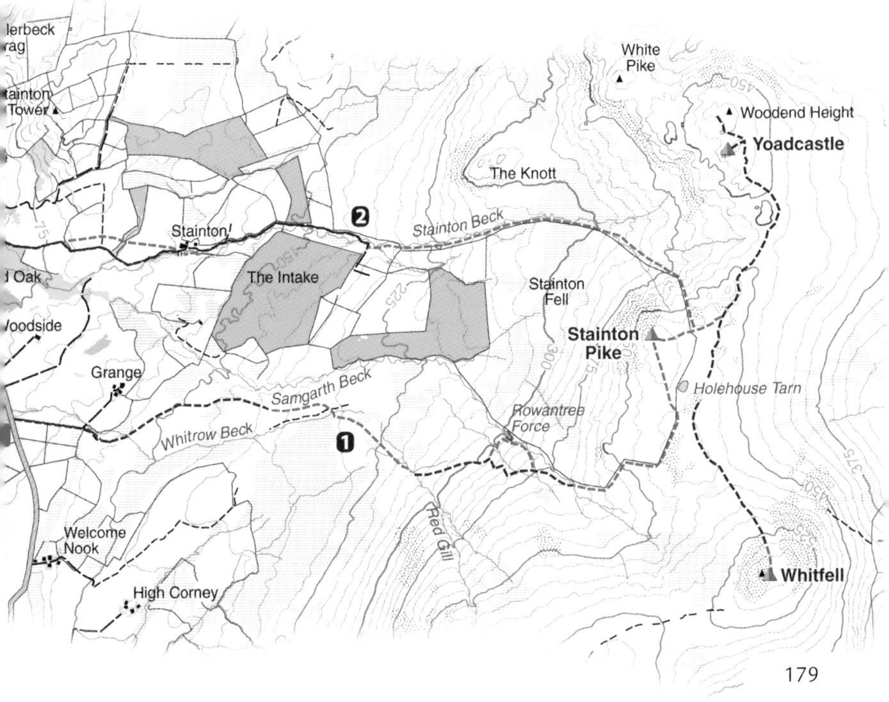

lerbeck
rag
White Pike
Woodend Height
Yoadcastle
tainton Tower
The Knott
2
Stainton
Stainton Beck
The Intake
Stainton Fell
d Oak
Voodside
Stainton Pike
Grange
Samgarth Beck
Holehouse Tarn
Whitrow Beck
Rowantree Force
1
Red Gill
Welcome Nook
High Corney
Whitfell

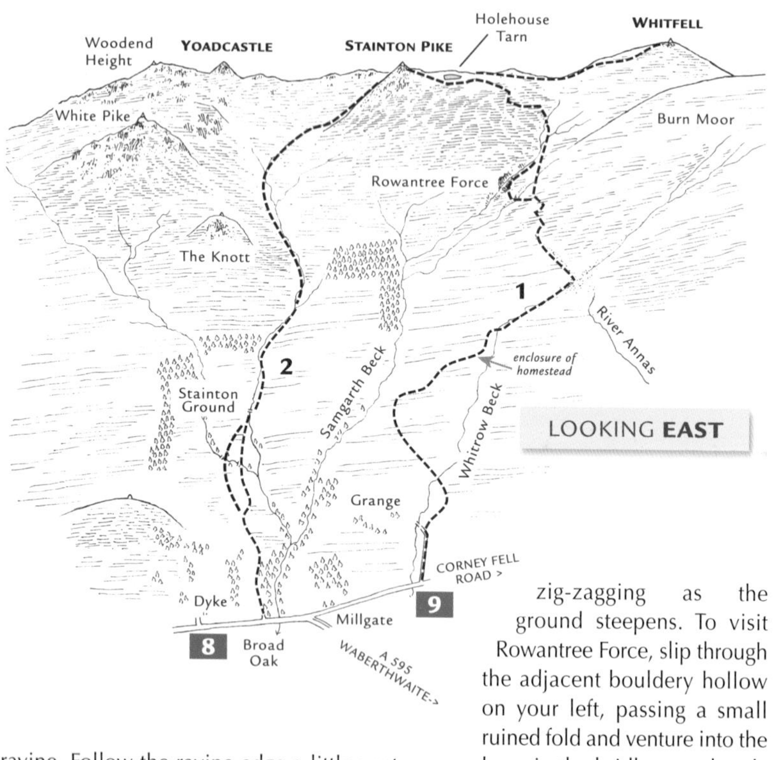

zig-zagging as the ground steepens. To visit Rowantree Force, slip through the adjacent bouldery hollow on your left, passing a small ruined fold and venture into the ravine. Follow the ravine edge a little upstream and regain the bridleway, already indistinct as it skirts the Withe Bottom mire. For ease of walking, keep up left and follow the fence, crossing over Sergeant Crag. As the fell levels out, cross the fence near Holehouse Tarn and follow a spidery path NW to the summit knoll.

Via Stainton Ground

4km/2¼ miles

2 This route along Stainton Beck makes a natural descent on a round trip. Park by the telephone kiosk opposite Broad Oak Farm, cross the cattle grid and follow the farm access track to Stainton Ground. Although there is a footpath, complete with stiles, it is preferable to follow the farm track, unless you wish to wade through the knee-high water at the Black Beck ford. Cross a ladder-stile right and an unusually broad footbridge, immediately before the farmyard gate. Embark on a footpath that hugs Stainton Beck by two fence-stiles, pass Stainton Ground and continue with gorse and marshy ground for comfort. Reach the open fell by two ladder-stiles and an intermediate low fence-stile. Beat a way through the bracken, without a path. Keep the fence close right as it climbs to a saddle, just east of the summit, finally crossing it to reach the cairn.

Rowantree Force

Looking west to the Cumbrian coast over the Rowantree Force ravine

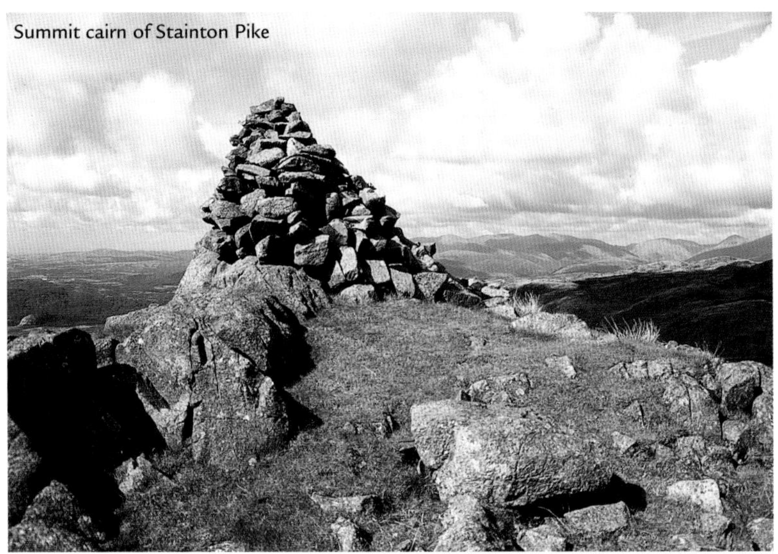
Summit cairn of Stainton Pike

THE SUMMIT

A broad north–south ridge culminates in a splendid flourish of rock on a modest outcrop north-west of Holehouse Tarn. It is surmounted with a neat edifice befitting a pike. Make sure you take time to linger and enjoy your visit.

SAFE DESCENTS

With a fence straddling the plateau just below the summit you have some reassurance in mist, but only if you want to head west. The footpath by Stainton Beck is invisible and painfully rough in places, but the way is clear at all times.

RIDGE ROUTES

WHITFELL	↓6m/20ft	↑75m/250ft	1.6km/1 mile
YOADCASTLE	↓65m/220ft	↑60m/190ft	2km/1¼ miles

Cross the plain fence (E) again to join the narrow ridge path running E of Holehouse Tarn. Go N to Yoadcastle and S to Whitfell. It's that simple!

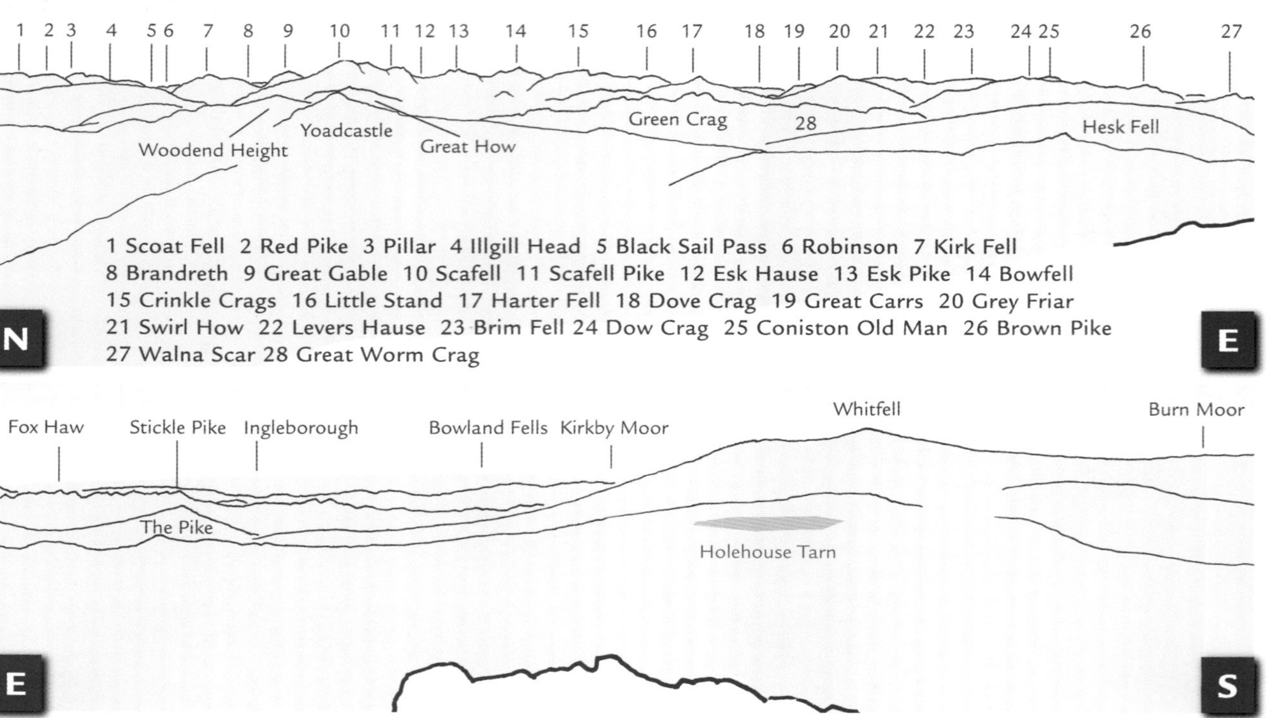
PANORAMA
1 2 3 4 5 6 7 8 9 10 11 12 13 14 15 16 17 18 19 20 21 22 23 24 25 26 27
Woodend Height
Yoadcastle
Great How
Green Crag
28
Hesk Fell
1 Scoat Fell 2 Red Pike 3 Pillar 4 Illgill Head 5 Black Sail Pass 6 Robinson 7 Kirk Fell
8 Brandreth 9 Great Gable 10 Scafell 11 Scafell Pike 12 Esk Hause 13 Esk Pike 14 Bowfell
15 Crinkle Crags 16 Little Stand 17 Harter Fell 18 Dove Crag 19 Great Carrs 20 Grey Friar
21 Swirl How 22 Levers Hause 23 Brim Fell 24 Dow Crag 25 Coniston Old Man 26 Brown Pike
27 Walna Scar 28 Great Worm Crag
N
E
Fox Haw
Stickle Pike
Ingleborough
Bowland Fells
Kirkby Moor
Whitfell
Burn Moor
The Pike
Holehouse Tarn
E
S

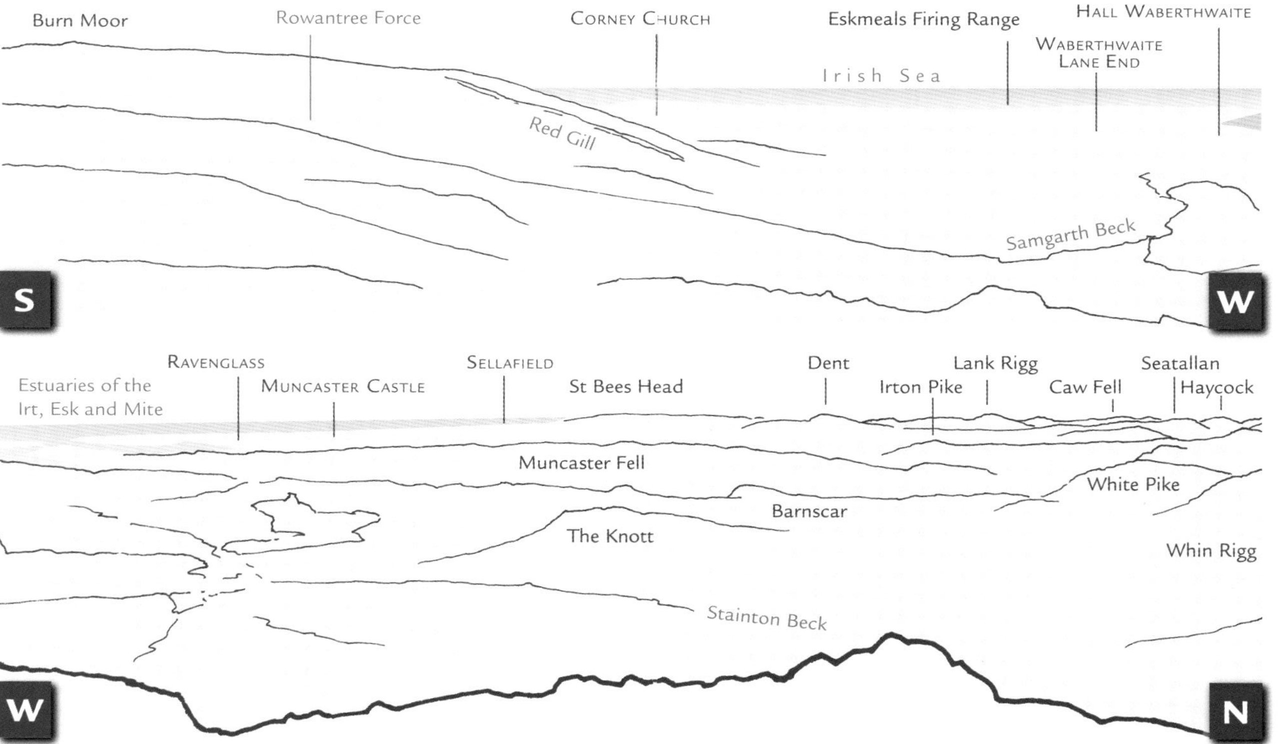
Burn Moor
Rowantree Force
Corney Church
Eskmeals Firing Range
Hall Waberthwaite
Waberthwaite Lane End
Irish Sea
Red Gill
Samgarth Beck
S
W
Ravenglass
Sellafield
Dent
Lank Rigg
Seatallan
Estuaries of the Irt, Esk and Mite
Muncaster Castle
St Bees Head
Irton Pike
Caw Fell
Haycock
Muncaster Fell
White Pike
Barnscar
The Knott
Whin Rigg
Stainton Beck
W
N

17 STICKLE PIKE *(376m, 1234ft)*

The hamlet of Hall Dunnerdale lies in the Duddon Valley and the Dunnerdale Fells are defined as the south-western slopes of Stickle Pike. But Dunnerdale Beck flows into the River Lickle at Broughton Mills which should surely make this side valley, east of Stickle Pike, the real Dunnerdale, and the main valley the Duddon? Whatever their names, both are beautiful and made the more so by the shapely presence of Stickle Pike and its associated tops. Adding to the general confusion, the parallel ridge, enclosing Dunnerdale Beck to the right, actually contains a higher summit, Fox Haw, superior by just under 10m. (How many of us remember the heights of fells, but that of Stickle Pike is certainly memorable (in imperial measurements at least), at 1234ft (Walla Crag was once deemed to hold this honour but no longer), and Great Stickle, its lower summit, is exactly 1000ft above sea level.) Most visitors are content to pick off the fell blithely from the open road summit at Kiln Bank Cross, but there is a good deal more to appreciate.

ASCENT FROM KILN BANK CROSS (23)

Direct 117m/384ft 0.5km/¼ mile

1 This ascent is a brief one. Park at Kiln Bank Cross and follow the beaten path curving up the shallow combe from south to south-west. The ground steepens and Stickle Tarn does its level best to hide, but seek it out to enjoy a moment's quiet contemplation at

 ↑ Great Stickle and Stickle Pike from Wallrigg

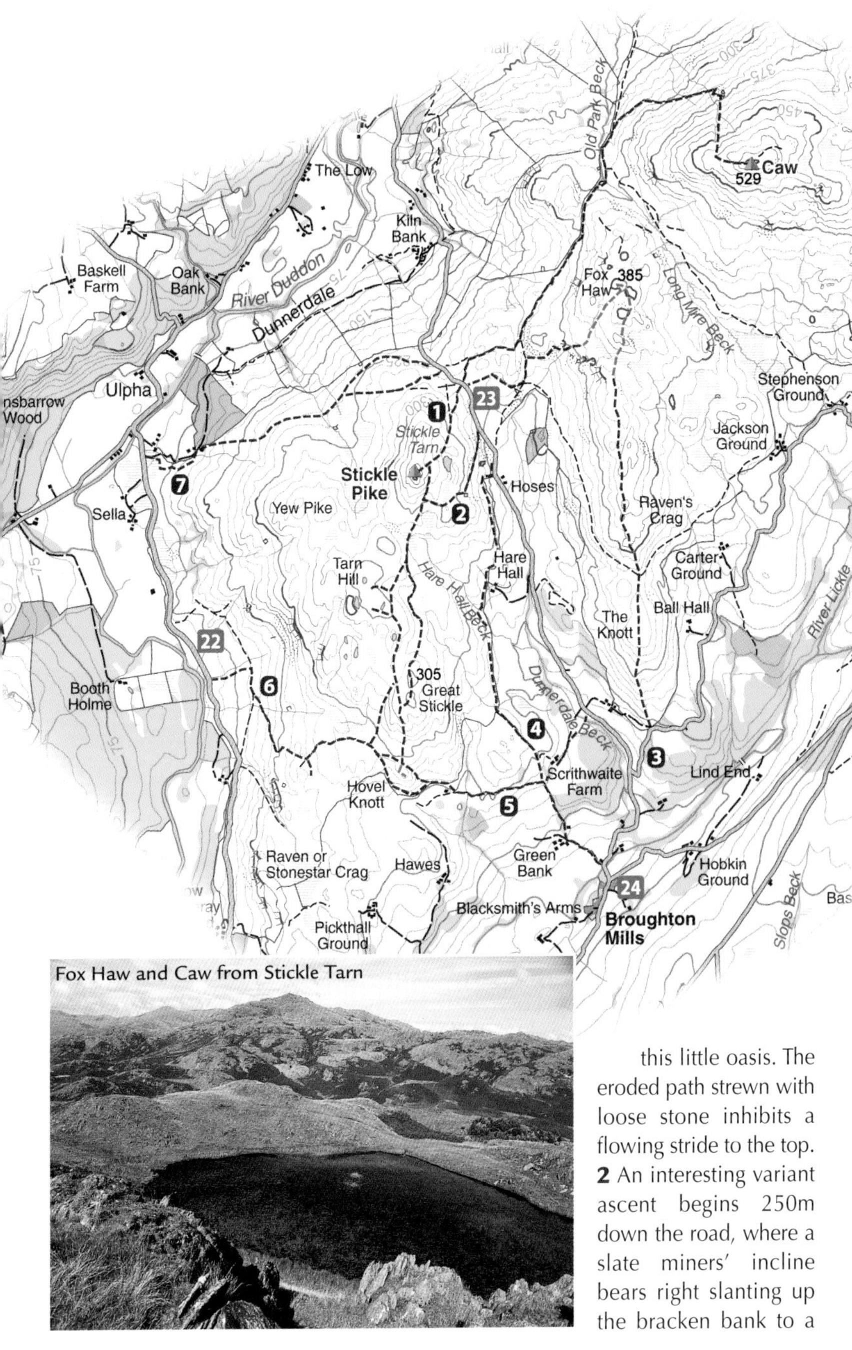

Fox Haw and Caw from Stickle Tarn

this little oasis. The eroded path strewn with loose stone inhibits a flowing stride to the top. **2** An interesting variant ascent begins 250m down the road, where a slate miners' incline bears right slanting up the bracken bank to a mine level. Pass up right by a workshop ruin to join the ridge path emanating from Great Stickle. Cut up right to link with the direct route at a high saddle.

ASCENT FROM BROUGHTON MILLS (24)

Via Fox Haw 425m/1395ft 5.2km/3¼ miles

3 The fell has obvious circular route potential, the best option being the horseshoe 'Dunnerdale Beck skyline' walk, taken anti-clockwise from The Blacksmith's Arms – a perfect destination to return to: real ales, scrumptious food in a setting of stone flagged floors, wooden panelling, old tables and open fires. Either follow the road crossing the Lickle, and then take the next two right forks to reach the ladder-stile on the left at the foot of The Knott ridge. Or, just over the river, fork left to Green Bank, and right through rustic Scrithwaite, crossing the clapper footbridge and then the dale road. Cross into the lane approach to and through Knott End, through gates, to reach that ladder-stile.

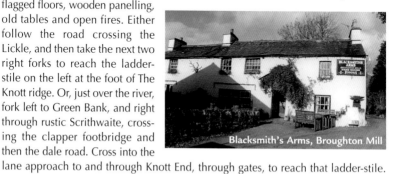

Blacksmith's Arms, Broughton Mill

A clear path leads up the ridge, through the bracken, onto the brow of The Knott, with a cairn almost on the highest point. Follow the ridge path north, crossing a broken wall and the bridleway at the saddle. This drove-way contours left directly to Kiln Bank Cross but skyliners keep up the broken edge ahead, drawing by a rock-girt pool onto Raven's Crag. Strategically sited cairns mark good viewpoints overlooking the white-washed Hoses to Stickle Pike. The ridge path dwindles at a depression and the route onto the raised headland of Fox Haw is undefined. Again the summit rock rib has a cairn with views to merit the effort, to Stickle Pike, and to the peak of Caw. Descend the southern slopes south-west to join an old quarry track associated with the two gaping hollows of the old Stainton Ground slate quarry. This slate is hard, markedly different from its Welsh counterpart in not forming smooth regular plane surfaces. Notice the holly growing from the mouth of the lower level. Join the Park Head Road green-way, a useful approach route to Stickle Pike from Seathwaite, and after 100m branch up right, leaving the track as it goes down to the road-gate at Hoses. Pass a slate mine level – internal railings preventing entry into what appears to be a nasty black hole – and reach the open parking space at Kiln Bank Cross.

Path to Kiln Bank Cross via Hare Hall 3.2km/2 miles

4 The Green Bank route passes a cottage as it enters woodland and soon emerges again at a hand-gate. It rises to a contemporary 'Ross's Camp' (see MUNCASTER FELL Route 9 (page 175)), a wooden picnic bench with the most favoured of views down the Lickle Valley to the coast. Follow the footpath rising north along a

Fox Haw and Caw from Stickle Pike

broken-walled lane, entering the fell enclosure at a gate and then accompanying the intake wall brushing through bracken above Hare Hall to join the road at Hoses.

Via Great Stickle 368m/1207ft 2.7km/1¾ miles

5 The skyline route bears left from the bench (Route 4), the walled lane rising and dipping to a gate, with stone stoups adjacent. The trackway passes by a stone barn and rises to a gate. The continuing green track sweeps around Hovel Knott, but the prime route branches up through the bracken on a clear path. Aim for the saddle to the right of Hovel Knott, a lovely little viewpoint in its own right. Bear up right from the narrow col. A path weaves over Little Stickle to the fading white-washed OS pillar on Great Stickle – a handsome viewpoint for the lower Duddon and Lickle Valleys. The northward connection to Stickle Pike has two basic variations, either forge swiftly on on the slightly lower level, crossing the marshy hollow, or hold to the ridge (to the left), passing the various attractive pools and puddles that characterise Tarn Hill.

ASCENT FROM ULPHA (22)

Via Tarn Hill 358m/1175ft 3km/1¾ miles

There are various small parking places where the rocky river and open road come close. Visitors of all ages revel in this lovely stretch of free-flowing water, not seen so well since Cockley Beck, way upstream between Wrynose and Hardknott. The rough skyline of Yew Pike shields Stickle Pike with no promise of a comfortable walk. Two paths make effective connections with the spine of the ridge, both fending off the all-too-evident bracken with unexpected ease, and they can be combined to make a really good scenic circular walk. **6** The footpath from Broughton Mills crossing over

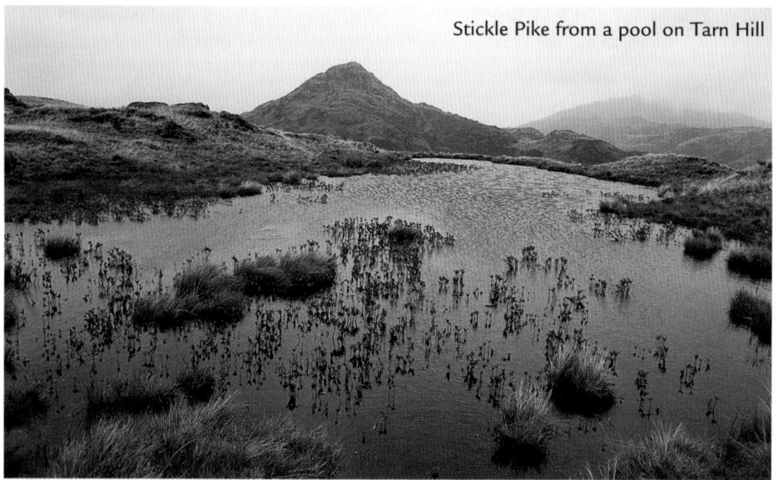
Stickle Pike from a pool on Tarn Hill

Stickle Pike summit cairn

the ridge by Hovel Knott reaches the Duddon at GR201917. A signed path steps off the road here by a small gill bridge and weaves up the fellside, drifting right. As the climb eases, skirt a hollow and angle left into the ridge-top saddle, just north of Great Stickle, to join Route 5.

Via Low Birks 308m/1010ft 2.5km/1½ miles

7 Less than a mile up the main road, at Ulpha bridge, a strip of tarmac leads from the valley road, close to the old school, and rises to the attractively located cottage at Low Birks. There are two bridleways. The one on the open fell, setting off for Kiln Bank Cross, shows off the Duddon valley to its best. To follow this, mount the bank by the water tank with the wall on your left. Veer away from the wall to negotiate damp ground, the path briefly indistinct. Pass a large quartz-streaked outcrop and soon after ford a headstream, amid juniper bushes. The path splits indistinctly, the clearer path joining the wall on the left to meet the road above the cattle grid sign, just on the Duddon side of the road pass. Turn right along the road and right again (Route 1) to complete the ascent.

THE SUMMIT

No wonder people race up from the road pass. Stickle Pike has a lovely little summit, with two tops, and a view that would cheer the most despondent.

SAFE DESCENTS

Cheered as you may be, don't treat the descent with frivolity. Keep tight to the one way up as it is the one way down, especially to the first shoulder.

RIDGE ROUTE

CAW ↓150m/480ft ↑300m/960ft 3.6km/2¼ miles

Follow the popular path N to the open road at Kiln Bank Cross. Head straight across and take one of two green paths leading NE down to the Park Head Road bridleway. After about half a mile, you come alongside a wall and the bridleway from Long Mire merges from the right. Watch for the obvious Caw Quarry slate miners' incline branching right. Ascend to the mine and climb the rake directly above to reach the OS pillar.

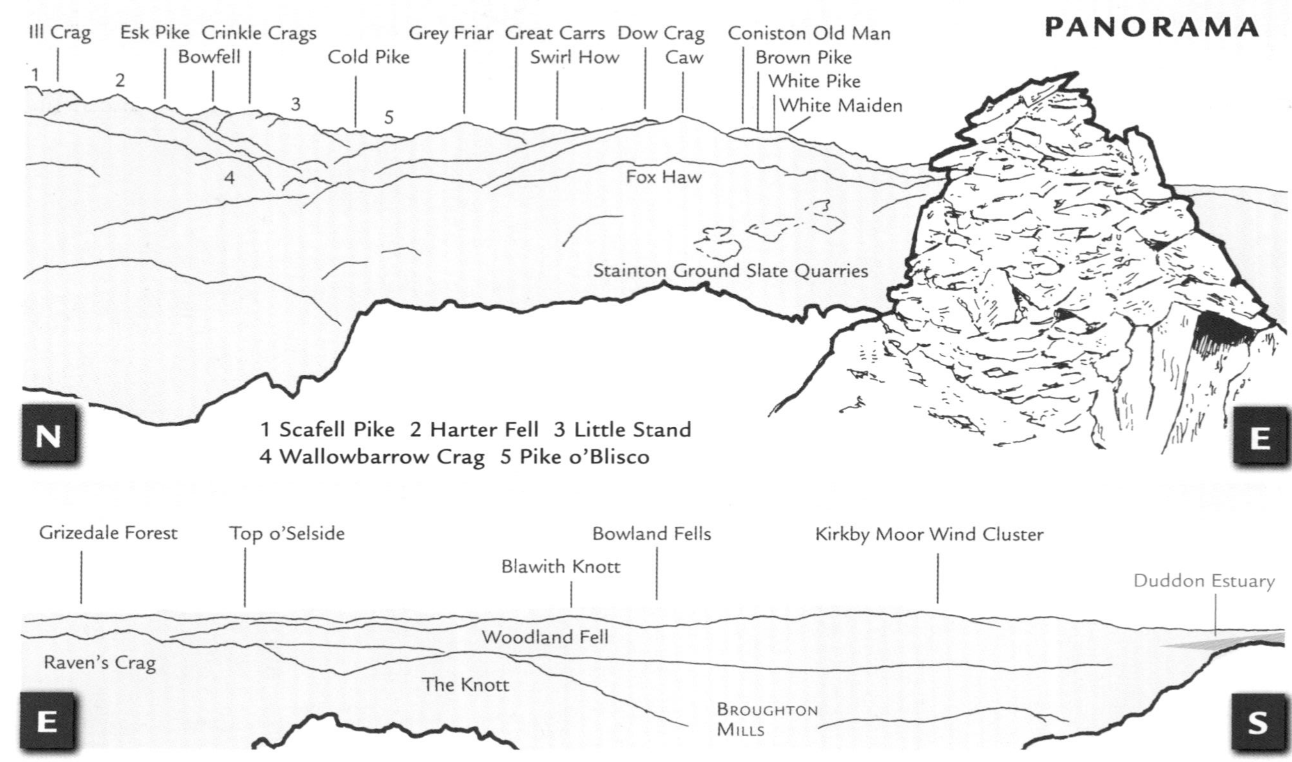
PANORAMA
Ill Crag
Esk Pike
Crinkle Crags
Bowfell
Cold Pike
Grey Friar
Great Carrs
Swirl How
Dow Crag
Caw
Coniston Old Man
Brown Pike
White Pike
White Maiden
1
2
3
4
5
Fox Haw
Stainton Ground Slate Quarries
N
E
1 Scafell Pike 2 Harter Fell 3 Little Stand
4 Wallowbarrow Crag 5 Pike o'Blisco
Grizedale Forest
Top o'Selside
Blawith Knott
Bowland Fells
Kirkby Moor Wind Cluster
Duddon Estuary
Woodland Fell
Raven's Crag
The Knott
Broughton Mills
E
S

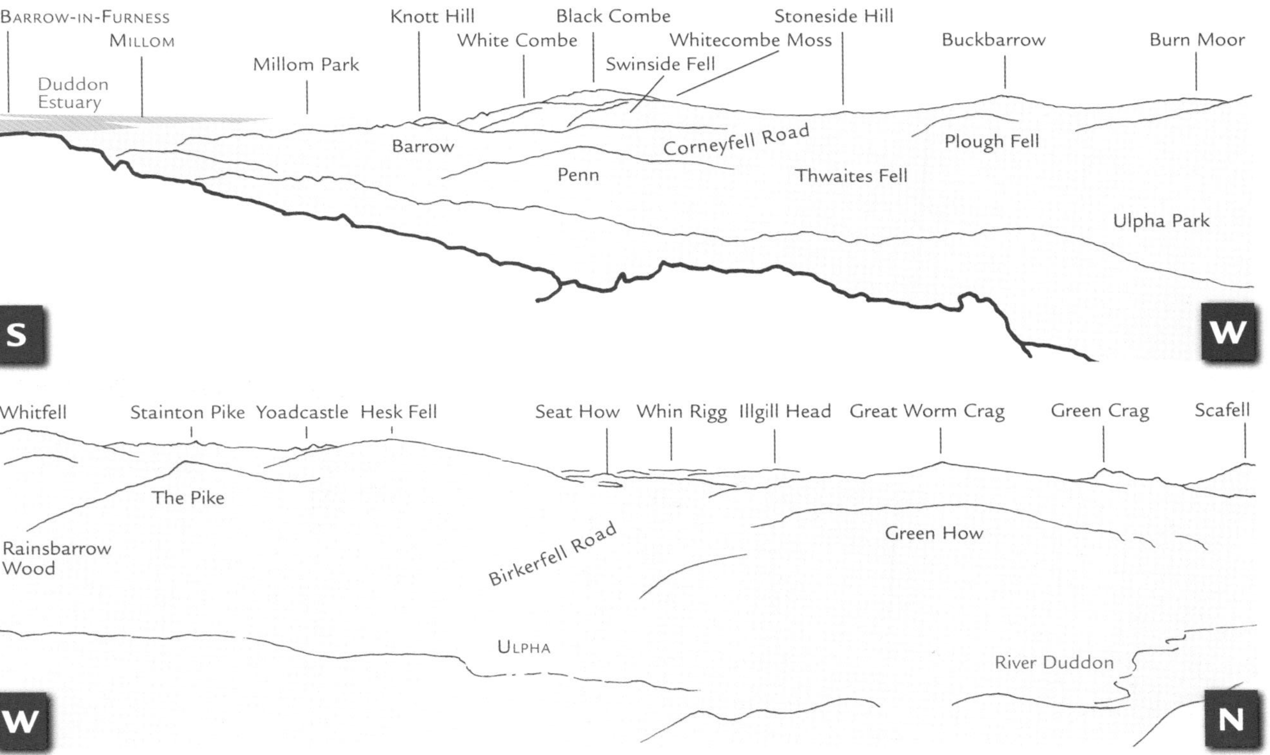
Barrow-in-Furness
Millom
Duddon Estuary
Millom Park
Knott Hill
White Combe
Black Combe
Swinside Fell
Whitecombe Moss
Stoneside Hill
Buckbarrow
Burn Moor
Barrow
Corneyfell Road
Plough Fell
Penn
Thwaites Fell
Ulpha Park
S
W
Whitfell
Stainton Pike
Yoadcastle
Hesk Fell
Seat How
Whin Rigg
Illgill Head
Great Worm Crag
Green Crag
Scafell
The Pike
Rainsbarrow Wood
Birkerfell Road
Green How
Ulpha
River Duddon
W
N

18 SWIRL HOW *(804m, 2638ft)*

The Old Man gets the plaudits and crowds; Swirl How gets the genuine fellwalker – and the nod in height, by a mere metre. (Such things are important to committed peak baggers!) This is the focal summit of the Coniston group, out from which three major ridges swirl. The ridge that climbs out of Little Langdale with its high-level connection with the Mid-Western Fells on Wrynose Pass, may be generally considered part of Great Carrs, but in truth its ultimate goal is Swirl How. Southward another ridge runs steadily down to Levers Hawse, en route to Brim Fell and the Old Man. Eastward stretches Prison Band, an exhilarating rock group. While Wetherlam dominates north-eastern perspectives, Swirl How makes

Wetherlam from Prison Band

 ↑ Swirl How from Raven Tor

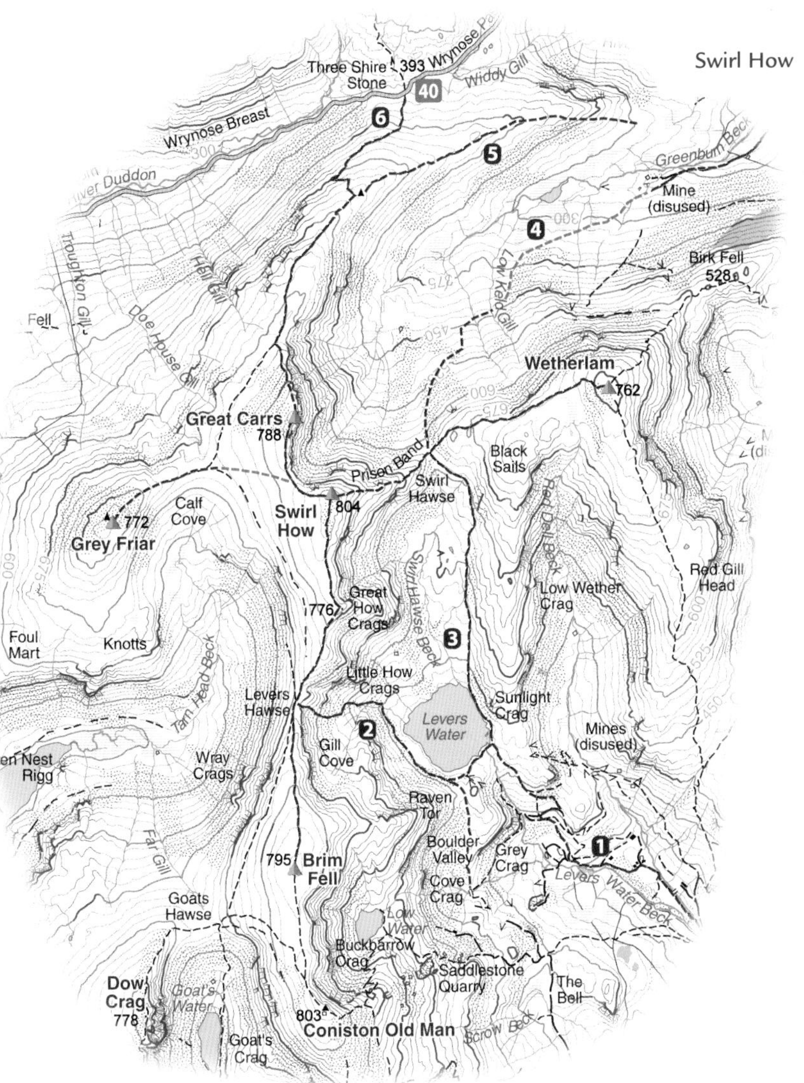

a graceful culmination to the Greenburn valley. The Prison Band commands the ridge approach from Black Sails and Great How Crags dominate the landscape from the top of Raven Tor on Brim Fell, a personal favourite viewpoint. Great and Little How Crags are the exclusive preserve of rock climbers, hence the white-painted notice on the east side of Great How's crest, warning walkers from attempting a descent. The wanderer, however, will enjoy the quest for the goose bield (fox trap) located tight under these crags, which can be safely conducted from the climbers' approach path above Levers Water.

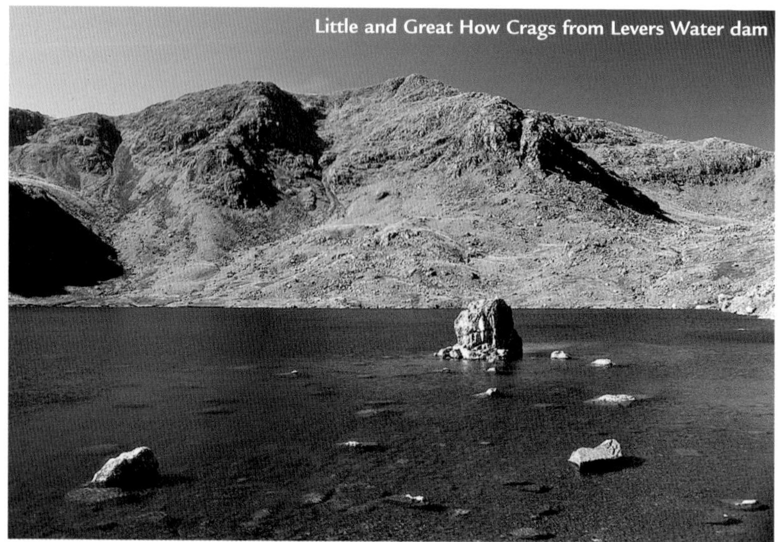
Little and Great How Crags from Levers Water dam

ASCENT FROM CONISTON (29 – OFF MAP SE)

Via the Coppermines Valley 744m/2440ft 5km/3 miles

1 The regular track, still industrially used by Burlington's slate lorries and United Utilities' vehicles heading for the Paddy End waterworks, advances up the Church Beck valley from Coniston. The approach is level to the superbly sited Coppermines Youth Hostel, followed by a brief steady rise, and then, after the concrete mass of the waterworks, zig-zags up to the outflow of Levers Water. Two routes to the summit are at once available. Both have their merits and they make a worthy round trip if combined.

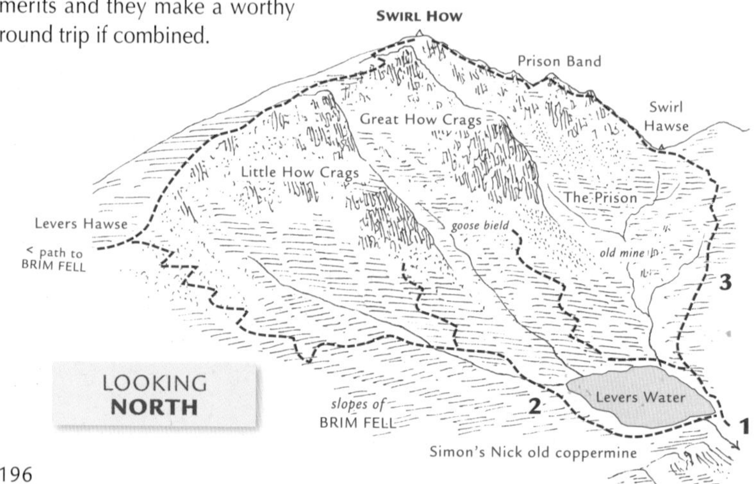

2 Bear left, crossing the dam causeway to cross the broken ground associated with the old Simon's Nick coppermine workings. The collapsed portion looks forbidding, and would be without the ropes needed for a proper speleological investigation. The Boulder Valley path merges from the left, as the rough path contours round, well above the southern and western shore of Levers Water. Ford Cove Beck and follow the cairns on a well-maintained path that climbs steadily towards Levers Hawse. The path towards Gill Cove is intermittently pitched, more so the higher one gets. Avoid the stony gully to the right and keep to the solid footing. When you eventually reach the saddle, turn right (north). Two paths head northwards. Follow the ridge path proper for the better views back, notably the fabulous view of Brim Fell, which graces the cover of this book, as seen from the little rocky top of Great How Crags. **3** The path to Swirl Hawse from Levers Water has grown in popularity over the years. It can be damp but it is a good route. Those of a wandering inclination might be tempted to venture up the slope of Great How Crags to inspect the goose bield, situated on a shelf beneath the large boulders. Reached via the left-hand side of a shallow rigg, this is the climbers' approach to the crag. This tiny pen would have had a cantilever plank bated with a goose at its tip. The fox would walk the plank, fall into the pen and starve. Goose bields were an effective control for fell foxes, although sentimental walkers would hardly stand for such a

Cotton-grass fringed pool in The Prison

Great How Crags and Levers Water from Swirl How

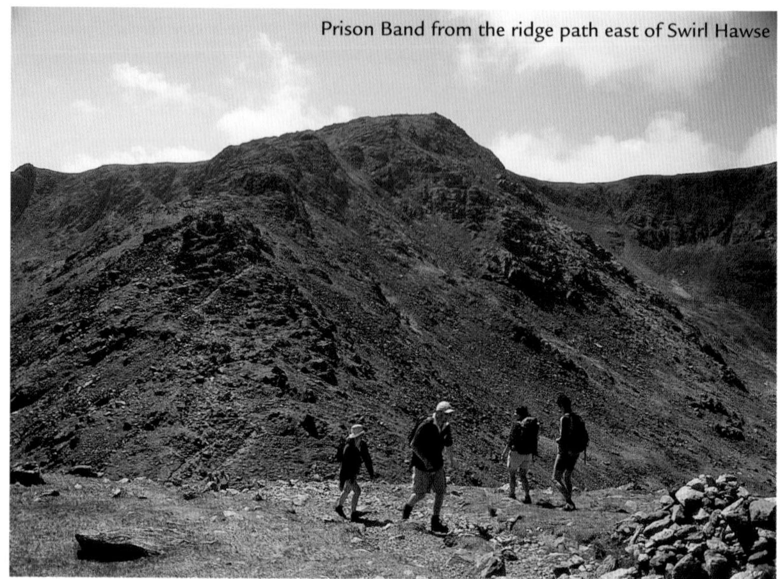
Prison Band from the ridge path east of Swirl Hawse

Swirl Hawse

practice today! Alternatively, you might be tempted to trek upstream with Swirl Hawse Beck, visiting the adjacent rigg with its pools and mine, and the coarse roche moutonée, pock-marked and banded with layers of volcanic rock. The upper cove is thoroughly hemmed in by crags. The miners called it The Prison with good reason, which is how the enclosing rocky ridge rising steeply from Swirl Hawse became known as the Prison Band. There is only the most modest amount of scrambling required in the ascent and, by and large, it's fun.

ASCENT FROM LITTLE LANGDALE (37 – OFF MAP NE)

Via Greenburn Beck **680m/2230ft 5.2km/3¼ miles**

There are two prime routes out of the Brathay valley. The more direct heads up Greenburn Beck. **4** From the hamlet of Little Langdale, begin by visiting Slater Bridge. Whatever else your day may hold in store, simply to step onto this little footbridge brings a special magic to your outdoor adventure. It's a work of art that has stood the test of time – a visual and tactile exhibition of the beauty of local slate.

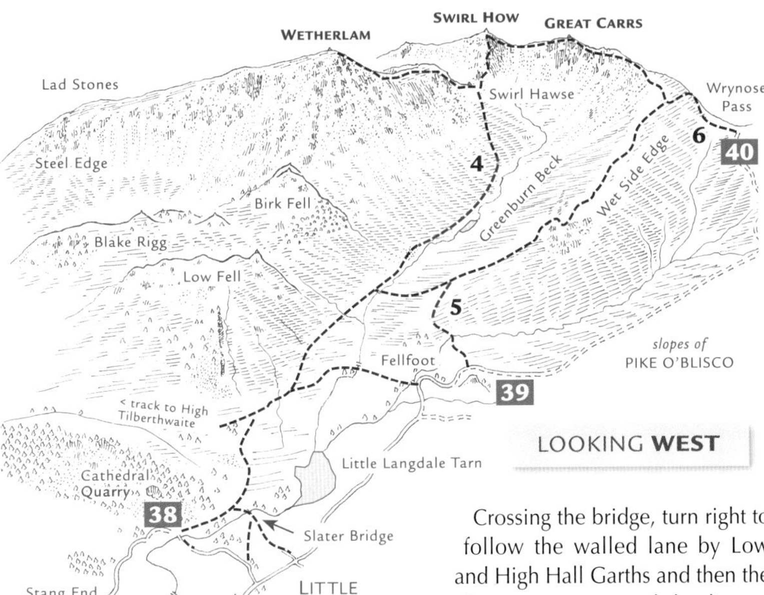

Crossing the bridge, turn right to follow the walled lane by Low and High Hall Garths and then the subsequent open track leading to the old Greenburn Coppermine, the site of which is now a protected monument. Thereafter, walkers take differing lines up the valley. A feeble path only emerges well up the valley side, after crossing High Keld Gill, bound for Swirl Hawse and the Prison Band ridge.

Via Wet Side Edge 685m/2250ft 6km/3¾ miles

5 Ridge walks are always the best of endeavours and the Great Carrs ridge is a classic highway. Start from Fellfoot via Bridge End and the Greenburn track, crossing a footbridge after the intake wall gate to clamber onto the low ridge heading for Rough Crags and Wet Side Edge. (You can also approach from Castle Howe, fording the infant Brathay to step onto the Hollin Crag ridge end – see GREAT CARRS Route 1 (page 103)).

ASCENT FROM WRYNOSE PASS (40)

Direct 411m/1350ft 2.5km/1½ miles

6 The first tourists were guided to the 'awful' summits on pony back, and it's no bad idea to use whatever horse power is at your disposal to save your legs and reduce the ascent by starting from the top of the Wrynose Pass. (See GREAT CARRS Route 4 (page 107)). The one disadvantage is that it does limit your choice of circular walks.

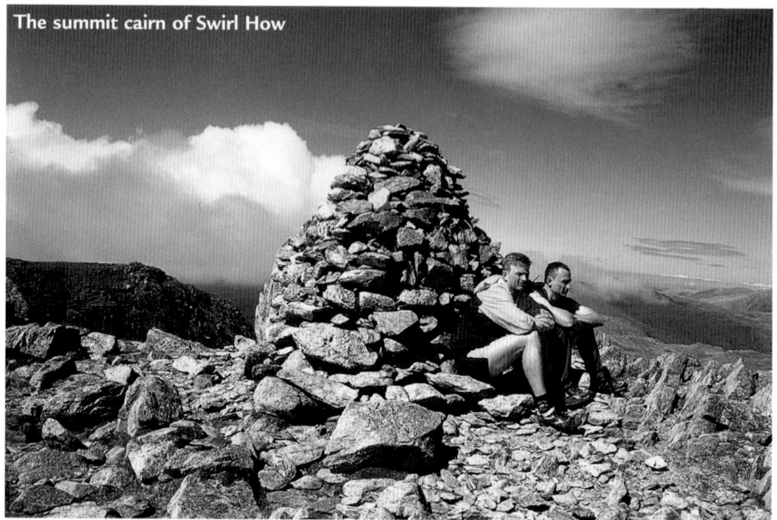
The summit cairn of Swirl How

THE SUMMIT

The place of congregation at the top of Swirl How is a small, flat plateau. Most visitors bound up in a skyline walk from Coniston are pleased to have made it to the highest point on their round and ready to face either the Old Man or Wetherlam. The rugged cairn, built close to the northern downfall into the depths of the Greenburn valley, provides a navigational fix and a place for happy relaxation after the strenuous climb. The view over Wetherlam and across Great Carrs to the Scafells (see photograph) gives a great sense of space. (From here, the Isle of Man sits precisely on top of Grey Friar.)

Great Carrs from Swirl How

SAFE DESCENTS

The Prison Band is steep, but unless conditions are icy it is a secure route to Coniston, turning right at Swirl Hawse for Levers Water. The ridge path S leads to the Levers Hawse depression, and is another good route to Coniston. The ridge N curving round by Great Carrs is a straightforward descent along Wet Side Edge for Wrynose Pass or into Little Langdale.

RIDGE ROUTES

BRIM FELL ↓120m/390ft ↑110m/360ft 2.4km/1½ miles

Follow the broad ridge S, climbing to the summit from the depression of Levers Hawse.

GREAT CARRS ↓40m/130ft ↑20m/65ft 0.5km/¼ mile

Go downhill W from the summit, curving N round the rim of Broad Slack.

GREY FRIAR ↓110m/370ft ↑80m/265ft 1.6km/1 mile

Descend W on grass into the broad Fairfield saddle, joining the ridge path that rises SW onto the summit plateau, passing the Matterhorn Rock.

WETHERLAM ↓190m/620ft ↑145m/480ft 2km/1¼ miles

Take care right from the start. Descend E down the rocky Prison Band ridge. It is straightforward but requires care in places in wet, windy or icy conditions. A large cairn marks Swirl Hawse, from where the ridge path climbs easily NE, avoiding the top of Black Sails, then E to the top.

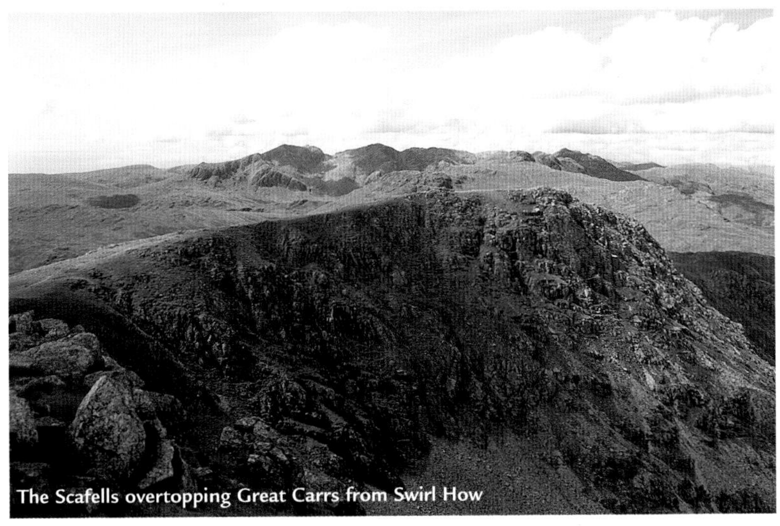

The Scafells overtopping Great Carrs from Swirl How

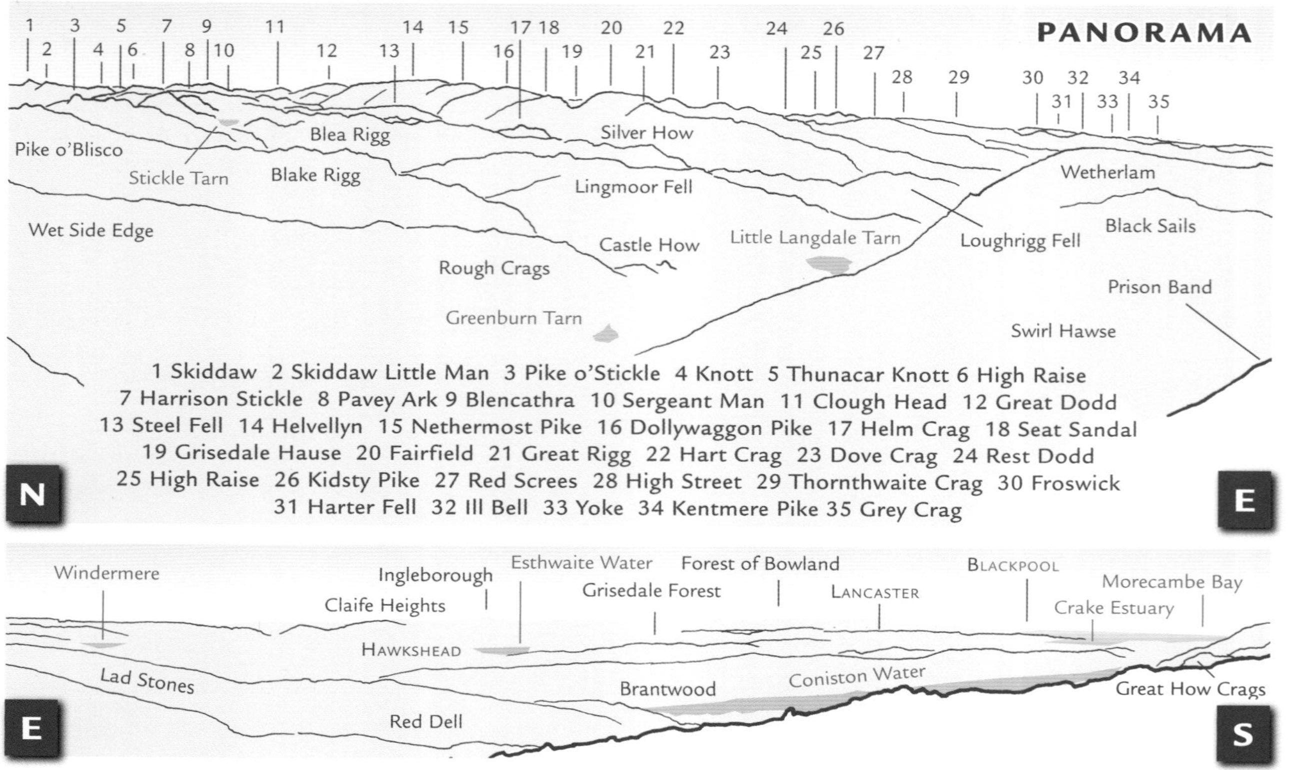
PANORAMA
1 2 3 4 5 6 7 8 9 10 11 12 13 14 15 16 17 18 19 20 21 22 23 24 25 26 27 28 29 30 31 32 33 34 35
Pike o'Blisco
Stickle Tarn
Blea Rigg
Blake Rigg
Silver How
Lingmoor Fell
Wet Side Edge
Castle How
Rough Crags
Little Langdale Tarn
Greenburn Tarn
Wetherlam
Loughrigg Fell
Black Sails
Prison Band
Swirl Hawse
1 Skiddaw 2 Skiddaw Little Man 3 Pike o'Stickle 4 Knott 5 Thunacar Knott 6 High Raise
7 Harrison Stickle 8 Pavey Ark 9 Blencathra 10 Sergeant Man 11 Clough Head 12 Great Dodd
13 Steel Fell 14 Helvellyn 15 Nethermost Pike 16 Dollywaggon Pike 17 Helm Crag 18 Seat Sandal
19 Grisedale Hause 20 Fairfield 21 Great Rigg 22 Hart Crag 23 Dove Crag 24 Rest Dodd
25 High Raise 26 Kidsty Pike 27 Red Screes 28 High Street 29 Thornthwaite Crag 30 Froswick
31 Harter Fell 32 Ill Bell 33 Yoke 34 Kentmere Pike 35 Grey Crag
N
E
Windermere
Ingleborough
Claife Heights
Esthwaite Water
Hawkshead
Forest of Bowland
Grisedale Forest
Lancaster
Blackpool
Morecambe Bay
Crake Estuary
Lad Stones
Brantwood
Coniston Water
Great How Crags
Red Dell
E
S

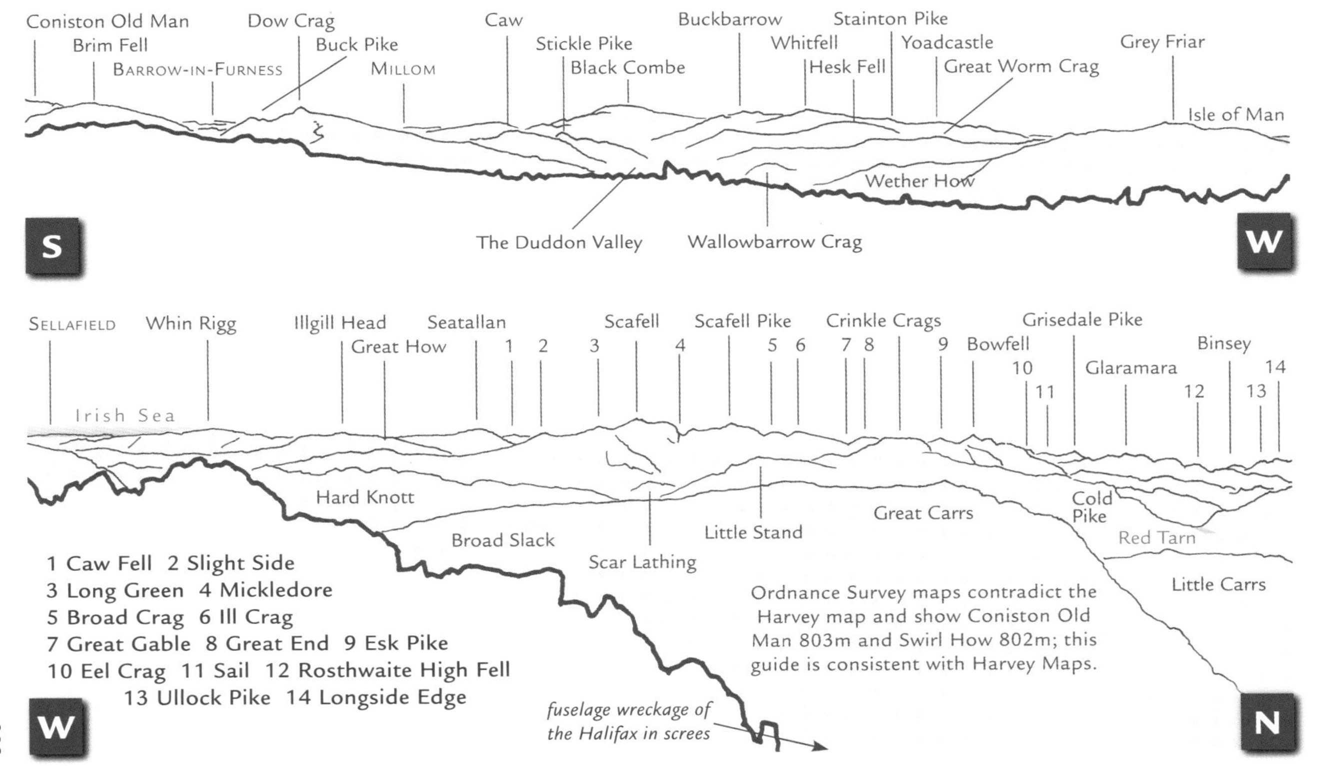
Coniston Old Man
Brim Fell
Barrow-in-Furness
Dow Crag
Buck Pike
Millom
Caw
Stickle Pike
Black Combe
Buckbarrow
Whitfell
Hesk Fell
Stainton Pike
Yoadcastle
Great Worm Crag
Grey Friar
Isle of Man
Wether How
The Duddon Valley
Wallowbarrow Crag
S
W
Sellafield
Whin Rigg
Illgill Head
Great How
Seatallan
1
2
3
Scafell
4
Scafell Pike
5
6
Crinkle Crags
7
8
9
Bowfell
10
11
Grisedale Pike
Glaramara
12
Binsey
13
14
Irish Sea
Hard Knott
Broad Slack
Scar Lathing
Little Stand
Great Carrs
Cold Pike
Red Tarn
Little Carrs
1 Caw Fell 2 Slight Side
3 Long Green 4 Mickledore
5 Broad Crag 6 Ill Crag
7 Great Gable 8 Great End 9 Esk Pike
10 Eel Crag 11 Sail 12 Rosthwaite High Fell
13 Ullock Pike 14 Longside Edge
Ordnance Survey maps contradict the Harvey map and show Coniston Old Man 803m and Swirl How 802m; this guide is consistent with Harvey Maps.
fuselage wreckage of the Halifax in screes
W
N

19 WALLOWBARROW CRAG *(292m, 958ft)*

Wallowbarrow Crag is a heather-capped wood-shawled little craggy eminence. This harmony of crag and gorge is exciting to the senses, and for just this one moment brings to the Duddon something of the drama and magic normally accorded exclusively to Castle Crag and the Jaws of Borrowdale. Greatly appreciated by rock climbers for its sunny, and therefore quick-drying, easily accessed crags, it is largely unknown to fellwalkers, in the main bypassed and thought of simply as one side of the famous gorge. This massive fist of magma, the remnant plug of a geologically ancient volcano vent, is, in fact, the Duddon's focal viewpoint. During August it is draped with the most luxuriant carpet of purple heather. Access onto its rough top is confined to one narrow trod and one heather-choked gully, both rising from the bridleway as it draws up to the low saddle on its west side.

Enjoy Wallowbarrow Crag. Ramble round through the gorge to Fickle Steps, ascend to Grassguards and track back along the bridleway, only then to step onto the crag and appreciate its unique Duddon credentials.

 ↑ Wallowbarrow Crag from Seathwaite

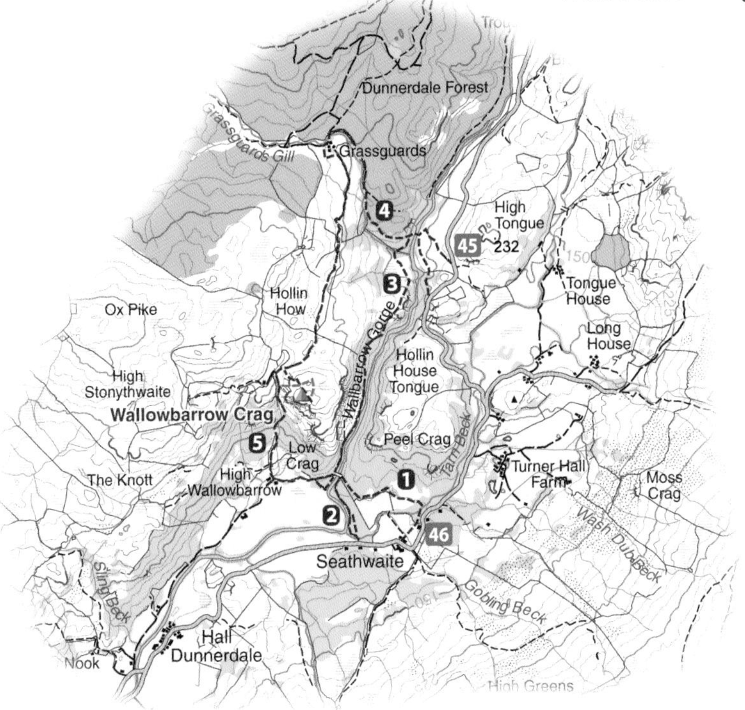

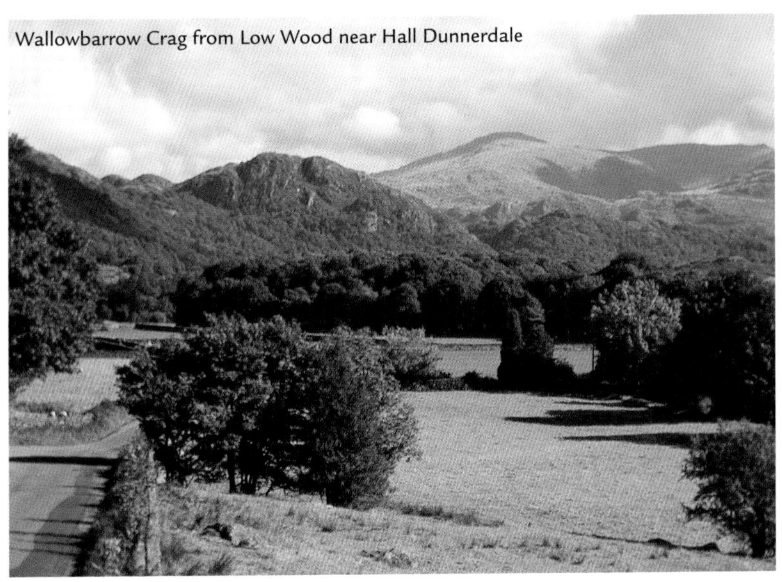
Wallowbarrow Crag from Low Wood near Hall Dunnerdale

ASCENT FROM SEATHWAITE (45 & 46)

Circuitous route via Wallowbarrow Gorge 232m/760ft 3.7km/2½ miles

1 Opposite The Newfield Inn a footpath leads, through gates, to a small footbridge spanning Tarn Beck. The path passes a small weir, skirts a marsh and comes alongside a wall before arriving at the memorial footbridge. (The seat, up to the right, does not, sadly, indicate a secret route onto Pen, its top hidden beyond in the trees.) **2** The bridge can also be reached from a footpath that leaves the valley road opposite the old school house, again crossing a Tarn Beck footbridge and weaving through woodland, passing the Duddon/Tarn Beck confluence on the way. **3** From the memorial bridge, venture up the gorge to your right. Progres through a fantasy world of rock and native woodland over stiles. The boulder scree spilling from the high crag is particularly impressive. The path climbs, then dips to a wooden footbridge over Grassguards Gill and advances to Fickle Steps. **4** A path from the open common descends to cross the Fickle Steps stepping stones (not always easy, being prone to submersion). On the far bank another path angles up the woodland half-left to rock steps then through a hand-gate, following the gill to the forest track access to Grassguards. Cross the footbridge to the left. A permissive path orbits the farmhouse and buildings on the right through hand-gates. Follow the bridleway beside a short thick-walled lane and an enclosure protected by deer gates until you reach the faint path leading, left, onto the top.

The Duddon from the Grassguards track

Wallowbarrow Gorge

Direct from High Wallowbarrow Farm 187m/615ft 1km/½ mile

Reach the memorial bridge (Routes 1 or 2), and head directly for High Wallowbarrow Farm by wood and meadow. **5** Follow the bridleway left from the barn-end and ascend through gates. Climbing up from beneath the mighty crag veer left to come alongside a wall. As this nears the top either look for the weakness up a gully to the right (no path) or, higher, find a thin path onto the top... and feel exulted!

SAFE DESCENTS

It is imperative that you leave the top of Wallowbarrow Crag on a NNW bias. No other line of descent is remotely tenable, nor safe! There is no single path down the heather banks but the various options all lead to the bridle track.

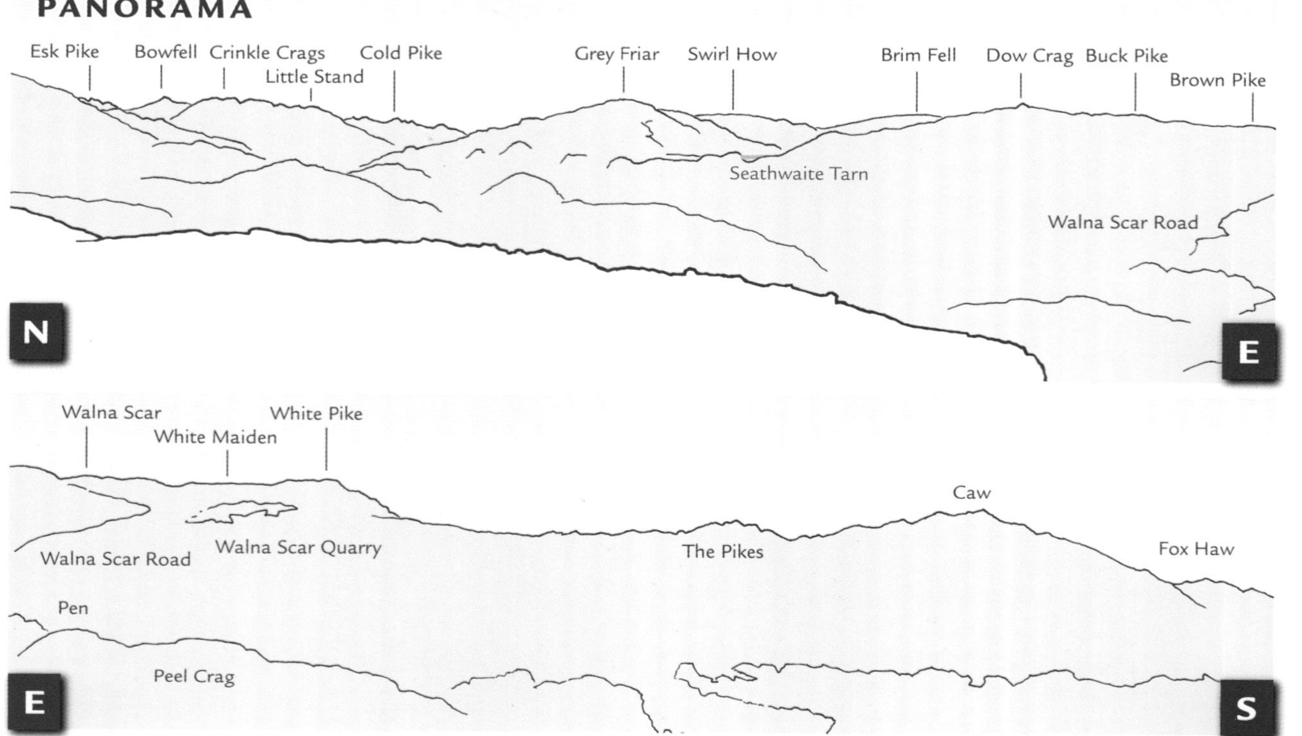
PANORAMA
Esk Pike
Bowfell
Crinkle Crags
Little Stand
Cold Pike
Grey Friar
Swirl How
Brim Fell
Dow Crag
Buck Pike
Brown Pike
Seathwaite Tarn
Walna Scar Road
N
E
Walna Scar
White Maiden
White Pike
Caw
Walna Scar Road
Walna Scar Quarry
The Pikes
Fox Haw
Pen
Peel Crag
E
S

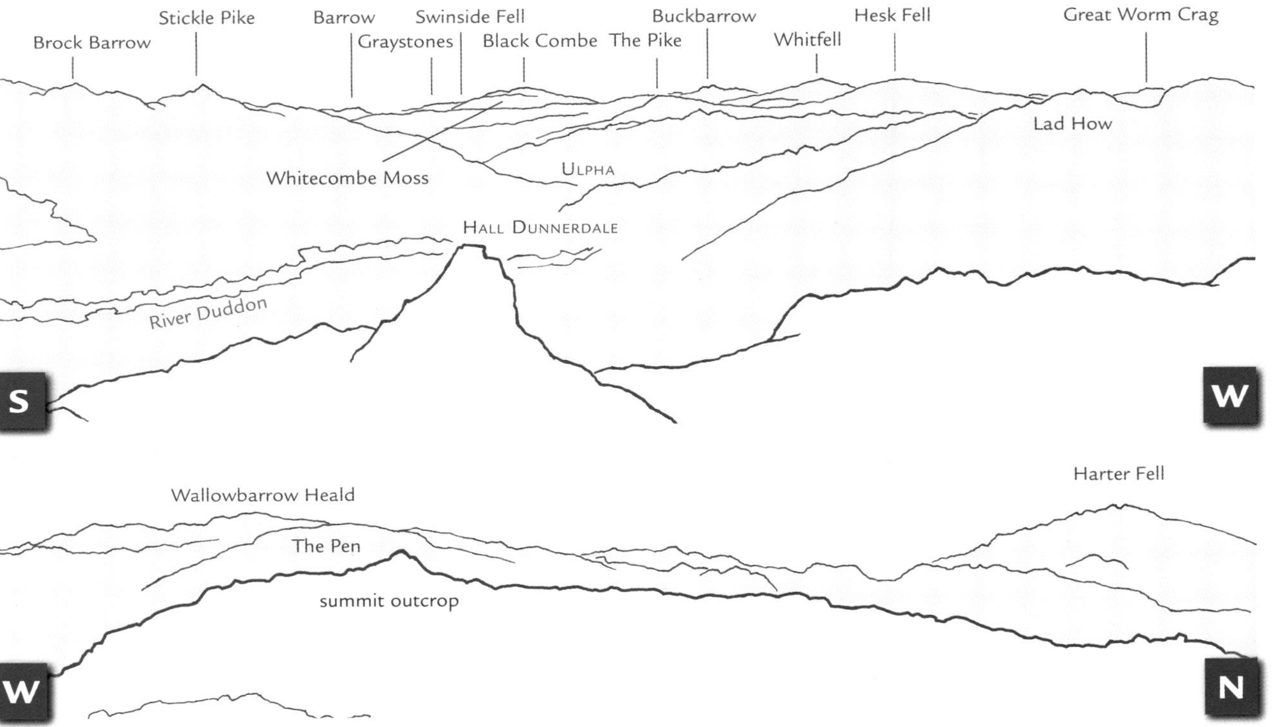
Brock Barrow
Stickle Pike
Barrow
Graystones
Swinside Fell
Black Combe
The Pike
Buckbarrow
Whitfell
Hesk Fell
Great Worm Crag
Lad How
Whitecombe Moss
Ulpha
Hall Dunnerdale
River Duddon
S
W
Wallowbarrow Heald
The Pen
summit outcrop
Harter Fell
W
N

20 WALNA SCAR *(621m, 2037ft)*

Off to climb Walna Scar... the rough road that crosses the high pass between Coniston and Seathwaite? The age-old highway loved to this day by walkers, cyclists and motorbikers alike? No, the fell! Stand in the bar at The Newfield Inn at Seathwaite and look down at the regular, striated dark and light slate flag floor. This tells of another side of Walna Scar's more recent history, as a source for excellent building stone. Gaping quarries might be said to 'scar' the western slope of the fell. Walna Scar completes the Dow Crag ridge to the south. Its highest point, a grassy hummock, is bettered as a summit by both White Maiden and White Pike. Although it can be easily 'bagged' from the old road, the fell has excellent approaches over wild country to suit the fell-wandering connoisseur.

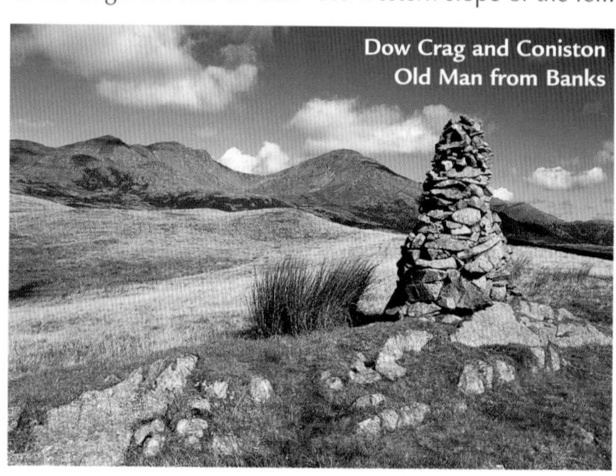

Dow Crag and Coniston Old Man from Banks

 ↑ White Pike and White Maiden from the Lickle Valley

ASCENT FROM CONISTON (29 – off map NE) AND THE FELL-GATE (28)

From the fell-gate via Walna Scar Road 390m/1280ft 3.2km/2 miles

1 The Walna Scar Road springs from the centre of Coniston (1 mile and 170m/560ft from the fell-gate). Climb on an initially steep gradient,

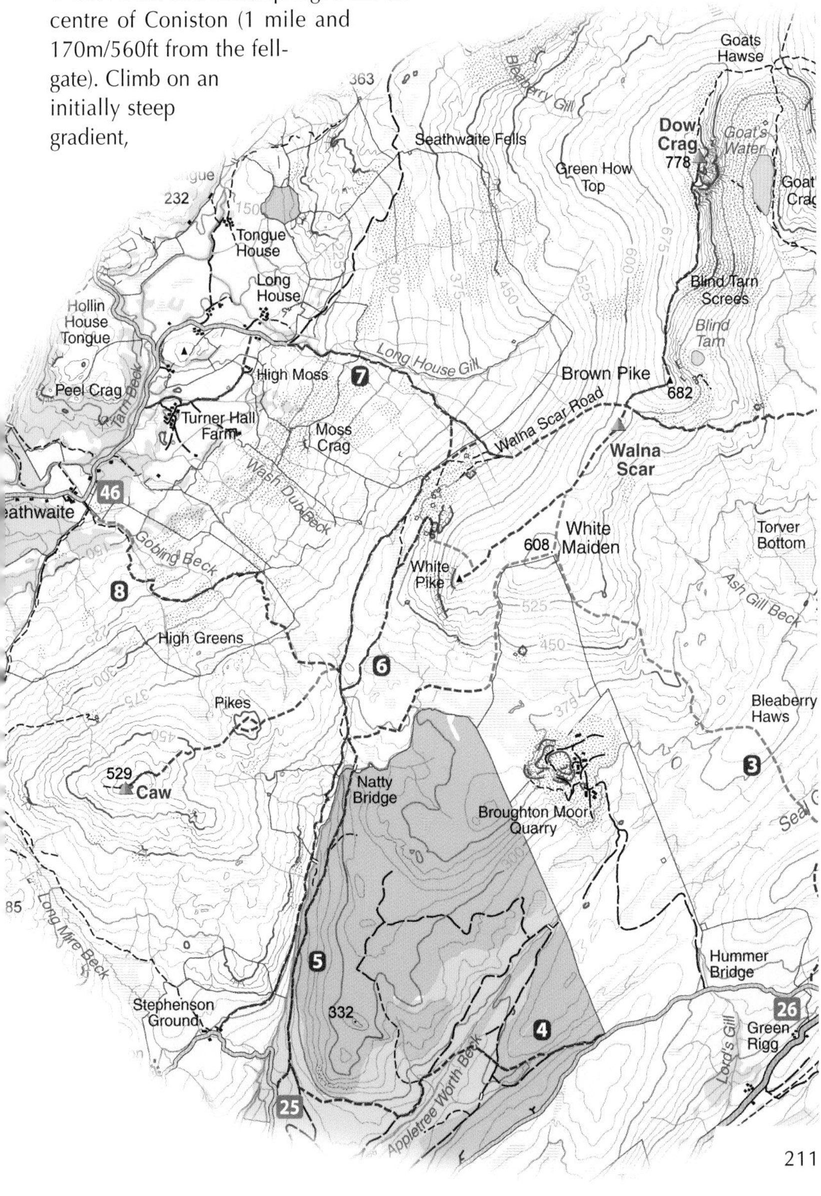

Map continues p212

pass the old station. The toil eventually abates, thank goodness, and progress becomes more leisurely in the country lane, rising to the fell-gate onto the common, where most car-borne walkers park and embark. A minority of 4x4 drivers park beyond Boo Tarn. Gone are the days when they could consider driving over the pass. The track climbs through two stone cuttings,

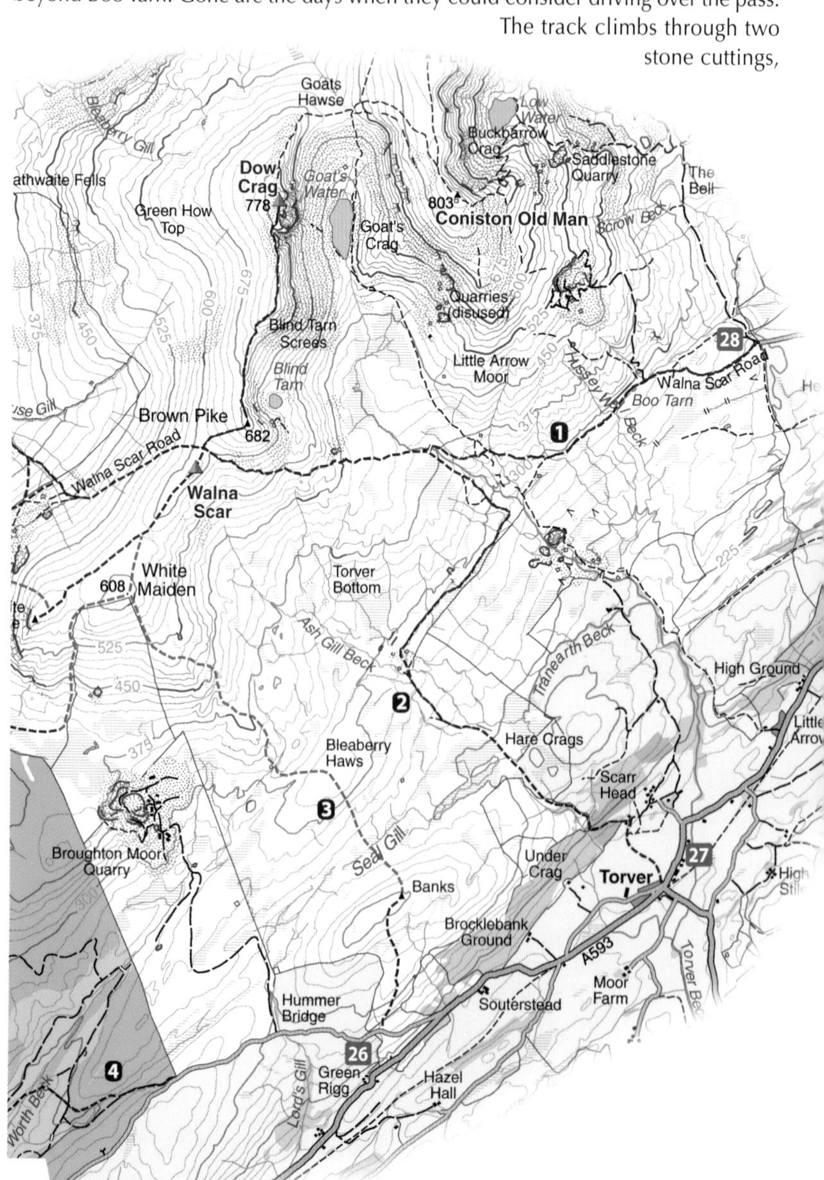

Map continued from p211

Brown Pike from the marsh below High Pike Haw

crosses Cove Bridge and mounts the steep flank of Brown Pike. The ingenious sentry box shelter gives a moment's cause to pause, prior to reaching the saddle. Turn left (south) at the saddle and climb onto the gentle apex of the fell.

ASCENT FROM TORVER (27)

Via Ashgill Quarry 6.4km/4 miles

2 Start from the Wilson Arms and follow the footpath lane rising via High Torver Park through woodland and up an old trackway onto the fell via gates and stiles leading to Ashgill Quarry. Traverse right to rise on an old path by Torver Beck to reach Cove Bridge and join Route 1.

ASCENT FROM HUMMER LANE (26)

Via Bleaberry Haws 500m/1640ft 4.2km/2½ miles

3 The small access point, off Hummer Lane above Torver, is the starting point for a most enjoyable, if unconventional approach. The only path of the ascent leads via Green Rigg Bank to the handsome standard cairn (see photograph page 210) prominently sited on the eastern shoulder of Banks, a Torver village landmark. Cross over the grassy ridge, and descend north-westward into the curiously named damp hollow of Plattocks. Thread a way up through the impending bracken, taking an old wall as your guide, past a small quarry to the cairn surmounting Bleaberry Haws. Slip through the next narrow valley depression with its small quarry ruin, to embark on the real climb of the day, checking out the oddly eroded, steeply pitched, bedrock as you clamber over High Pike Haw. Pass up by a marshy hollow to a sheepfold tucked under Dropping Crag. (Note the subterranean gill in the boulders above.) Step through the outcrops onto the broad ridge to join the rising wall to White Maiden.

ASCENT FROM THE LICKLE VALLEY (25)

This is the perfect approach to Walna Scar, as the valley-head mountain. Reversed, this route may also be woven into a circular expedition using the well-marked bridleway through the Broughton Moor forest (**4**) as the means of getting back to the Hummer Lane start of Route 3.

Valley approach 460m/1510ft 3.7km/2¼ miles

5 Either follow the forest track direct from the recessed forest gate at GR238928, advancing to the stile and wooden footbridge through the ravine at Natty Bridge or, alternatively, cross Water Yeat Bridge and follow the minor road up to Stephenson Ground to find the gated bridleway up the western side of the Lickle gorge, a lovely approach focused on White Pike. Where this then crosses the continuing footpath from Natty Bridge, go forward (east) following the grooved path weaving onto Caw Moss, crossing a small flag bridge with White Pike dominant. The occasional fell-walker keeps the path discernible as it leads on towards a gateway in a wall with a tarn beyond. Ignore the path and take off up the fellside, keeping this wall close right. This is a simple pathless means of getting onto White Maiden and a safe escape route off the ridge in bad weather too.

Via Walna Scar Quarry 444m/1455ft 4km/2½ miles

6 Alternately, from Natty Bridge, you can walk on to the natural destination of the Lickle head path – the Walna Scar Road – across the base of the spoil banks of Walna Scar Quarry. As the bridleway reaches the brow, a little after the turn-off for Route 5, you come to a fork. Neither path has a mastery of the marshy ground here, and bikers have damaged the surface in places. The more commonly followed footpath leads straight on by Dawson's Pike, comes under the slate spoil and follows the intake wall direct to the 'Road'. The right-hand bridleway takes you up among the quarry workings and so is the preferred option. The vast quantity of slate tip suggests a major hollowing of the fell, and sure enough this is what has happened. (If you are lured into the main quarry, the only way out is the way you went in!) Keep up the

Access to derelict Walna Scar Quarry slate workings

White Pike from Caw Moss

right-hand side of the workings to get the most stupendous, perhaps fearful, view into the cavity. You cannot look at things like this without being aware of what they represent in terms of human toil (long before the protection of trade unions). The rest of the ascent is straightforward, if pathless. On reaching the plateau top, slant right to visit the cairn on White Pike and an excellent viewpoint down the Lickle Valley to the sea.

ASCENT FROM SEATHWAITE (46)

Via Walna Scar Road 520m/1705ft 3.5km/2¼ miles

7 Walkers from the Duddon side can use Walna Scar for a short day trip, useful if the cloud rules out any chance of a view from Dow Crag. The Walna Scar Road branches from the valley road half a mile north of The Newfield Inn, above Seathwaite Bridge. There is also a well-marked field-path route via Turner Hall and High Moss (Rucksack Club Hut), which takes a great slice out of road walking. The road becomes a rough track after a gate and climbs to a further gate, with a slate tip close at hand. Centuries of wear compounded by modern traffic, and motorbikes in particular, have taken their toll.

Via Gobling Beck 3.7km/2¼ miles

8 An off-road route can be followed almost directly from The Newfield Inn. Embark upon the Park Head Road and then bear left up the old drove-way. From the hurdle gate at the top, cross Yaud Mire, pass Dawson's Pike by the large quartz outcrop, linking up with Route 6 leading by Walna Scar Quarry.

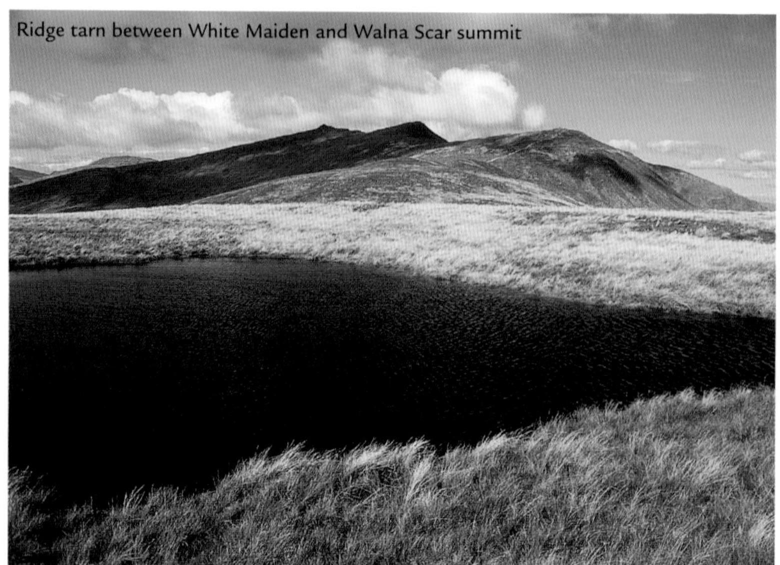
Ridge tarn between White Maiden and Walna Scar summit

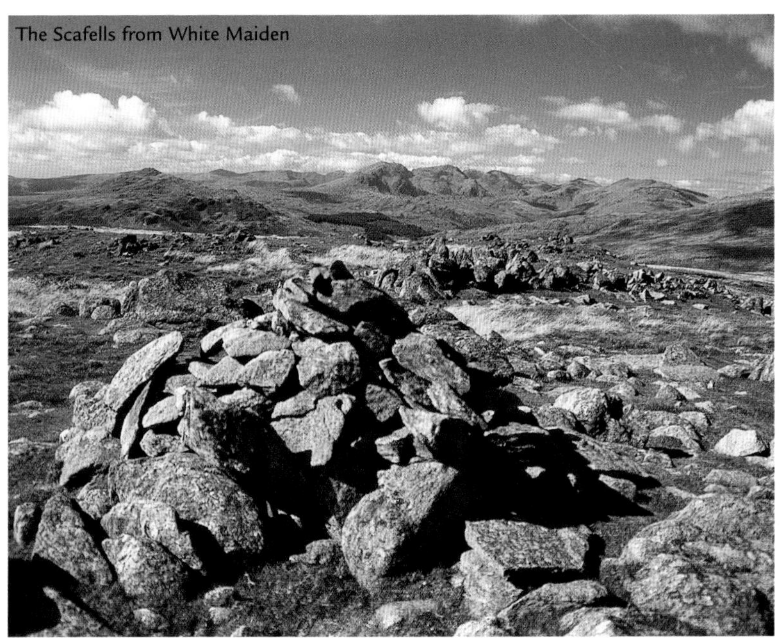
The Scafells from White Maiden

THE SUMMIT

An apology for a cairn marks the top of a grassy pillow rise but the view is excellent, if constricted by Brown Pike to the north. Tick this one off and speed on to rocky White Maiden (see photograph) and the prow end of the ridge at White Pike for the best fell-top sensations.

SAFE DESCENTS

The Walna Scar Road is the obvious option E or W. Should you be tempted to descend off White Pike, watch out for crags but do not head NW towards the slate quarries. An ability to fly will be your only salvation from the unprotected edge.

RIDGE ROUTES

CAW ↓85m/270ft ↑60m/190ft 4km/2½ miles

Follow the ridge SW, passing the pool in the dip then accompany the wall off White Maiden. Traverse Caw Moss heading SW onto the ridge via The Pike.

DOW CRAG ↓20m/70ft ↑180m/585ft 1.6km/1 mile

Go N over the Walna Scar pass, climbing past cairns on Brown and Buck Pikes. Follow along the exciting edge to the cliff-top summit battlement – holding on to your hat in a gale will be the least of your concerns!

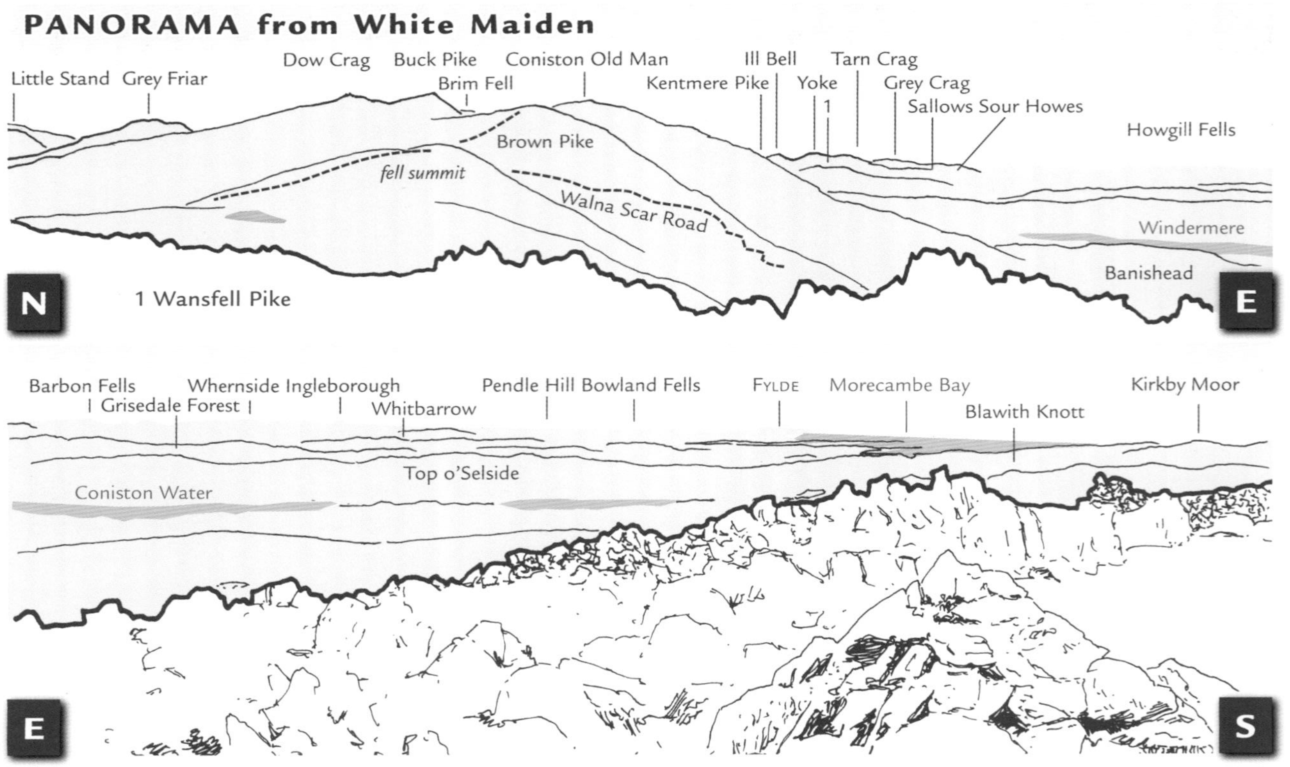
PANORAMA from White Maiden
Little Stand
Grey Friar
Dow Crag
Buck Pike
Brim Fell
Coniston Old Man
Kentmere Pike
Ill Bell
Yoke
1
Tarn Crag
Grey Crag
Sallows
Sour Howes
Howgill Fells
Brown Pike
fell summit
Walna Scar Road
Windermere
Banishead
N
1 Wansfell Pike
E
Barbon Fells
Grisedale Forest
Whernside
Ingleborough
Whitbarrow
Pendle Hill
Bowland Fells
Fylde
Morecambe Bay
Blawith Knott
Kirkby Moor
Top o'Selside
Coniston Water
E
S

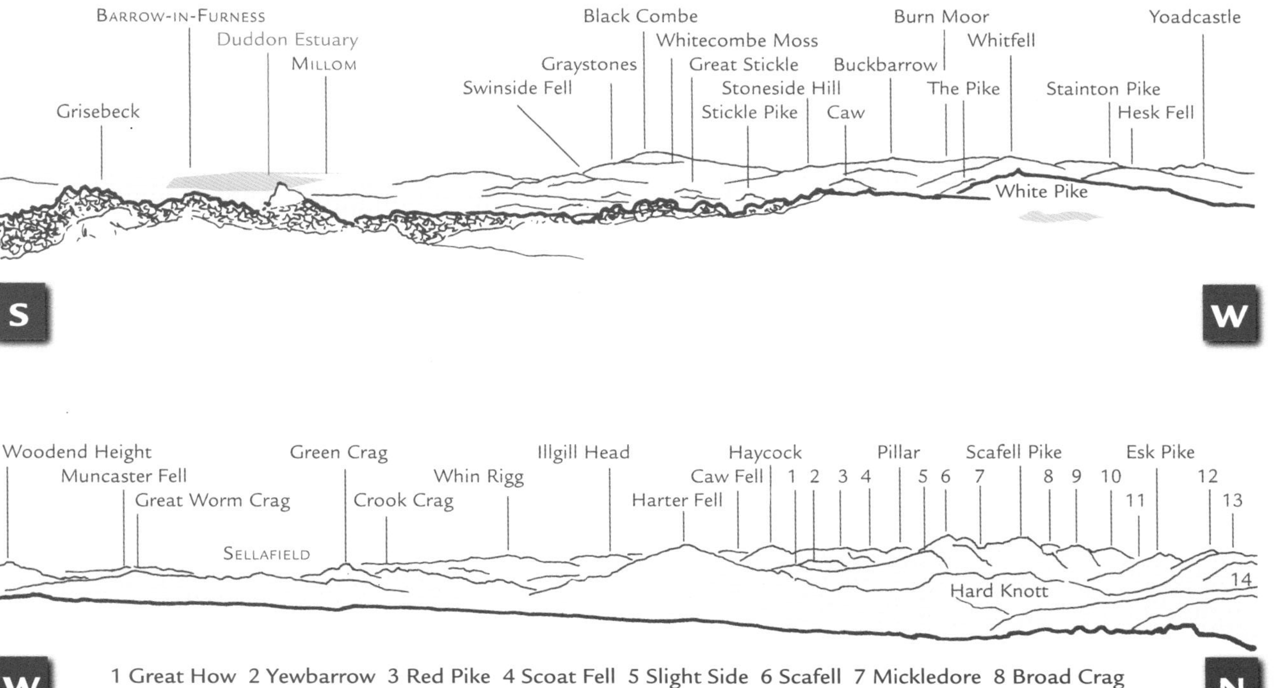
Barrow-in-Furness
Duddon Estuary
Millom
Grisebeck
Black Combe
Whitecombe Moss
Graystones
Great Stickle
Swinside Fell
Stoneside Hill
Stickle Pike
Caw
Burn Moor
Buckbarrow
Whitfell
The Pike
Stainton Pike
Hesk Fell
Yoadcastle
White Pike
S
W
Woodend Height
Muncaster Fell
Great Worm Crag
Sellafield
Green Crag
Crook Crag
Whin Rigg
Illgill Head
Harter Fell
Haycock
Caw Fell
1
2
3
4
Pillar
5
6
7
Scafell Pike
8
9
10
11
Esk Pike
12
13
14
Hard Knott
W
N
1 Great How 2 Yewbarrow 3 Red Pike 4 Scoat Fell 5 Slight Side 6 Scafell 7 Mickledore 8 Broad Crag
9 Ill Crag 10 Great End 11 Esk Hause 12 Bowfell 13 Crinkle Crags/Long Top 14 Little Stand

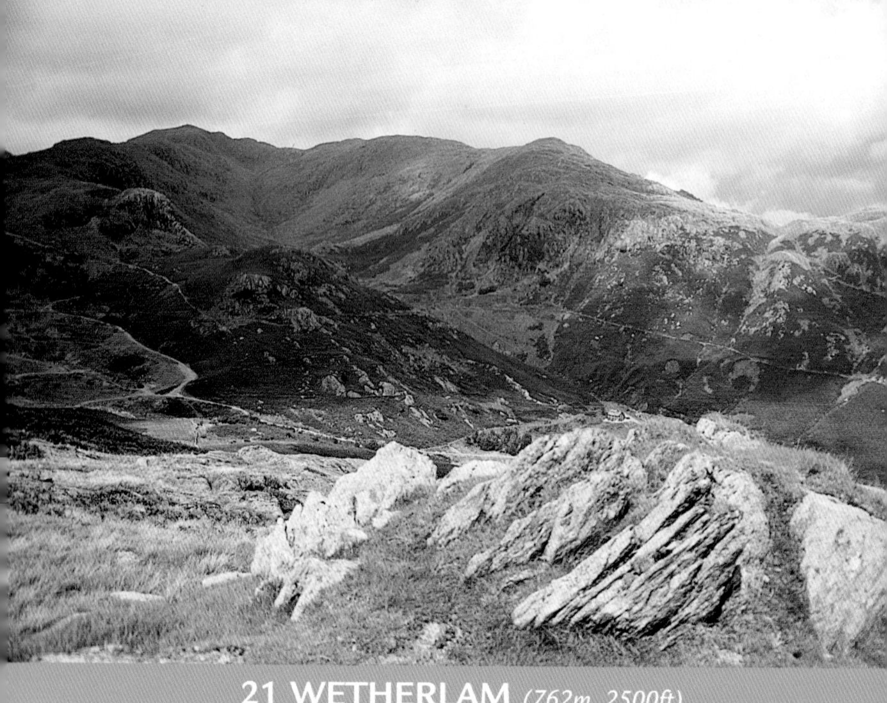

21 WETHERLAM *(762m, 2500ft)*

Glances to the southern quarter of Lakeland frequently fall upon Wetherlam, a prominent marker for the Coniston Fells. Whether first viewed from across Windermere or, most strikingly, from Elterwater Common on the Red Bank road near High Close, the fell exhibits an elegant mass. Wetherlam is one of the most complex mountains in the district, not so much in terms of surface features, but rather in its hidden depths from its mining past. It also has the greatest array of route choices of any among the Southern Fells. Boldly individual, few can reach this summit on a decent day with any sense of disappointment.

It is much more than bulky mass. Down the centuries its wealth of copper and dense fine-grained slate has attracted the attention of industrious man. Deep shafts, levels and open quarries penetrate into its colourful interior. None of these are safe for the average inquisitive fell wanderer – we can only examine these cavities from the surface. Those mines with easiest access have been tightly fenced but in recent decades several incautious folk have met their deaths here.

The four aspects of Wetherlam are quite distinct. The northern slopes, tumbling as crags and scree into the Greenburn valley, are steep and austere. The tenacity of copperminers who worked this flank is quite breathtaking. Waters feeding the Brathay here flow into Windermere. The eastern slopes, initially no less steep, are given extra spice by the imposition of Tilberthwaite Ghyll. The upper ravine, draped

 ↑ Wetherlam from The Bell

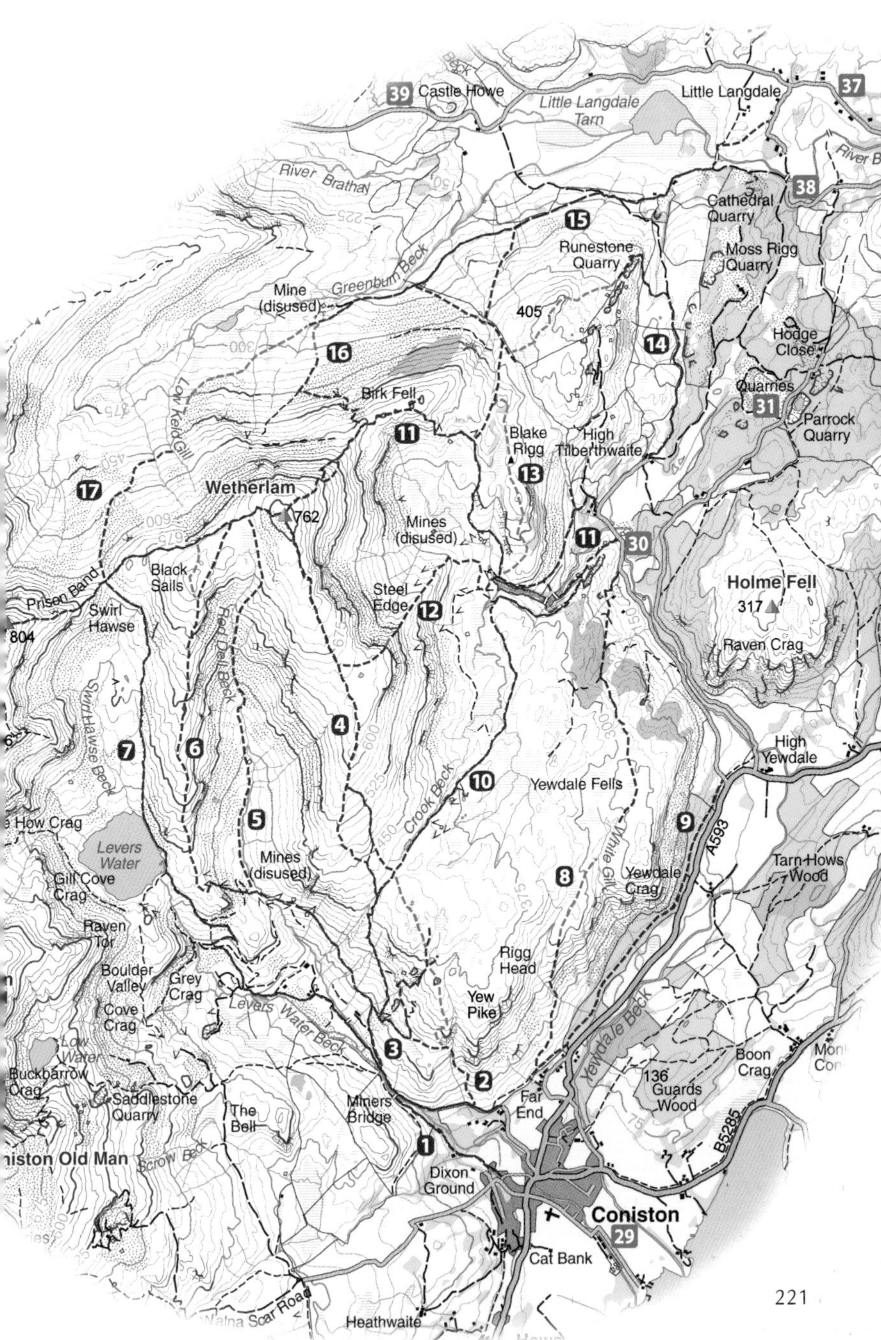
Castle Howe
Little Langdale Tarn
Little Langdale
River Brathay
Greenburn Beck
Mine (disused)
Runestone Quarry
Cathedral Quarry
Moss Rigg Quarry
Hodge Close
Quarries
Parrock Quarry
405
Birk Fell
Blake Rigg
High Tilberthwaite
Low Keld Gill
Wetherlam
762
Mines (disused)
Black Sails
Prison Band
Swirl Hawse
804
Steel Edge
Holme Fell
317
Raven Crag
Red Dell Beck
Swirl Hawse Beck
Crook Beck
Yewdale Fells
High Yewdale
How Crag
Levers Water
Gill Cove Crag
Mines (disused)
White Gill
Yewdale Crag
A593
Tarn Hows Wood
Raven Tor
Boulder Valley
Grey Crag
Cove Crag
Rigg Head
Yew Pike
Levers Water Beck
Low Water
Buckbarrow Crag
Saddlestone Quarry
The Bell
Miners Bridge
Far End
Yewdale Beck
Boon Crag
136
Guards Wood
B5285
Coniston Old Man
Scrow Beck
Dixon Ground
Coniston
Cat Bank
Walna Scar Road
Heathwaite

Wetherlam from Raven Tor

Wetherlam Edge from Yewtree Farm

alpine fashion in larch and flanked by slate quarries, leads up into shallow coves with the undulating indefinite massif of the Yewdale Fells to its south. Irregular shapely ridges run from its north down by Low Fell towards Slater Bridge in Little Langdale. The southern perspective is dominated by two great ridges. The Yewdale Fells form the first craggy rebuff from the village of Coniston, but, above this, the Lad Stones ridge rises imperiously to the summit. Immediately west of this is the wild recess of Red Dell and Black Sails' strangely neglected ridge. From Swirl How, the pivotal summit on the main ridge, the Prison Band ridge leads east and a curious saddle, Swirl Hawse, makes the connection with Wetherlam.

It is not the highest peak but is so placed as to feature in the plans of many grand horseshoe walks. In the normal course of events, Coniston Old Man will be the initial prize. Once upon the ridge Brim Fell and Swirl How quickly succumb. A few walkers will descend Prison Band and be tempted to sidle down to Levers Water, but the inclusion of Wetherlam gives the outing a real flourish.

ASCENT FROM CONISTON (29)

Aspirations normally focus on gaining the high Lad Stones ridge, the natural start/finish to the perennially popular Coniston skyline walk embracing Swirl How, Brim Fell and Coniston Old Man. There are three lead-in routes to the Hole Rake gap, where the ridge effectively begins.

Via Sweeten Crag and Lad Stones 730m/2395ft 5.2km/3¼ miles

1 Turning right above the Sun Hotel, a short walk up the road from the bridge, follow the path from Dixon Ground, which leads to Miners Bridge. Cross the bridge and go left on the main valley track and, as it levels, fork right on the old quarry track. Be sure to take the third left turn in a zag-zag course, on an incline path to Hole Rake. **2** Follow the road access into the Coppermines Valley from beyond the Black Bull and the Ruskin Museum. It soon becomes a rough track. Beyond a cattle grid branch off up the Mouldry Bank slope, contouring round from an old cairn under Rascal How to link with Route 1. Or **3** bear up the old quarry path right, taking care where the quarry has collapsed and removed a chunk of the track. This route winds up through the upper portion of the Blue Quarry onto the fell above. Here, either climb over Sweeten Crag or find the green path leading north-west by Kitty Crag to Hole Rake. (Sweeten Crag is the high point of the undulating rough fell alp which

Coppermines Youth Hostel and cottages backed by the Black Sails ridge

runs from Yew Pike to Yewdale Crag – an absorbing place to wander if relieved of the desire or need to get to the top of Wetherlam.)

4 Two paths have developed to the Lad Stones ridge: one starts short of the top of the pass, dipping through the gill and weaving onto the ridge-end; the other, a more cautious path, departs over stepping stones before the rushy tarn, north of the rake. It mounts assuredly onto the ridge north-westward through early slabs, turning at a large block of bedrock. On the ridge top the two paths join and proceed to the summit. It takes far longer than expected, over two pronounced steps in the ridge.

Via Red Dell and Black Sails 715m/2345ft 6.5km/4 miles

An unprotected copper mine shaft below Kennel Crag

5 Take Route 1 to the point where it turns off up to Hole Rake, and continue on the quarry track to reach a row of quarrymen's terraces, known as Irish Row. Just past here a path leads right towards Red Dell. This is coppermines country sure enough. Above the cascading Red Dell Beck are leats (water channels) and water-wheel pits. The Thriddle incline, which pitches due west up the north side of Kennel Crag, is evidence of long-abandoned deep workings beneath into the Bonsor vein. Bracken fronds grow around their gaping mouths like lures to a death trap. It's a landscape full of interest and considerable danger! A path leads on past the site of a 17th-century copper ore grinding mill into the Red Dell valley. Pass a large erratic and then a sheepfold before fording the gill. At its head climb on the east side. A faint trod guides up to cairns leading to the peaty hollow, just to the west of the summit.

6 The neglected Black Sails ridge provides a gem of an ascent. Climb the Thriddle incline, pass a mine level halfway up with two gate-grilled levels at the top. Go left to the saddle and follow naturally right up the ridge, with faint evidence of a path. You can also join the ridge from the outflow of Levers Water. Look out for the narrow banded rocks (see photograph page 233) from where there is a superb view back over Levers Water to Raven Tor and the Old Man. The path tends to avoid the ridge top, although there is no good reason to do so. (Notice the intensity of lichen

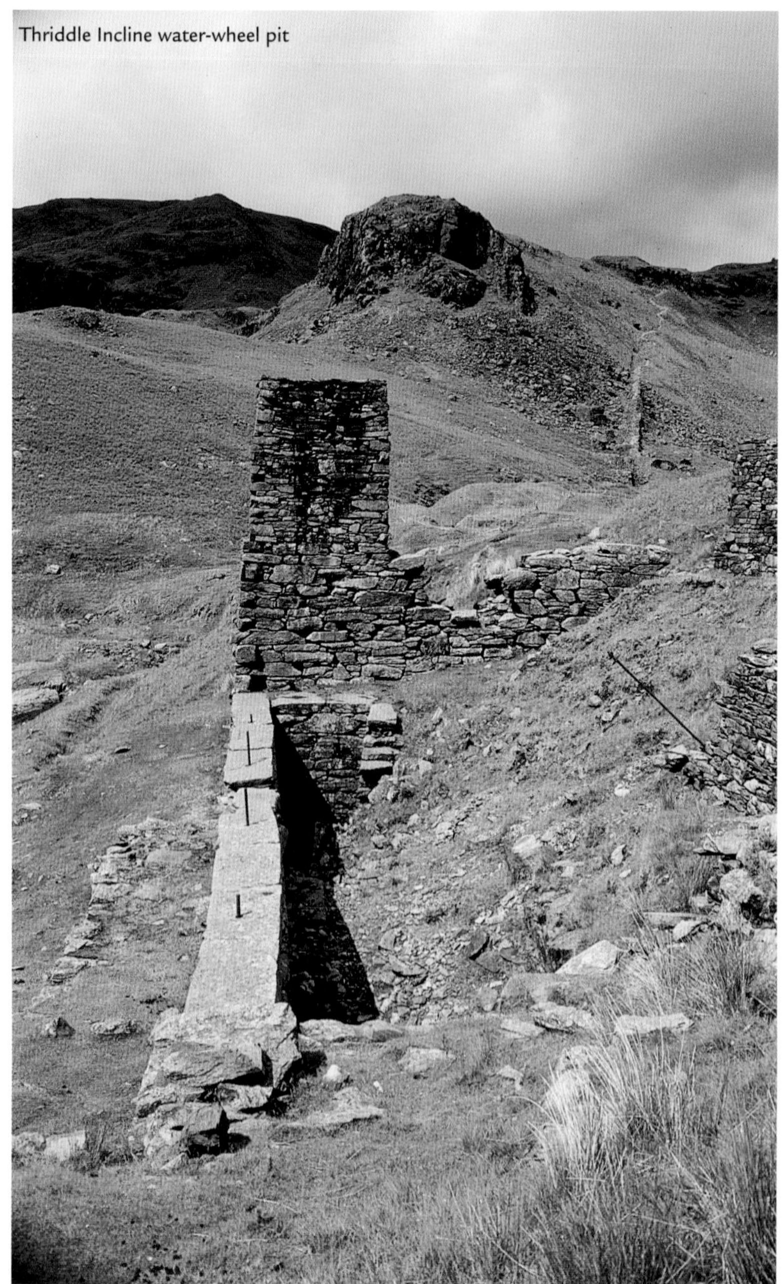

Thriddle Incline water-wheel pit

growth.) At the top the ridge constricts to give a fine view back down Red Dell. You can clamber up to the cairn on Black Sails or slant half-right to join the main ridge path, from Swirl Hawse, to reach the summit.

Via Swirl Hawse 660m/2165ft 7km/4¼ miles

7 The steady route up Wetherlam, suitable when poor conditions require a less exposed line or for easy descent, continues up the Swirl Hawse Beck valley from the outflow of Levers Water. (See SWIRL HOW Route 1 (page 196) for the route up to Levers Water.) Marshy ground is the only hazard to the saddle's cairn. At the saddle, a path goes on into the Greenburn Beck valley ahead, a minor trod by comparison with the worn trail at your feet. Go right (east) traversing the north slope of Black Sails to reach the summit and consistently enjoying the fabulous views to the north.

To Tilberthwaite Gill via the Yewdale Fells 255m/835ft 2.5km/1½ miles

Two paths from Coniston make good approaches to Tilberthwaite Ghyll, extending the exploration of Wetherlam's eastern foothills. **8** At the northern end of the village, on a loop off the A593, is Holly How Youth Hostel. Pass by the hostel and turn up a path to the left beside Far End Cottages to join a lateral path from the Coppermines valley access track as it becomes a rough track. Go through the hand-gate to follow a path climbing directly opposite. The climb, identified by small cairns, is unexpectedly steep and interesting and has a marvellous outlook. Cross the

Far End, Coniston

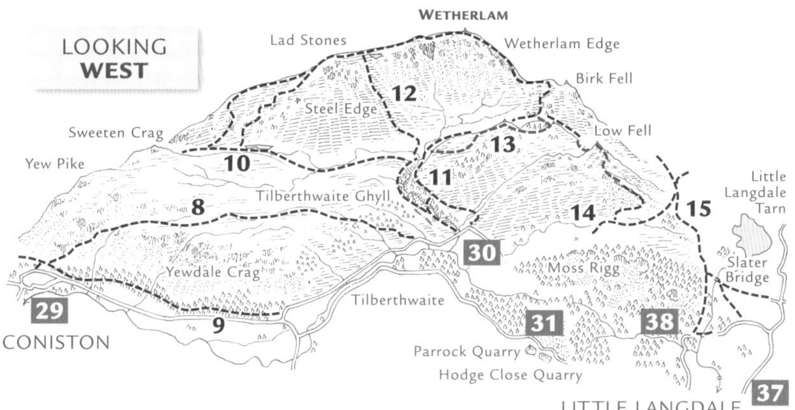

headstream of White Gill (a striking water-slide feature from Yewdale), perhaps detouring briefly to visit the Yewdale Crag headland, before weaving down through juniper and Penny Rigg slate quarry/mine to the Tilberthwaite road. **9** Alternatively, a gentle path threads through the woodland at the foot of the Yewdale Crag scarp. Fording White Gill you may notice on your right, at the edge of the pasture close to the road, a 19th-century lime kiln, which exploited the narrow band of mountain limestone here for quick-lime. In season, the continuing path is renowned for its deep-pile carpet of bluebells.

ASCENT FROM LOW TILBERTHWAITE (30) AND LITTLE LANGDALE (37)

Ask any fellwalker how many ways there are to the top of Wetherlam, and you may get the answer of no more than four. But once you start looking an array of options emerge, particularly from the east and north.

Via Steel Edge and Birk Fell Hawse 640m/2100ft 3.5km/2¼ miles

Paths ascend either side of Tilberthwaite Ghyll, and connect to one another halfway up via a scenic footbridge. **10** The path on the south side of the ghyll leads up through minor slate sites worthy of brief inspection and on along Hole Rake to connect with Route 4. **11** The path to the north starts from High Tilberthwaite itself and curves slowly round towards the ghyll, meeting it above the footbridge at an area of very old coppermines at the head of the ravine. The main route to Birk Fell and Wetherlam Edge goes north, leading round the two shallow combes of Dry Cove with further evidence of old coppermines. On a newly pitched path, step

Low Tilberthwaite

Wetherlam Edge from Hawk Rigg

onto Birk Fell and find a cairn with a lovely view off to the right. From Birk Fell Hawse the high prow of Wetherlam Edge looms. The climb includes several rocky steps, but nothing extraordinary. The erosion suggests that the pitching repair work needs to continue, however. **12** Alternatively, at the head of the ravine, cross the footbridge and turn right, then left, onto the base of the Steel Edge ridge. Starting as a grassy rigg it narrows impressively to culminate in a spot of hands-on scrambling of the easiest kind, up to the Lad Stones ridge-top, near a perfect horseshoe-shaped pool. A word of warning: if you choose to descend by this ridge, do not be lured into the gully on the north side. This looks to be the way but most definitely is not. Its loose angular scree is horrid. **13** As a variation on Route 11, from the point that the main path on the north side of the ghyll turns north, you can step onto the low ridge on the right, without a path, and hold to the skyline via the little cairned knoll-tops of Blake Rigg and Hawk Rigg, then easily turn right (north) back onto the main route.

Via Low Fell 720m/2360ft 5km/3 miles

14 From High Tilberthwaite two tracks proceed north. Take the left-hand option. Copper and slate were once ferried along here by pack mules from Little Langdale. The track begins to descend an old quarry track and forks left. Follow this up to the ridge-end slate tip through a gate. Climb to the mid-point of Runestone Quarry (the name means naturally inscribed slate with a runic look). Branch right and climb pathless to the summit of Low Fell, which has a wonderful carpet of bilberries and an excellent view of Little Langdale, through the Blea Tarn gap to the Langdale Pikes. It's a hilltop to spend idle time on. A spidery path leads west from the summit descending Great

The Langdale Pikes from Low Fell

Intake to a ladder-stile. Find a path linking over a small saddle, north of Hawk Rigg, back down south-west to the popular path. Go right to climb onto Birk Fell (Route 11).

Via Greenburn Mine 660m/2170ft 5.2km/3¼ miles

15 Wetherlam dominates Little Langdale and the climb is irresistible. From the Three Shires Inn make for Slater Bridge. Among the trees above you at this point is Cathedral, or Little Langdale, Quarry, which is well-worth investigating, but be careful and heed the signs if you go in via the tunnel. Pass along the narrow lane by Low and High Hallgarths. Shortly after the old road from Tilberthwaite comes in, the track forks.

Greenburn coppermine

Take the left fork, which rises with a wall to the right. Pause and take a good look north over Bridge End to the Langdale Pikes. As the wall drifts away a narrow path can be followed left up the bracken slope of Great Intake to a ladder-stile bound for the saddle next to Hawk Rigg, or you can turn left after the gate in the next wall to follow the wall up to the saddle.

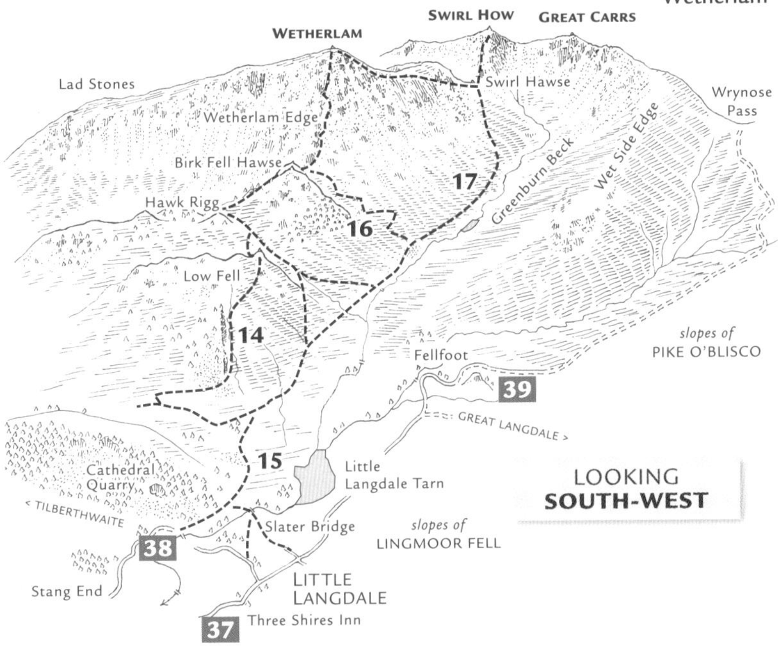

SWIRL HOW
GREAT CARRS
WETHERLAM
Lad Stones
Swirl Hawse
Wrynose Pass
Wetherlam Edge
Wet Side Edge
Greenburn Beck
Birk Fell Hawse
17
Hawk Rigg
16
Low Fell
14
slopes of PIKE O'BLISCO
Fellfoot
39
GREAT LANGDALE >
15
Cathedral Quarry
Little Langdale Tarn
LOOKING SOUTH-WEST
< TILBERTHWAITE
Slater Bridge
slopes of LINGMOOR FELL
38
Stang End
LITTLE LANGDALE
37
Three Shires Inn

Old coppermine path climbing to the old workings below Birkfell Hause

16 However, the best option is to stay with the valley track alongside Greenburn Beck rising to the old Greenburn Coppermine (see photograph). It's a protected monument, so inspect it respectfully. Dependent on the mountain's mood, Wetherlam looms either impressively or dauntingly above this scene of past industry. Many walkers blithely stride on up the valley giving only the briefest thought to the old workings but it is worth making a more thorough inspection and seeking out the associated remains higher up. (The mining and quarrying history of the fell warrants an exclusive walking guide for the inquisitive surface explorer. Practical itineraries by local mine expert Eric G Holland can be found in his *Coniston Copper Mines: A field guide* published by Cicerone Press.)

Once past the ruins, angle half-left, finding a gap in the bracken to find an engineered miners' path slanting left up the steep fellside. An early cairn indicates a branch path leading half-right up to the Long Crag Level. The main grass path climbs to Pave York Levels. There are three mine adits here (entrances), one above the other. Traces of the rail incline remain by which the ore was conveyed to the crushing mill and dressing floor below (the bottom of this incline, the central feature in the picture on the previous page). Weave up the fell glancing at each dark dank level in turn, the top one probably the most intriguing. A fellwalker's path continues above, rising to Birk Fell Hawse, and then onto the popular path climbing Wetherlam Edge.

Via Swirl Hawse **660m/2165ft** **7km/4¼ miles**

17 The more usual approach to Wetherlam is to continue up the dale from Greenburn Mine and bear half-left from the reservoir dam. Go up the fellside. There is only evidence of a path once Low and High Keld Gills have been forded. Climb the dry slope beneath the scree to the Hawse.

THE SUMMIT

The highest ground is a gentle dome with small rocky protuberances, the unruly summit cairn itself taking advantage of one low plinth. The site deserves a far more elegant pile – send up the man who created the Low Tilberthwaite fold and see what he can do! Certainly it's a place to consider a wide Lakeland landscape, the deep furrow of Greenburn ensuring an uninhibited prospect. In imperial measurements, the height of the fell has a pleasing neatness – 2500ft.

Summit of Wetherlam

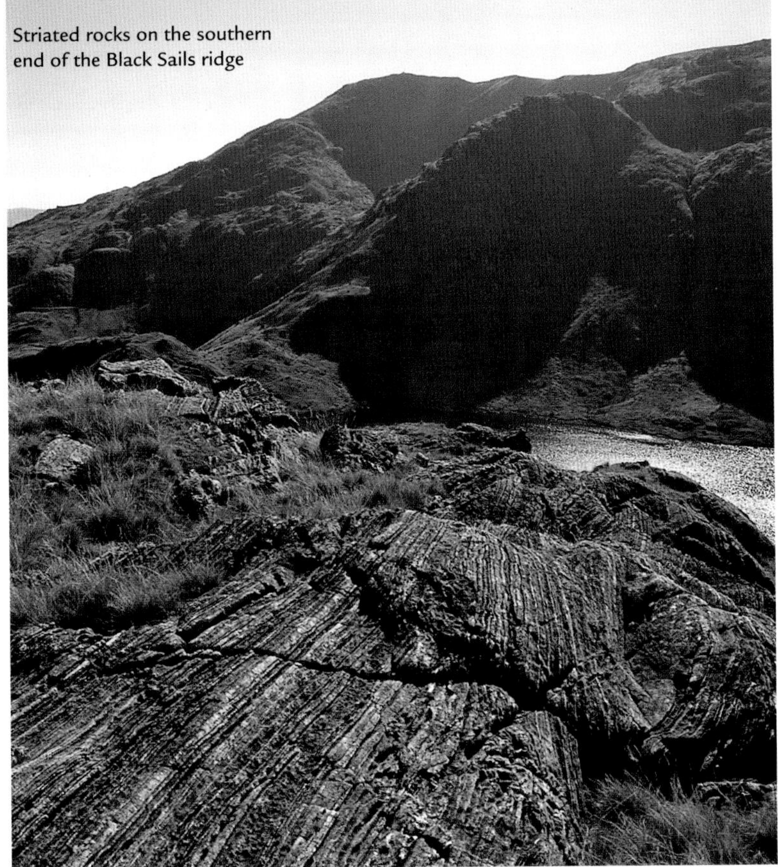
Striated rocks on the southern end of the Black Sails ridge

SAFE DESCENTS

The ground falls innocently away to the W and S but matters to the N and E need careful attention. The rocky steps of Wetherlam Edge face into a biting winter gale but are otherwise non-too-troublesome. The easier routes are S down the Lad Stones ridge or W to Swirl Hawse.

RIDGE ROUTE

SWIRL HOW ↓145m/480ft ↑190m/620ft 2km/1¼ miles

Head W down an early stony slope. Two paths converge to cross peaty ground on the shallow plateau hollow at the head of Red Dell. The clear stony path drifts across the northern flank of Black Sails before descending more steeply to Swirl Hawse (at 625m (2033ft) clearly identified by its large cairn. The Prison Band ridge looks tough but is meekly overcome via a series of mock towers. Note one particularly strikingly banded specimen a third of the way up.

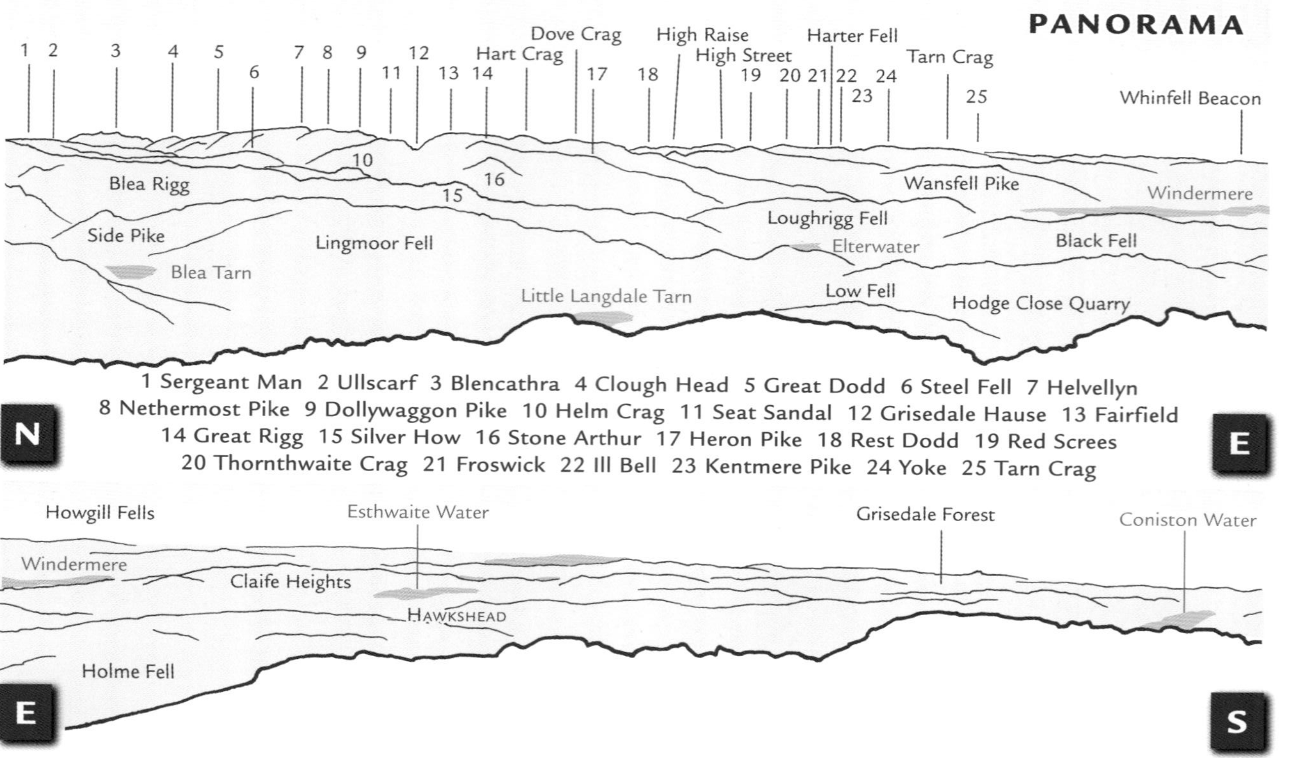
PANORAMA
1 2 3 4 5 6 7 8 9 11 12 13 14 17 18 19 20 21 22 23 24 25
Dove Crag
Hart Crag
High Raise
High Street
Harter Fell
Tarn Crag
Whinfell Beacon
10
16
15
Blea Rigg
Side Pike
Blea Tarn
Lingmoor Fell
Little Langdale Tarn
Wansfell Pike
Loughrigg Fell
Elterwater
Low Fell
Windermere
Black Fell
Hodge Close Quarry
1 Sergeant Man 2 Ullscarf 3 Blencathra 4 Clough Head 5 Great Dodd 6 Steel Fell 7 Helvellyn
8 Nethermost Pike 9 Dollywaggon Pike 10 Helm Crag 11 Seat Sandal 12 Grisedale Hause 13 Fairfield
14 Great Rigg 15 Silver How 16 Stone Arthur 17 Heron Pike 18 Rest Dodd 19 Red Screes
20 Thornthwaite Crag 21 Froswick 22 Ill Bell 23 Kentmere Pike 24 Yoke 25 Tarn Crag
N
E
Howgill Fells
Esthwaite Water
Grisedale Forest
Coniston Water
Windermere
Claife Heights
HAWKSHEAD
Holme Fell
E
S

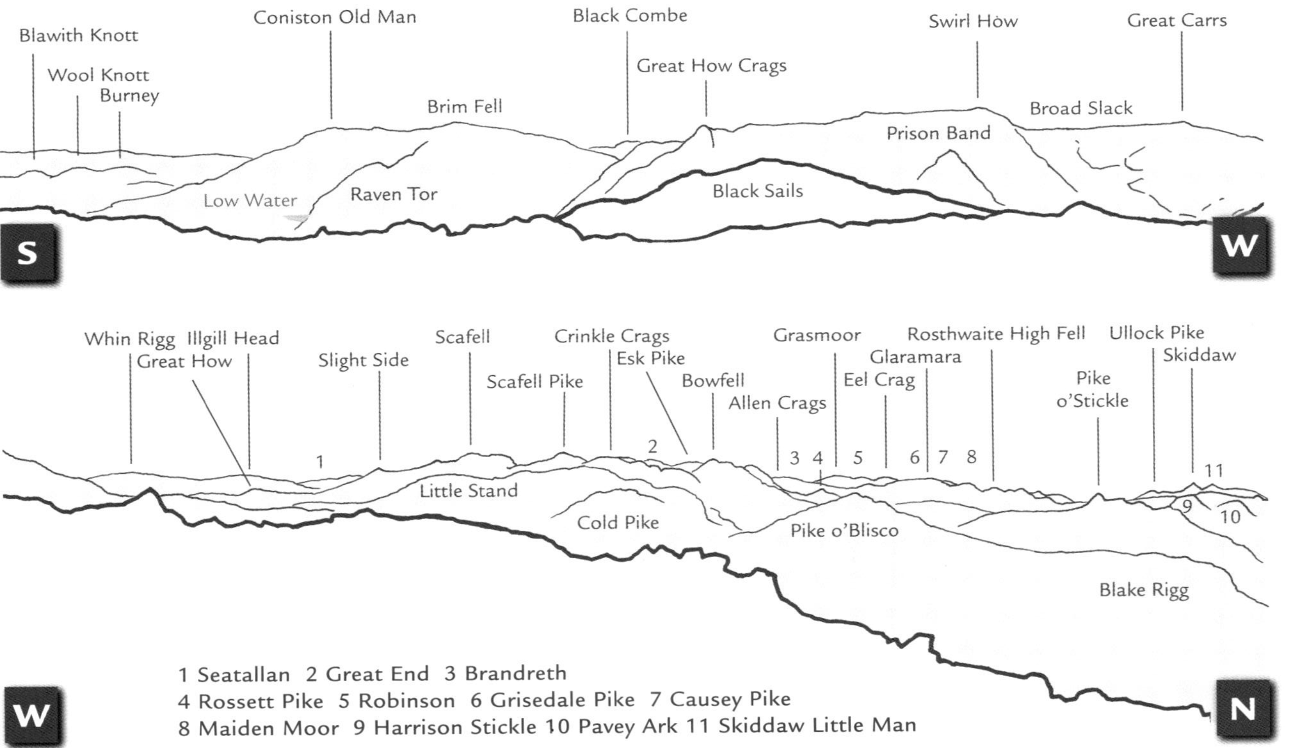
Blawith Knott
Wool Knott
Burney
Coniston Old Man
Brim Fell
Low Water
Raven Tor
Black Combe
Great How Crags
Black Sails
Swirl How
Prison Band
Broad Slack
Great Carrs
S
W
Whin Rigg
Illgill Head
Great How
Slight Side
1
Scafell
Scafell Pike
Little Stand
Crinkle Crags
Esk Pike
2
Cold Pike
Bowfell
Allen Crags
3
4
Grasmoor
5
Eel Crag
Glaramara
6
7
8
Pike o'Blisco
Rosthwaite High Fell
Pike o'Stickle
Ullock Pike
Skiddaw
11
9
10
Blake Rigg
W
N
1 Seatallan 2 Great End 3 Brandreth
4 Rossett Pike 5 Robinson 6 Grisedale Pike 7 Causey Pike
8 Maiden Moor 9 Harrison Stickle 10 Pavey Ark 11 Skiddaw Little Man

22 WHITFELL *(573m, 1880ft)*

The south-westerly rippling ridge that springs from Harter Fell and terminates on Black Combe is focused on Whitfell. A rounded, elegant sentinel, keeping guard over an ancient bridleway, it is the natural target for a fell climb or a long ridge traverse. It has the kind of summit that walkers find engaging – a stout cairn built upon an archaic gathering of stones, whose cultural significance has long been lost. The feminine grace of the main fell contrasts with the chunky mass of Burn Moor tagged on to its west – a Te Kanawa and Pavarotti double act.

Whitfell from Withe Bottom

 ↑ Whitfell from the bridleway through the cattle pasture above Bigert Mire

ASCENT FROM BRACKENTHWAITE (20)

Direct 373m/1225ft 3.7km/2½ miles

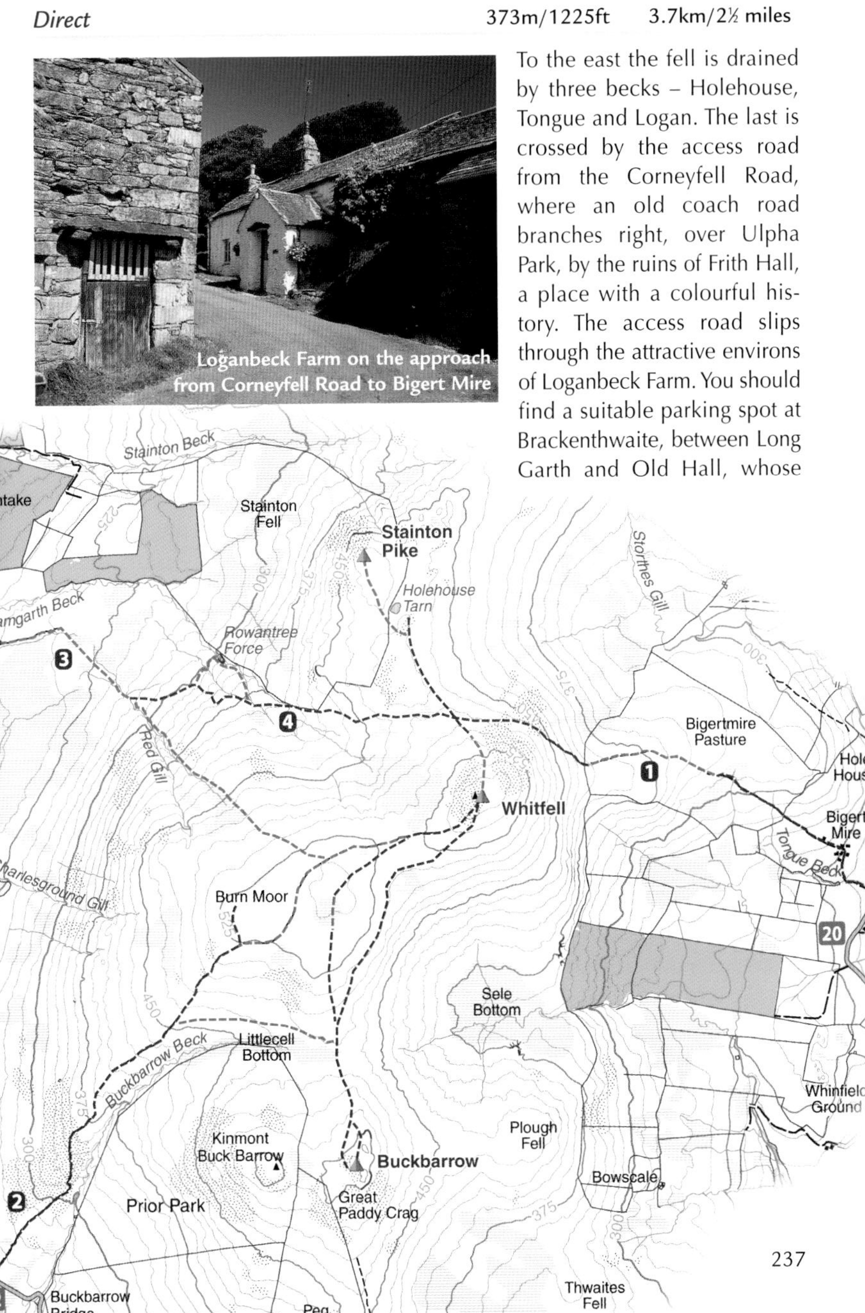

Loganbeck Farm on the approach from Corneyfell Road to Bigert Mire

To the east the fell is drained by three becks – Holehouse, Tongue and Logan. The last is crossed by the access road from the Corneyfell Road, where an old coach road branches right, over Ulpha Park, by the ruins of Frith Hall, a place with a colourful history. The access road slips through the attractive environs of Loganbeck Farm. You should find a suitable parking spot at Brackenthwaite, between Long Garth and Old Hall, whose

The Pike from Bigert Pasture

ruined peel tower serves as a grandiose sheep pen. From this Duddon side there is only one approach. **1** A bridleway traverses the ridge from Bigert Mire, a very tidy community with six cottages huddling together where once just one farm stood. There is space for one parked car at a pinch. Walk through to the gate, and bear up left on the bridle track, passing a lone standing barn. The track enters Bigertmire Pasture at a gate and begins purposefully enough – well used by a tractor carrying feed to livestock – but the line of the path fades as it rises up the great pasture. Stride up to a kissing-gate in the fence, which seems to be strengthening the broken intake wall, and the path reappears on the other side. Rise to the cairn at the top of the pass, bear left, now with the ridge path, to the summit tumulus.

ASCENT FROM CORNEYFELL ROAD (11 & 12)

Via Fell Lane or Burn Moor 353m/1160ft 4.5km/2¾ miles

2 From the Corneyfell Road at GR132904 a bridle track climbs to the cairn on Hare Raise then apparently stops. It was an old peat-cutters' track. However, the table-top summit has no impediment to a simple traverse other than tough grass and you can visit the prominent cairn en route. **3** The Fell Lane approach (see STAINTON PIKE Route 1 (page 179)) is the western limb of the bridleway from Bigert Mire. Follow this up Whitrow Beck as far as the gullied foot of Red Gill. From this point you can bear right to follow the left-hand edge of this deeply gullied forked gill onto Burn Moor. Sheep trods give some assistance to the saddle, where you pass a small exposure of peat, the proverbial Peakland 'grough', and climb onto easier ground leading to the summit. **4** Alternatively, the bridleway, an engineered green-way, climbs the steeper ground eastward, and allows a quick detour left to visit Rowantree Force. The path is lost as the ground levels in the broad basin of Withe Bottom but restored as you rise to the small cairn at the highest point of the pass. Join the ridge path and climb right (south) to the summit.

THE SUMMIT

Rising to a gentle dome, the fell culminates in an ancient cairn. This is a low, round pile of rocks some 18 strides wide upon which has been built a rustic, yet quite noble, cairn. Inevitably visitors have further adapted the handy stones to fashion a wind shelter, tucked in on the leeward side. Sandwiches consumed, gaze east and south into the Duddon and its spreading estuary. An old Ordnance Survey pillar (see photograph) stands forlornly on a flat patch of ground to the north-east.

RIDGE ROUTE

BUCKBARROW ↓95m/310ft ↑70m/230ft 2.4km/1½ miles

A path descends SW, traversing the E slopes of Burn Moor. Cross the marshy edge of Littlecell Bottom S, onto the emerging rocky edge.

STAINTON PIKE ↓75m/250ft ↑6m/20ft 1.6km/1 mile

Descend N. A path materialises as you cross the old bridleway (now NW) onto the low ridge. Branch half-left to cross the plain fence before Holehouse Tarn. A narrow trod leads to the summit knoll.

Whitfell summit, a large cairn resting on a massive tumulus

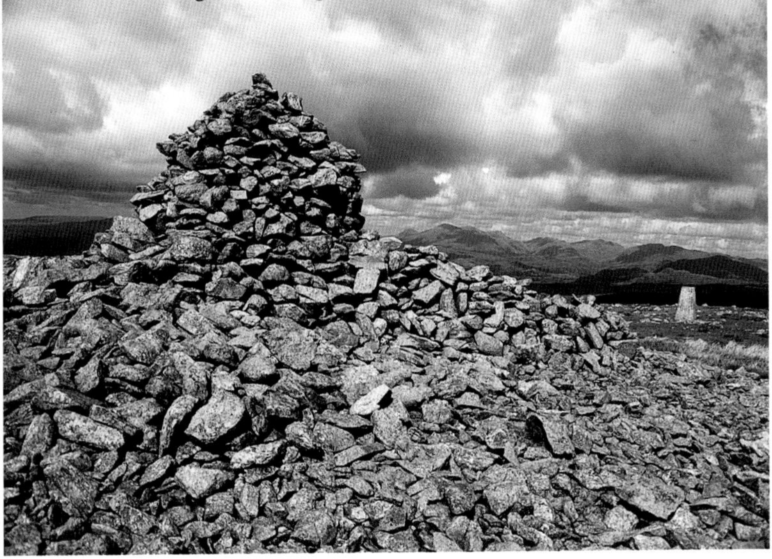

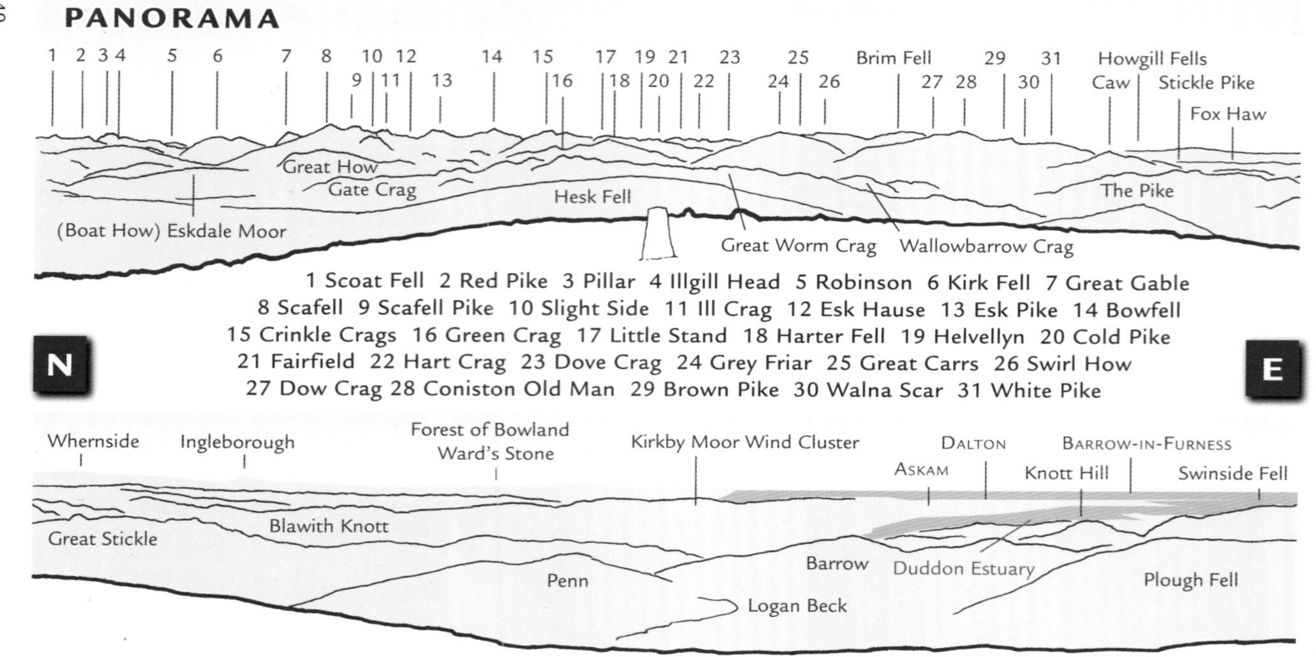

At your feet is an accumulation of stones, the remains of an ancient cairn, possibly an elevated Bronze Age burial site.

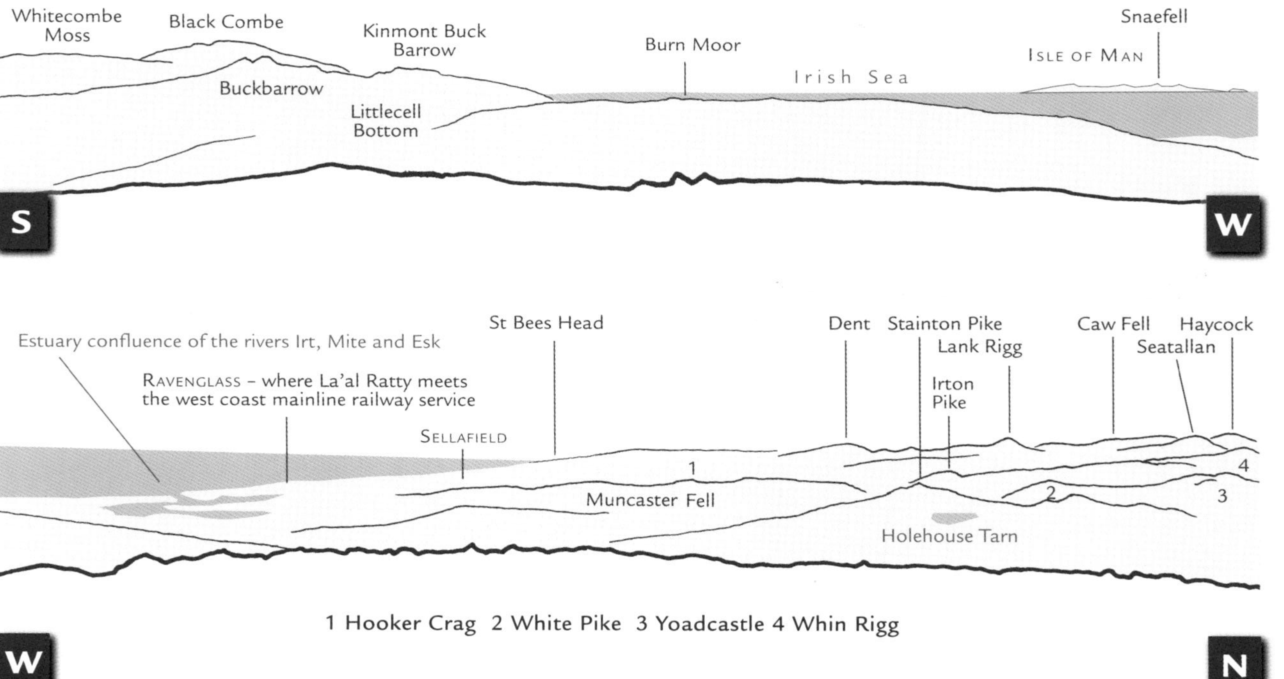

1 Hooker Crag 2 White Pike 3 Yoadcastle 4 Whin Rigg

23 YOADCASTLE *(494m, 1621ft)*

Motorists with an eye for a scenic drive scan their atlases and quickly home in on the Birkerfell Road, delighting in the moorland traverse between Eskdale Green and Ulpha with the thrilling backdrop of the Scafells in grand perspective. On a good day it can be hard to keep driving, frequent laybys tempting you to pull in and gaze with admiration at the Lakeland alps. Those that park up and wander to the lonely shores of Devoke Water find serenity and solace in the timeless wilderness setting. Devoke Water reflects a blue sky as well as any Lakeland tarn, being open if not bare. But most folk will tell you that it is a black lake. (The tarn-name means 'the little black one', from the effect the peaty waters have on its native stock of brown trout which remain small and very dark.) The discerning wanderer, with the boots and the will, takes to the fellsides and reaps rich rewards from the discovery of the numerous cairned tops surrounding the lake: Seat How, Rough Crag, Water Crag, Brantrake Crag, Garner Bank, White Pike and the cairnless Rowantree How, visited on the climb to Woodend Height and scenically the best of the bunch. Nonetheless, although set back and hidden from the immediate arena, Yoadcastle – aloof and inviting – must be considered the ultimate goal of the well-rounded expedition.

↑ Yoadcastle from the Stainton Pike ridge path

ASCENT FROM DYKE AND BROAD OAK (10)

Via Barnscar 472m/1550ft 7.2km/4½ miles

1 A small section of old road may be used for parking at the entrance to Dyke Farm. (The squat, pepperpot tower on the hilltop above the farm, associated with Nether Stainton, was erected as a summer house and there is no public access.) Follow the farm track through the farm buildings. Rising beyond, watch for a gate on the left. The bridleway emerges from the more obvious farm lane. Keep within the walled lane, admiring the pink stonework. (Note two combination sheep creeps and shepherd's

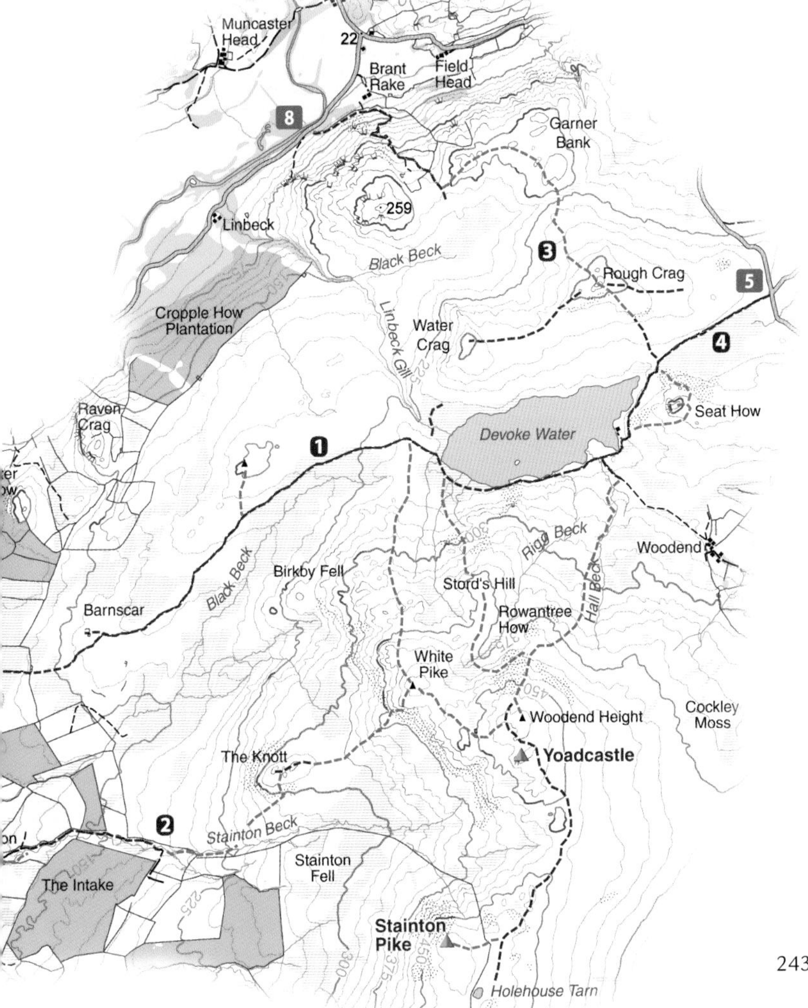

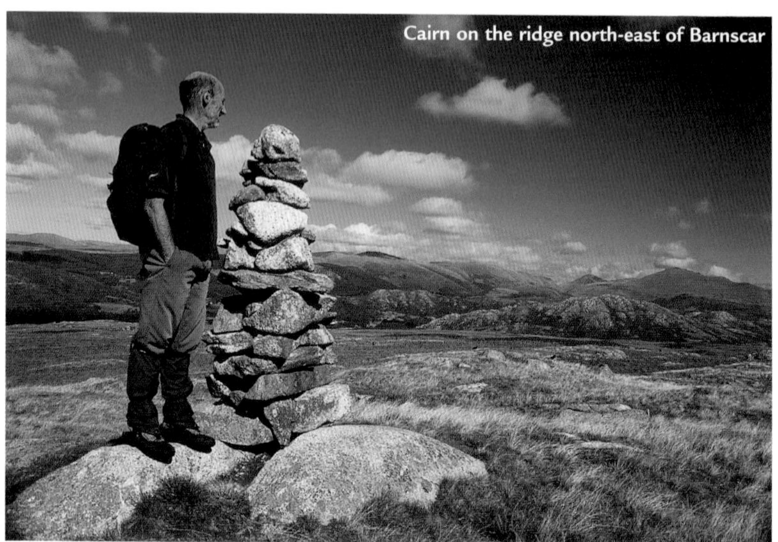
Cairn on the ridge north-east of Barnscar

wall-stiles.) A further gate spells a change but not for the better! The next enclosure is traversed by both a bridleway and a footpath. The ground is so rough and wet that horseriders have been re-directed onto the footpath, making the walkers' lot nigh on impossible. Cling on to the wall and hop from tuft to tuft. The fun and games only partially dies down as the path turns right, away from the wall, with the dampest bit paved. But thankfully matters finally improve after the next gate!

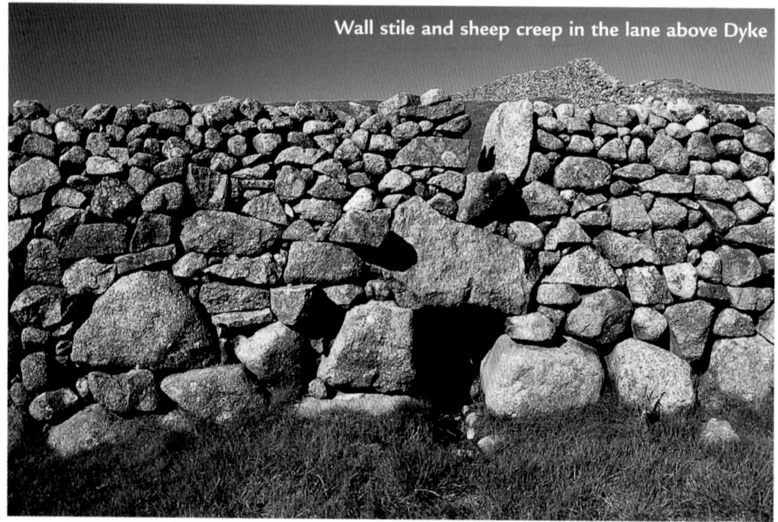
Wall stile and sheep creep in the lane above Dyke

Devoke Water backed by Harter Fell and Seat How

A clear green way rises easily by the obscure remains of the Bronze Age native settlement of Barnscar, traces of field walls and huts lying beneath a dense cover of bracken. The cairned path leads on, with a low ridge on the left, crowned by a cairn – a tempting distraction. A sequence of paired stone markers guide the old path, over wet ground, towards the western end of Devoke Water, overlooked by two Bronze Age cairns, and the path continues just above the southern shore.

Taking the line that most appeals bear off right onto either White Pike or Stord's Hill. If you choose Stord's Hill, make sure to climb onto the subsidiary top of Rowantree How on your way to the great cairn on Woodend Height. **2** White Pike may also accessed from Broad Oak (see STAINTON PIKE Route 2 (page 180)). Leave the Stainton Pike route to climb up onto The Knott and then, more steeply, to the handsome cairn (see photograph page 247). There is not the slightest hint of a path. It's up to you.

ASCENT FROM BRANTRAKE (8)

Via Rough Crag and Seat How 560m/1840ft 6km/3¾ miles

3 A small parking area beside the River Esk is a handy springboard. From the hand-gate almost opposite, keep beside the wall under the mightily rough fellside of Brantrake Crags. Coming above the old farm, begin a series of hairpins, the original 'brant rake' or steep steps climbing to a saddle where the old peat track dissolves into the combe of Brantrake Moss. Ford the gill, left, and follow on over the cairned top to the east, traipsing round to a large boiler-plate slab composed of a pale rock typical hereabouts. Head south slipping through a narrow defile at the head of Hare Gill. Pass a pair of spruces heading up to the cairn on Rough Crag – a fine viewpoint.

Visitors often walk round Devoke Water taking in the neighbouring cairned top of Water Crag to the west, although Linbeck Gill can be deep and troublesome to ford. From Rough Crag descend south-east to the boathouse approach track.

ASCENT FROM BIRKERFELL ROAD (5)

Via Devoke Water 256m/840ft 3.7km/2¼ miles

4 By parking at the minor junction, on the Birkerfell Road at GR171977, you can join the track leading south-west to the tarn, thus avoiding the Brantrake section of the ascent (Route 3). As a novel addition, you could include Seat How. Access to the top is only possible from the east. This rocky knot, commanding a view down the lake, has old enclosure walling on this side too. The track terminates at the ruined Victorian lakeside boathouse. A path continues round the southern shore, contending with wet ground. The third beck flowing into the tarn, Rigg Beck, is the clue to the ascent. Climb south over Rowantree How onto Woodend Height. There are no paths to begin with, symptomatic of all Yoadcastle approaches, but once the high ground is made there they are, naturally!

THE SUMMIT

On the ground the summit is obvious, although maps tend to be a little vague and the whole mass of adjacent ground carries no distinguishing name. The abrupt summit outcrop is easily mounted to get to a small top with only the tiniest of cairns. All

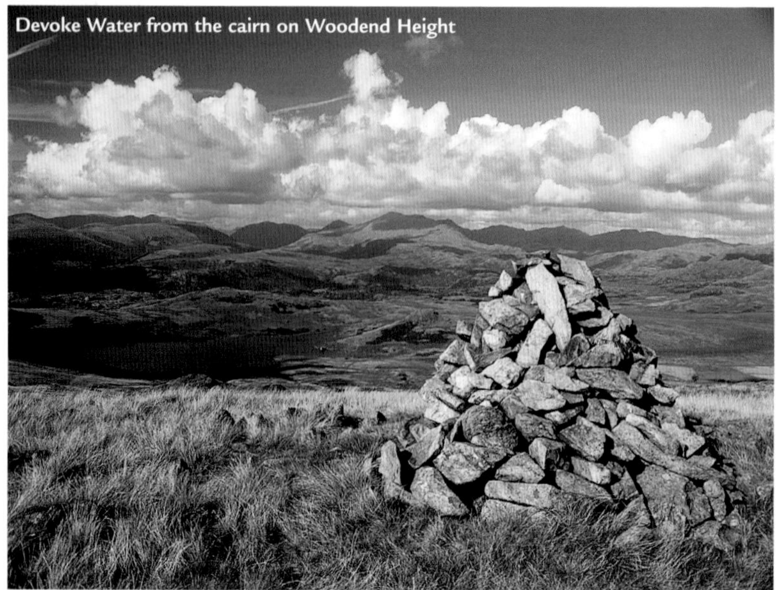

Devoke Water from the cairn on Woodend Height

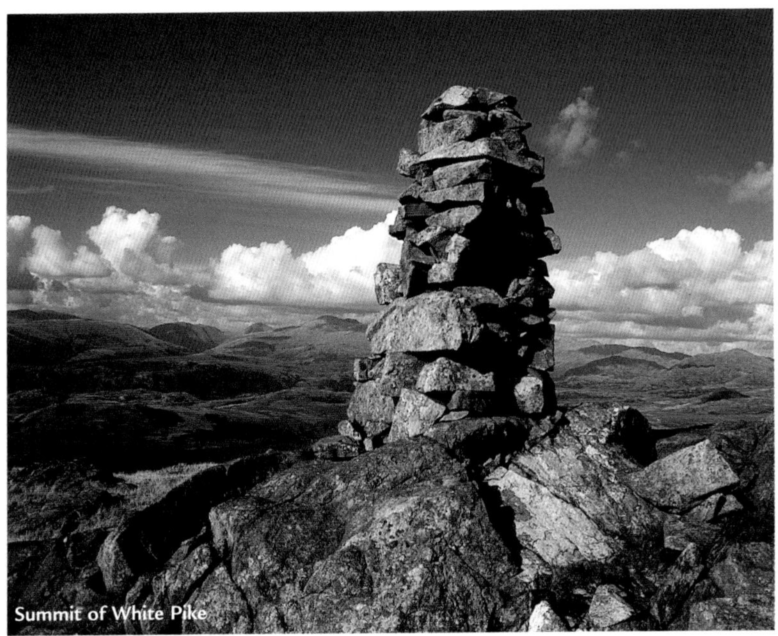
Summit of White Pike

cairn-building effort has apparently been exhausted in creating Woodend Height's sturdy cairn, which is the obvious second port of call, followed by White Pike.

SAFE DESCENTS

Be wary of the outcrops that form a battlement to White Pike. Otherwise all crags are minor and, while there are no paths off the fell, the gills are universally open-coursed and easy to follow.

RIDGE ROUTE

STAINTON PIKE ↓60m/190ft ↑65m/220ft 2km/1¼ miles

A path little better then a sheep track leads on a gentle curving line S. Crossing a broad saddle it mounts a shallow bank from where you need to branch right by a cairn and cross the plain fence to reach the solitary summit cairn, set a little further west than Yoadcastle.

HESK FELL ↓120m/390ft ↑100m/330ft 2.5km/1½ miles

Walk E without the benefit of a tangible path into the broad and exceedingly damp depression at the head of the great bowl of Storthes Gill. Gaining firmer ground, begin the ascent of Hesk Fell, drifting SE onto the featureless top to locate the small heap of stones marking the summit.

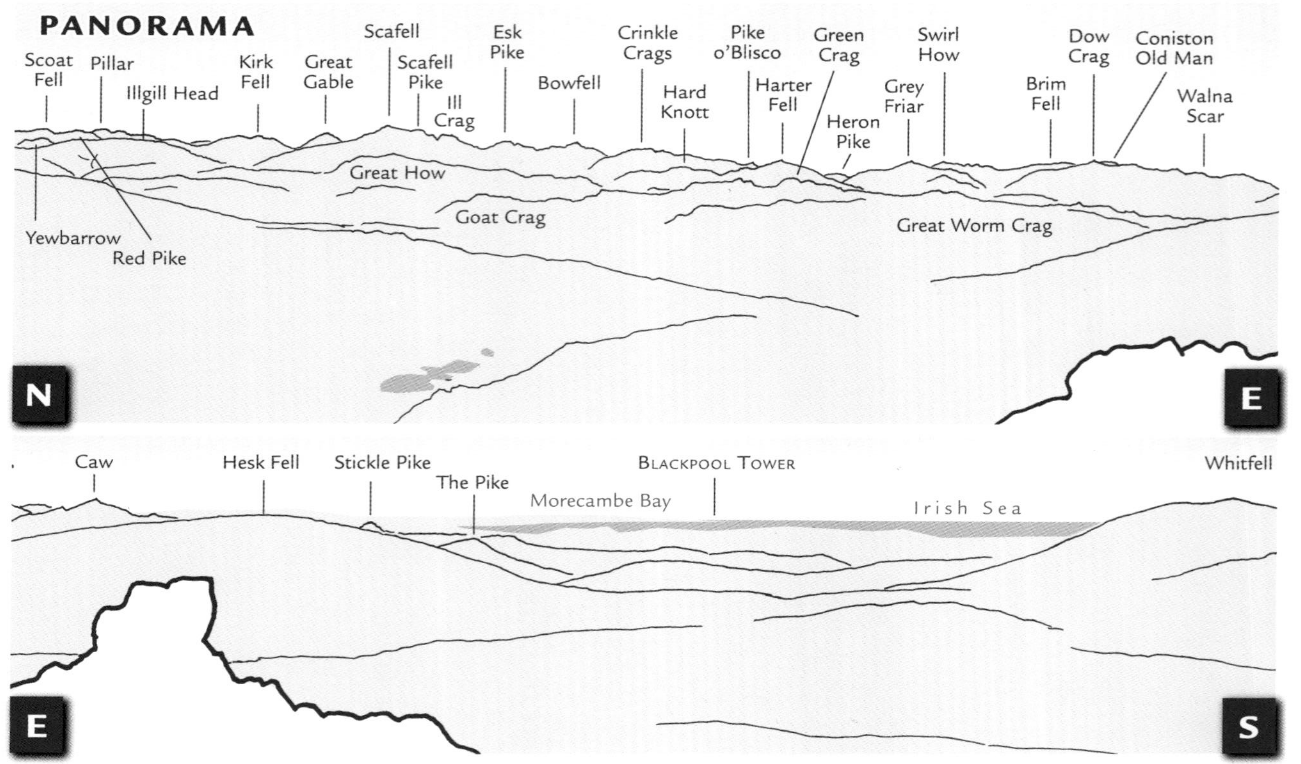
PANORAMA
Scoat Fell
Pillar
Illgill Head
Kirk Fell
Great Gable
Scafell
Scafell Pike
Ill Crag
Esk Pike
Bowfell
Crinkle Crags
Hard Knott
Pike o'Blisco
Harter Fell
Green Crag
Heron Pike
Grey Friar
Swirl How
Brim Fell
Dow Crag
Coniston Old Man
Walna Scar
Great How
Goat Crag
Great Worm Crag
Yewbarrow
Red Pike
N
E
Caw
Hesk Fell
Stickle Pike
The Pike
Morecambe Bay
Blackpool Tower
Irish Sea
Whitfell
E
S

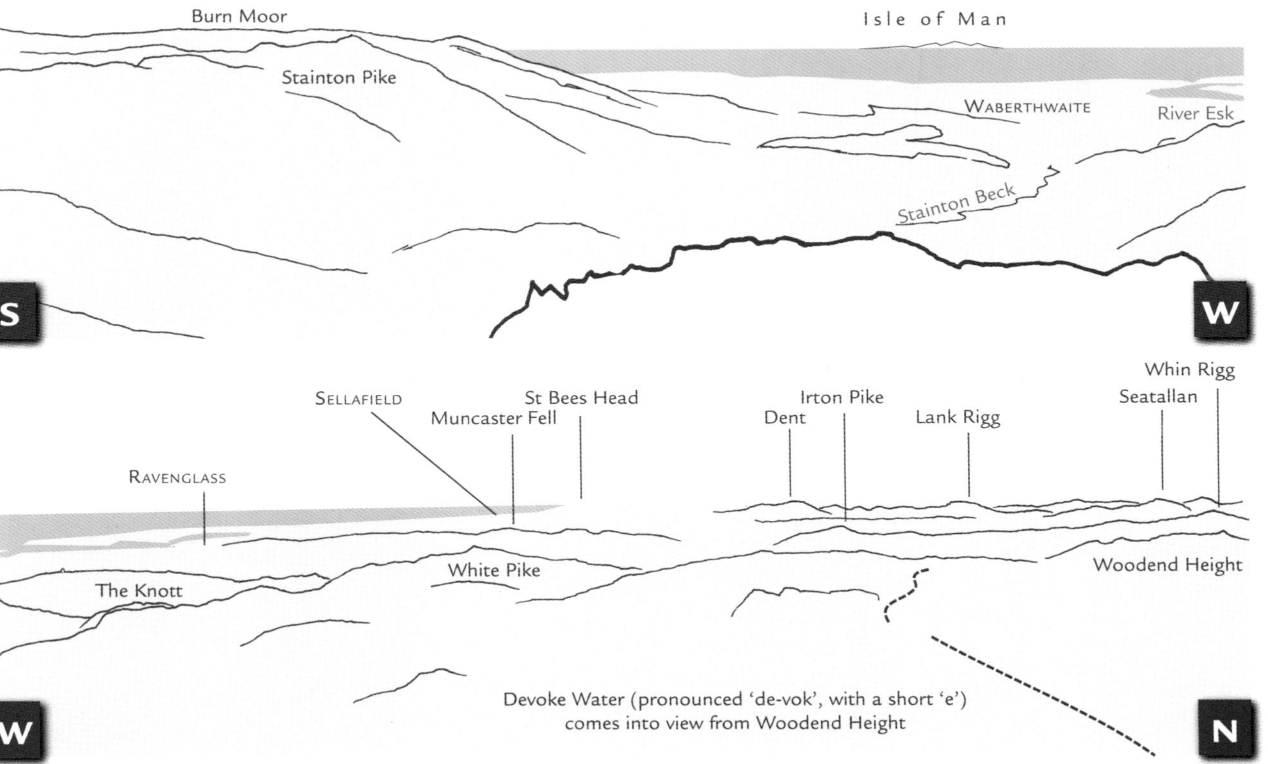
Burn Moor
Isle of Man
Stainton Pike
Waberthwaite
River Esk
Stainton Beck
S
W
Whin Rigg
Sellafield
St Bees Head
Irton Pike
Seatallan
Muncaster Fell
Dent
Lank Rigg
Ravenglass
Woodend Height
White Pike
The Knott
Devoke Water (pronounced 'de-vok', with a short 'e')
comes into view from Woodend Height
W
N

Helicopter delivering path-building rock on the steep slopes of Dollywaggon Pike

FIXING THE FELLS FOR THE FUTURE

In preparing this guide I am ever more keenly aware of the work being done to secure the fell paths, making the whole fell environment visually a better place. The National Park Authority in conjunction with the National Trust are playing crucial roles within the structure of the Fix the Fells Project (visit: www.fixthefells.co.uk).

A huge amount of work has been devoted to stabilising paths, including intelligent pre-emptive work. Capital projects, too, have seen mechanical diggers carried high onto the fells at key points to heal sorely worn paths. Huge quantities of path-pitching stone is carried most economically by helicopter. Sadly worn paths of Wainwright's day have been given a new lease of life. While some walkers may gripe that the hard pitching is tough on the ankles and knees, at least it's not so tough on the mountains themselves – which has to be good.

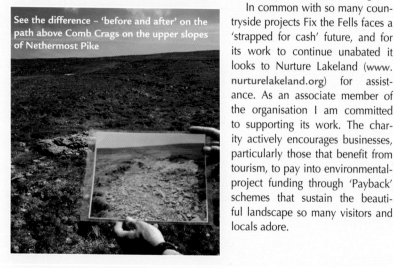

See the difference – 'before and after' on the path above Comb Crags on the upper slopes of Nethermost Pike

In common with so many countryside projects Fix the Fells faces a 'strapped for cash' future, and for its work to continue unabated it looks to Nurture Lakeland (www.nurturelakeland.org) for assistance. As an associate member of the organisation I am committed to supporting its work. The charity actively encourages businesses, particularly those that benefit from tourism, to pay into environmental-project funding through 'Payback' schemes that sustain the beautiful landscape so many visitors and locals adore.

INDEX

Bold indicates Fell Chapters

Southern Fells

LISTING OF CICERONE GUIDES

BRITISH ISLES CHALLENGES, COLLECTIONS AND ACTIVITIES

The End to End Trail
The Mountains of England and Wales: 1&2
The National Trails
The Relative Hills of Britain
The Ridges of England, Wales and Ireland
The UK Trailwalker's Handbook
The UK's County Tops
Three Peaks, Ten Tors

UK CYCLING

Border Country Cycle Routes
Cycling in the Cotswolds
Cycling in the Hebrides
Cycling in the Peak District
Cycling in the Yorkshire Dales
Cycling the Pennine Bridleway
Mountain Biking in the Lake District
Mountain Biking in the Yorkshire Dales
Mountain Biking on the North Downs
Mountain Biking on the South Downs
The C2C Cycle Route
The End to End Cycle Route
The Lancashire Cycleway

SCOTLAND

Backpacker's Britain
  Central and Southern
    Scottish Highlands
  Northern Scotland
Ben Nevis and Glen Coe
Great Mountain Days in Scotland
Not the West Highland Way
Scotland's Best Small Mountains
Scotland's Far West
Scotland's Mountain Ridges
Scrambles in Lochaber
The Ayrshire and Arran Coastal Paths
The Border Country
The Cape Wrath Trail
The Great Glen Way
The Isle of Mull
The Isle of Skye
The Pentland Hills
The Scottish Glens 2 – The Atholl Glens
The Southern Upland Way
The Speyside Way
The West Highland Way
Walking Highland Perthshire
Walking in Scotland's Far North
Walking in the Angus Glens
Walking in the Cairngorms
Walking in the Ochils, Campsie Fells and Lomond Hills
Walking in Torridon
Walking Loch Lomond and the Trossachs
Walking on Harris and Lewis
Walking on Jura, Islay and Colonsay
Walking on Rum and the Small Isles
Walking on the Isle of Arran
Walking on the Orkney and Shetland Isles
Walking on Uist and Barra
Walking the Corbetts
  1 South of the Great Glen
  2 North of the Great Glen
Walking the Galloway Hills
Walking the Lowther Hills
Walking the Munros
  1 Southern, Central and Western Highlands
  2 Northern Highlands and the Cairngorms
Winter Climbs Ben Nevis and Glen Coe
Winter Climbs in the Cairngorms
World Mountain Ranges: Scotland

NORTHERN ENGLAND TRAILS

A Northern Coast to Coast Walk
Backpacker's Britain
  Northern England
Hadrian's Wall Path
The Dales Way
The Pennine Way

NORTH EAST ENGLAND, YORKSHIRE DALES AND PENNINES

Great Mountain Days in the Pennines
Historic Walks in North Yorkshire
South Pennine Walks
St Oswald's Way and St Cuthbert's Way
The Cleveland Way and the Yorkshire Wolds Way
The North York Moors
The Reivers Way
The Teesdale Way
The Yorkshire Dales
  North and East
  South and West
Walking in County Durham
Walking in Northumberland
Walking in the North Pennines
Walks in Dales Country
Walks in the Yorkshire Dales
Walks on the North York Moors – Books 1 & 2

NORTH WEST ENGLAND AND THE ISLE OF MAN

Historic Walks in Cheshire
Isle of Man Coastal Path
The Isle of Man
The Lune Valley and Howgills
The Ribble Way
Walking in Cumbria's Eden Valley
Walking in Lancashire
Walking in the Forest of Bowland and Pendle
Walking on the West Pennine Moors
Walks in Lancashire Witch Country
Walks in Ribble Country
Walks in Silverdale and Arnside
Walks in the Forest of Bowland

LAKE DISTRICT

Coniston Copper Mines
Great Mountain Days in the Lake District
Lake District Winter Climbs
Lakeland Fellranger
  The Central Fells
  The Far-Eastern Fells
  The Mid-Western Fells
  The Near Eastern Fells
  The Northern Fells
  The North-Western Fells

The Southern Fells
The Western Fells
Roads and Tracks of the Lake District
Rocky Rambler's Wild Walks
Scrambles in the Lake District North & South
Short Walks in Lakeland
1 South Lakeland
2 North Lakeland
3 West Lakeland
The Cumbria Coastal Way
The Cumbria Way and the Allerdale Ramble
Tour of the Lake District

DERBYSHIRE, PEAK DISTRICT AND MIDLANDS

High Peak Walks
Scrambles in the Dark Peak
The Star Family Walks
Walking in Derbyshire
White Peak Walks
The Northern Dales
The Southern Dales

SOUTHERN ENGLAND

Suffolk Coast & Heaths Walks
The Cotswold Way
The North Downs Way
The Peddars Way and Norfolk Coast Path
The Ridgeway National Trail
The South Downs Way
The South West Coast Path
The Thames Path
Walking in Berkshire
Walking in Essex
Walking in Kent
Walking in Norfolk
Walking in Sussex
Walking in the Cotswolds
Walking in the Isles of Scilly
Walking in the New Forest
Walking in the Thames Valley
Walking on Dartmoor
Walking on Guernsey
Walking on Jersey
Walking on the Isle of Wight
Walks in the South Downs National Park

WALES AND WELSH BORDERS

Backpacker's Britain – Wales
Glyndwr's Way
Great Mountain Days in Snowdonia
Hillwalking in Snowdonia
Hillwalking in Wales: 1&2
Offa's Dyke Path
Ridges of Snowdonia
Scrambles in Snowdonia
The Ascent of Snowdon
The Ceredigion and Snowdonia Coast Paths
Lleyn Peninsula Coastal Path
Pembrokeshire Coastal Path
The Severn Way
The Shropshire Hills
The Wye Valley Walk
Walking in Pembrokeshire
Walking in the Forest of Dean
Walking in the South Wales Valleys
Walking on Gower
Walking on the Brecon Beacons
Welsh Winter Climbs

INTERNATIONAL CHALLENGES, COLLECTIONS AND ACTIVITIES

Canyoning
Europe's High Points
The Via Francigena (Canterbury to Rome): 1&2

EUROPEAN CYCLING

Cycle Touring in France
Cycle Touring in Ireland
Cycle Touring in Spain
Cycle Touring in Switzerland
Cycling in the French Alps
Cycling the Canal du Midi
Cycling the River Loire
The Danube Cycleway
The Grand Traverse of the Massif Central
The Rhine Cycle Route
The Way of St James

AFRICA

Climbing in the Moroccan Anti-Atlas
Kilimanjaro
Mountaineering in the Moroccan High Atlas
The High Atlas
Trekking in the Atlas Mountains
Walking in the Drakensberg

ALPS – CROSS-BORDER ROUTES

100 Hut Walks in the Alps
Across the Eastern Alps: E5
Alpine Points of View
Alpine Ski Mountaineering
1 Western Alps
2 Central and Eastern Alps
Chamonix to Zermatt
Snowshoeing
Tour of Mont Blanc
Tour of Monte Rosa
Tour of the Matterhorn
Trekking in the Alps
Trekking in the Silvretta and Rätikon Alps
Walking in the Alps
Walks and Treks in the Maritime Alps

PYRENEES AND FRANCE/SPAIN CROSS-BORDER ROUTES

Rock Climbs in the Pyrenees
The GR10 Trail
The Mountains of Andorra
The Pyrenean Haute Route
The Pyrenees
The Way of St James
Through the Spanish Pyrenees: GR11
Walks and Climbs in the Pyrenees

AUSTRIA

The Adlerweg
Trekking in Austria's Hohe Tauern
Trekking in the Stubai Alps
Trekking in the Zillertal Alps
Walking in Austria

EASTERN EUROPE

The High Tatras
The Mountains of Romania
Walking in Bulgaria's National Parks
Walking in Hungary

FRANCE

Chamonix Mountain Adventures
Ecrins National Park
GR20: Corsica
Mont Blanc Walks
Mountain Adventures in the Maurienne
The Cathar Way
The GR5 Trail
The Robert Louis Stevenson Trail
Tour of the Oisans: The GR54

Tour of the Queyras
Tour of the Vanoise
Trekking in the Vosges and Jura
Vanoise Ski Touring
Via Ferratas of the French Alps
Walking in the Auvergne
Walking in the Cathar Region
Walking in the Cevennes
Walking in the Dordogne
Walking in the Haute Savoie North & South
Walking in the Languedoc
Walking in the Tarentaise and Beaufortain Alps
Walking on Corsica

GERMANY
Germany's Romantic Road
Hiking and Biking in the Black Forest
Walking in the Bavarian Alps
Walking the River Rhine Trail

HIMALAYA
Annapurna
Bhutan
Everest
Garhwal and Kumaon
Kangchenjunga
Langtang with Gosainkund and Helambu
Manaslu
The Mount Kailash Trek
Trekking in Ladakh
Trekking in the Himalaya

ICELAND & GREENLAND
Trekking in Greenland
Walking and Trekking in Iceland

IRELAND
Irish Coastal Walks
The Irish Coast to Coast Walk
The Mountains of Ireland

ITALY
Gran Paradiso
Sibillini National Park
Stelvio National Park
Shorter Walks in the Dolomites
Through the Italian Alps
Trekking in the Apennines
Trekking in the Dolomites
Via Ferratas of the Italian Dolomites: Vols 1 & 2
Walking in Abruzzo
Walking in Sardinia
Walking in Sicily
Walking in the Central Italian Alps
Walking in the Dolomites
Walking in Tuscany
Walking on the Amalfi Coast
Walking the Italian Lakes

MEDITERRANEAN
Jordan – Walks, Treks, Caves, Climbs and Canyons
The Ala Dag
The High Mountains of Crete
The Mountains of Greece
Treks and Climbs in Wadi Rum
Walking in Malta
Western Crete

NORTH AMERICA
British Columbia
The Grand Canyon
The John Muir Trail
The Pacific Crest Trail

SOUTH AMERICA
Aconcagua and the Southern Andes
Hiking and Biking Peru's Inca Trails
Torres del Paine

SCANDINAVIA
Walking in Norway

SLOVENIA, CROATIA AND MONTENEGRO
The Julian Alps of Slovenia
The Mountains of Montenegro
Trekking in Slovenia
Walking in Croatia
Walking in Slovenia: The Karavanke

SPAIN AND PORTUGAL
Costa Blanca: West
Mountain Walking in Southern Catalunya
The Mountains of Central Spain
The Northern Caminos
Trekking through Mallorca
Walking in Madeira
Walking in Mallorca
Walking in Menorca
Walking in the Algarve
Walking in the Cordillera Cantabrica
Walking in the Sierra Nevada
Walking on Gran Canaria
Walking on La Gomera and El Hierro
Walking on La Palma
Walking on Tenerife
Walking the GR7 in Andalucia
Walks and Climbs in the Picos de Europa

SWITZERLAND
Alpine Pass Route
Canyoning in the Alps
Central Switzerland
The Bernese Alps
The Swiss Alps
Tour of the Jungfrau Region
Walking in the Valais
Walking in Ticino
Walks in the Engadine

TECHNIQUES
Geocaching in the UK
Indoor Climbing
Lightweight Camping
Map and Compass
Mountain Weather
Moveable Feasts
Outdoor Photography
Polar Exploration
Rock Climbing
Sport Climbing
The Book of the Bivvy
The Hillwalker's Guide to Mountaineering
The Hillwalker's Manual

MINI GUIDES
Alpine Flowers
Avalanche!
Navigating with a GPS
Navigation
Pocket First Aid and Wilderness Medicine
Snow

MOUNTAIN LITERATURE
8000m
A Walk in the Clouds
Unjustifiable Risk?